DEMOCRACY'S ANGELS

Democracy's Angels

The Work of Women Teachers

KRISTINA R. LLEWELLYN

McGill-Queen's University Press
Montreal & Kingston · London · Ithaca

© McGill-Queen's University Press 2012

ISBN 978-0-7735-4036-1 (cloth)
ISBN 978-0-7735-4050-7 (paper)

Legal deposit third quarter 2012
Bibliothèque nationale du Québec

Printed in Canada on acid-free paper that is 100% ancient forest free
(100% post-consumer recycled), processed chlorine free

This book has been published with the help of a grant from the Canadian
Federation for the Humanities and Social Sciences, through the Aid to
Scholarly Publications Program, using funds provided by the Social
Sciences and Humanities Research Council of Canada.

McGill-Queen's University Press acknowledges the support of the Canada
Council for the Arts for our publishing program. We also acknowledge the
financial support of the Government of Canada through the Canada Book
Fund for our publishing activities.

Library and Archives Canada Cataloguing in Publication

Llewellyn, Kristina, 1976–
Democracy's angels: the work of women teachers / Kristina Llewellyn.

Includes bibliographical references.
ISBN 978-0-7735-4036-1 (bound). – ISBN 978-0-7735-4050-7 (pbk.)

1. Women teachers – Canada – History – 20th century. 2. Democracy
and education – Canada – History – 20th century. 3. Gender identity in
education – Canada--History – 20th century. 4. Education – Social aspects
– Canada – History – 20th century. I. Title.

LC191.8.C2L64 2012   306.43'2097109045   C2012-901912-7

This book was typeset by Interscript in 10.5/13 Sabon.

Contents

Acknowledgments

This book was possible because of the support of extraordinary people. The women teachers who shared their homes, time, and memories are the heart of this project. I am grateful for their trust in me as a researcher and I admire their contributions to Canadian education. Veronica Strong-Boag supervised the original version of this project as a PhD dissertation at the University of British Columbia. She provided challenging and wise guidance through all aspects of my doctoral studies. She continues to be an inspiration for my scholarship and a dear friend. The other members of my thesis committee, Mona Gleason and Jean Barman, offered detailed readings of earlier drafts that have made this book much stronger. Providing a balance of rigorous scholarship and good humor, they demonstrated unwavering commitment to my academic success.

Research for this book was guided by library staff of the Ontario Institute for Studies in Education of the University of Toronto and archivists at the Toronto Board of Education and Vancouver City Archives. Records manager David Stange with the British Columbia Teachers' Federation went above and beyond his job to ensure my research was comprehensive. I would not have pursued my research on women teachers without the encouragement of Cecilia Morgan, Elizabeth Smyth, and Cathy James. Sharon Cook and Joel Westheimer enriched my understanding of citizenship education during my post-doctoral studies at the University of Ottawa. It is a privilege to have them as colleagues. Nolan Reilly and Alexander Freund deepened my commitment to oral history and the democratization of knowledge as co-editors for *Oral History Forum/d'historie orale*.

I also extend my appreciation to Deirdre Kelly, Gillian Creese, Sara Burke, and Paul Axelrod for their thoughtful comments on the thesis. Thank you to the anonymous reviewers from McGill-Queen's University Press for their meticulous feedback. Jacqueline Mason and Ryan Van Huijstee have been gracious and patient editors during the publication process. Susan Glickman provided skillful copyediting. I had time and resources for this project because of funding from the Social Sciences and Humanities Research Council of Canada. Thanks are extended to the Renison University College Research Support Program for additional funds. Portions of this book have been reproduced with permission from *Historical Studies in Education, Review of Education, Pedagogy and Cultural Studies, and Oral History Forum / d'histoire orale.*

It is my family to whom I must offer the greatest acknowledgment of thanks. I recognize in particular my grandmother Jean MacKay's gift of community storytelling. She gave me the privilege of conducting my first oral history with her. My grandfather Raymond MacKay taught me the art of listening carefully. He cherished the lessons of the past. My parents Karen MacKay Llewellyn and Hallett Llewellyn have shared and continue to share each step of my research and writing. I have learned from their life's work the fulfillment people can derive from passionate, political engagement in issues of social justice. This book would not have been possible without their guidance. My sister Jennifer Llewellyn is a moving example of an academic committed to social change. I have relied upon her encouragement and friendship throughout the writing process. The love of my partner Todd Arsenault ensured my dedication to this project. He has provided and continues to provide extraordinary support for my feminist research and activism. Thank you to our son Ethan Llewellyn Arsenault for allowing me to juggle publishing and parenthood. My admiration, love, and appreciation for my family run deep.

DEMOCRACY'S ANGELS

Introduction

THE RELATIONSHIP OF GENDER, EDUCATION, AND DEMOCRACY

The work of women teachers in postwar secondary schools reveals the limits of Canadian democracy. On the one hand, they were encouraged to participate in the increasingly democratized institution of the public secondary school and embraced as necessary participants in the labour market of the education system. The reconstitution of the "normal" social order depended upon their performance. On the other hand, traditional gender roles, disrupted by the trauma of war, were still heralded as women's primary contribution to the nation's stability. While women teachers acted within public institutions, their role remained defined by their private sphere "capabilities" and a gendered model of citizenship that promised security through the performance of educational democracy.

In the 1940s and 1950s, Canada's schools embraced democracy as their primary goal. At the beginning of the twenty-first century, that spirit seems to have returned. In response to perceived threats to national and global security, political officials and school administrators once again heighten the rhetoric of egalitarian rule, and tout policies for equal educational opportunities. Democracy is far more than a constitutional, legal, and political arrangement. It is also a social contract that presumes a common citizenship that transcends differences, including those based on ability, class, race, ethnicity, sexuality, and gender. The public school, particularly at the secondary level, has been and still is responsible for producing that binding social contract among the nation's future adults. Its role extends

beyond teaching a particular political system. Students are to acquire
and practice the knowledge, values, and attitudes consistent with
state laws and regulations, to live democratically.[1]

As it was understood and practiced in the years after the Second
World War, educational democracy failed to deliver fundamental
freedoms to students, teachers, and community. The dominant liberal ideology of the day promised that everyone could participate
equally in civic affairs. But throughout Canada's past, it has been
only those persons with privileged identities, including dominant
masculinities, who have had the power to assume the place of legitimate citizens. Our schools perpetuated this "nameless, faceless,
entity" that attempted to mask systemic inequalities.[2] Women, along
with groups identified as "Other," were acutely affected by these
abstract notions.[3] An examination of women teachers in the postwar era illustrates how educational "democracy" has too often failed
to deliver on its promises of freedom, autonomy, and equality.

Democracy's Angels provides an empirical application of the work
of feminist theorists, from political science to sociology, who in the
late twentieth century challenged historical definitions of gendered
citizenship. Recent studies examine how schooling shapes the concepts of democracy and citizenship according to gender and in relation to diverse social locations.[4] This book adds to the comprehensive
and critical analysis of the relationship among gender, education,
and democracy through an appraisal of the work of women teachers
in postwar Canada.

The masculine citizen has historically been at the centre of most
nations' liberal democratic projects. Carole Pateman's groundbreaking work demonstrates that the democratic social contract, constructed by European political philosophers, was founded upon a
sexual contract based on the distinction between public and private
spheres.[5] According to this contract, women's sexual, economic, and
political agency is dependent upon and excluded from men's prevailing power in the public world. Western philosophical tradition
asserted that the public/private divide was the natural order.
Women's "inherent" concerns for family, and thus women's agency
itself, are almost a sideshow, albeit always critical, to public debates
and the determination of national citizenship.

As Anne Phillips argues, the production of the masculine as synonymous with citizen has not only resulted in women's exclusion
from the state, but also their simultaneous secondary inclusion.[6]

Women are a critical "Other" in substantiating the perceived basis for ideal citizenship: the rational, objective, politically autonomous individual, the alpha male who can freely contribute to the production of a democratic order. The "universal, faceless historical citizen of public discourse was almost universally male" because the supposedly weak and irrational female could not, as decreed by nature itself, support roles beyond the private sphere.[7] Promises of autonomy, freedom, and equal membership within community do not then cut across the hierarchical structure of a diverse society.[8] Instead women, and others who cannot subcribe to dominant conceptions of masculinity, are marginalized.

Feminist socialist, post-colonial, and lesbian scholars have been particularly attuned to the need for complicating the public/private divide, illustrating that women, among themselves, live the effects of gender binaries in very different ways. Nira Yuval-Davis makes the case that nationalist rhetoric of democratic order not only legitimates the dominance of male super-ordinance but circumscribes all those who position themselves, or are positioned by cultural renderings of gender, on the margins of the state as "non-citizens."[9] She writes: "the study of citizenship should consider the issue of women's citizenship not only by contrast to that of men, but also in relation to women's affiliation to dominant or subordinate groups, their ethnicity, origin, and urban or rural residence."[10]

Social contract theory was most influential in shaping institutions from the 1840s to 1970s. Thereafter, various movements mobilized to fight for diversity of political representation and voice.[11] The implications for education have nonetheless been long-lasting. Liberal democracy's conceptions of privacy, sexuality, and marriage, as related to gender binaries, have significantly shaped contemporary education, framed as it is by public discourses of nationalist citizenship. Studies show pedagogy as a tool for phallocentric knowledge or social interactions in the classroom, the school's disciplining of the student body for particular subjectivities, specifically hetero-normativity, and the regulation of gender through selective educational reforms and accountability measures.[12] Researchers have addressed the ways students and school communities are exposed to definitions of the ideal citizen, from textbooks to technology. These definitions construct a view of political agency within a gendered civic sphere. Female students and women teachers learn the limitations of their political participation.

The schooling of "democratic" identities and the woman teacher's role in that process are produced through regulatory fictions. Valerie Walkerdine and Helen Lucey, examining "equal opportunity" rhetoric in British education from the postwar period to the 1980s, show how fictions of choice and autonomy serve to subordinate social identities that do not produce the ideal citizen: that is, the bourgeois male.[13] Children learn illusions of their free will, a non-coercive technique to manage a citizenry, from mothers and women teachers who, as "naturally" non-authoritarian nurturers, are responsible for safeguarding masculine models of democracy that lessen female political, social, and professional powers. Jo-Anne Dillabough illustrates the danger of democratic illusions for the political identification of British women teachers.[14] Their memories reveal women's lived paradox of being socially constructed as non-citizens due to their domestic ties, yet simultaneously responsible for the socialization of a new generation of citizens because of the service profession of teaching.

The symbolic, discursive practices and social, structural constraints of masculine narratives of democracy have been underexplored within the Canadian educational context. We do not know how these narratives intersect with those individuals, particularly women, who are charged with living out and/or reproducing citizenship. This book interrogates the relationship between the governance of gendered identities in Canadian education and women's shifting experiences of that governance. It simultaneously challenges the often abstract concept of democracy, which attempts to mask hegemonic power inequalities.

The pages that follow offer an educational history that deconstructs a contextually and temporally specific invocation of democracy. Democracy's Angels examines Canadian egalitarianism rhetoric from 1945 to 1960, a period especially preoccupied with the question of national identity. Toronto and Vancouver public secondary schools provide a regional comparison of nationalist rhetoric through the country's two largest English school boards. Although national discussions of education often include all levels of schooling, this work targets the objectives for secondary schools: the primary sites for citizenship gate-keeping. The secondary school was critical to ensuring collective security through its assumption of the superiority of Western political rule. In worried acknowledgement of this key function, Z.S. Phimister, Superintendent and Chief Inspector of Schools in Toronto, noted in 1947 that "People turn to the school after the war ... in the faint hope that the school may be able to do something which will make it possible for the next generation to avoid another calamity."[15] *Democracy's Angels* explains this hope and asks: how was educational democracy constructed as a universalizing narrative, and what were its specific meanings for the agenda of postwar schools? How did official, educational, and academic discourses construct privileged identities of citizenship and insert them into secondary schools, an increasingly common experience for Canadian youth? More specifically, how were master narratives of democracy gendered?

Official narratives from newspapers, school board minutes and reports, provincial commission reports, and teachers' federation newsletters are examined in relation to oral histories. The latter illustrate how women teachers saw themselves positioned as marginalized, private representatives for democracy and, contradictorily, included as potential agents of change in the production of the "egalitarian" platform for the school and the nation. In its centering of female professionals, this study poses the questions: how did masculine constructions of educational democracy function for women teachers whose capacity for authority and political power were tenuous in the postwar context? At a practical level, how did women teachers reconcile their public duty as agents for citizenship with a femininity relegated to the private sphere? How were the gendered contradictions these women experienced characterized by their social status of marriage, age, region, class, sexuality, and ethnicity, and affected by the subject matter, credentials, and promotion of their school-bound status? In answering these questions, this book addresses the shifts in and enactment of educational discourse and policy that occurred after the Second World War. In other words, it interrogates the enactment of a master narrative of masculine normality that shaped the teaching of the next generation of Canadian citizenry. In deconstructing the multiple messages of these years, this book illuminates both the democratic order and the ways that women teachers negotiated its boundaries.

Democracy was a regulatory discourse for women's lives despite the very contested and complex messages it enveloped. Regulatory discourses are, as Michel Foucault argues, historically contingent strategies whereby processes of differentiation and homogenizing label some qualities as good and others as bad.[16] If a regulatory discourse is successful then it becomes hegemonic. Hegemony, according to Antonio Gramsci, favours a ruling group who, though not always consciously, manufactures seemingly spontaneous consent from subordinate groups to guarantee social order.[17] In order for discourses to be hegemonic, they must contain conflicts by addressing counter-hegemonic ideals within the dominant consent.[18] The boundaries of a legitimate social order, in this case democracy, are unstable, temporary, and transgressive, and produce conflicting meanings. Within the context of postwar reconstruction, efforts to produce a stable and, thus, "superior" democratic nation necessarily embodied the consolidation of dissenting or conflicting ideals. Transgressive boundaries became an inherent part of a postwar social order that sought stability. In other words, the deviant or the forbidden were regularly in plain sight even as their existence was employed to justify the status quo.

Andrew Ross argues that no period better exhibits the creation of that consensus described by Gramsci's concept of hegemony than the decades after the Second World War in the United States.[19] The same can be said of Canada. This era is at times memorialized as golden. Cold War atomic threats, global decolonization movements, and agitations for civil rights sometimes barely seem to disturb its intrinsic harmony. Canadian historians have begun to explore the inequities of the postwar era and have found that the popularization of liberal democratic rhetoric emerged as a national defense against the uncertainties of the age.[20] These changes were the basis for the "Cold War mentality" of the era by which social authorities forwarded an agenda that acquiesced to reform only in so far as it contained dissension and radicalism. The primary model of internal defense was to champion national togetherness under the liberal pluralist banner of a fully democratic, egalitarian nation.[21] Commonality and stability were defined according to a desired, hegemonic norm: English, middle class, white, Protestant, and heterosexual citizenship.

Even as state reforms moved towards equity in the name of a stable and free nation, their invocation remained firmly set within conservative ideals. The postwar Canadian government sought to ensure public entitlements, including renewed social security initiatives such as health insurance, unemployment insurance, and workmen's compensation.[22] These initiatives included specific promises to women, including fair remuneration and the elimination of a marriage bar for female civic employees. Such Fordism, however, was premised on the independence of the private realm of the family, which was still very much consigned to women as the mothers of the nation.[23] By definition, women could only be quasi-citizens and thus secondary workers in the public world. Men were, by contrast, long-term participants in the labour market, with rights to authority and knowledge in the public world.[24]

Given the citizenship function of the secondary school, objectives for education reflected the progressive-conservatism of state initiatives. As such, a gender hierarchy, marked by class, race, and sexuality was an implicit part of the educational agenda for democracy. The woman teacher, as quasi-citizen, was designated a limited role in the implementation of this agenda. As with their treatment of the postwar period generally, historians have not typically highlighted changes from the traditional patterns of schooling.[25] Shifts toward the democratization of education are often characterized as the influence of progressivism.[26] There is a need to go beyond the typical progressive/traditional debate; adherents to both theories of education embraced postwar democratic rhetoric as the primary lesson for secondary schools. While these theories were certainly incompatible in many ways, their commonalities were pronounced for educators as they upheld both the nation's liberal social order and its conservative ideal of citizenship.

Secondary schools in Toronto and Vancouver responded to hegemonic and national calls for democratization. Major trends included: increased universal access to secondary education, with streamed programming to address individual learning needs; growth in social services for character education within the school; and increased participation by each member of the school community through decentralized decision-making initiatives. These reforms were the schools' visible commitment to equal opportunity, freedom of personal expression, and individual political autonomy. The ideal citizen produced through this programming was a knowledgeable worker who, through self-governance and the needs of the state, practiced Christian, capitalist, nuclear family values. Educational administrators across the political spectrum affirmed the separate spheres of the social contract for good citizenship: the school as a public institution was dedicated to the rational, autonomous, politically engaged subject.

"Woman" was not that subject. Women were critical to the nuclear family and thus private creatures who, obligated to children

and husbands, could not be astute political representatives of the
public world. Women teachers therefore were symbolically *excluded*
from educational democracy. Most school officials characterized
them as tenuous professionals, with a fundamental lack of commitment to public life and the potential irrationality of the weaker
sex.[27] At the same time, they were *included* not only as necessary
workers during a labour shortage, but as the motherly guardians of
moral order. School officials idealized the service of women teachers
even as they left the real power to produce and manage educational
democracy to men.

Women's oral histories illustrate their negotiations of the prevailing acceptance of the postwar idea of women's inferiority within
"democratic" education. Specifically, they comment on professional
discourses that barred them from knowledge claims and promotional credentials. They also speak to intense surveillance of their life
choices, especially marriage and motherhood, and their physical
appearance. Instances of commonality, quite often in the oral histories, exhibit the point at which national discourses meet local gender
subjectivities. As such, the women speak to public policies of gender
discrimination as they relate to more innocuous forms of discrimination concerning the private realm. They reveal, for example, how
their choice of dress was part of character education, and symbolic
of the nation's faith in heterosexual coupling for social stability.
Their oral histories also present individual variations shaped by
their specific positions in Toronto and Vancouver secondary schools.
Those who possessed graduate degrees, rather than temporary teaching certificates, were more confident in their claims to a "masculine,"
detached, and rational model of professionalism. Stories also demonstrate isolated cases of overt discrimination which differed according to social locations; primarily the interviewees are white, urban,
and middle-class women, but sexuality, ethnicity, and marriage
provide opportunities for tension and contradiction. Women who
embodied the white, middle-class, and heterosexual ideal of citizenship, as opposed to those who were Chinese, lesbian, or working-
class, appeared more comfortable taking on the role of moral
guardians for the school and, implicitly, the nation.

They were, therefore, neither the dupes of democracy nor radical
dissenters to prevailing codes. Their agency came through everyday
means rather than formal feminist action. They nonetheless sometimes broke the bounds of their private sphere "capabilities" to insert

themselves as stakeholders in public discourses of citizenship, albeit with limited powers.[28] They depicted their teaching selves as change-makers both structurally, in term of their postwar work lives, and symbolically, in terms of their representation during the interview process. For example, some women declared themselves to be the effective heads of departments within an all-woman subject area, like girls' physical education, even when they were denied official promotion. Other women described themselves as taking over the prescribed curriculum through their own pace, methods, and lessons. Agency was shaped by each woman's social and work context. Some women spoke of supportive colleagues, while others admitted to working in an atmosphere of harassment and intimidation. Talk of resistance also depended upon the availability of discourses for each woman to frame herself as a respectable teacher. A Chinese-Canadian interviewee argued that she not only struggled to prove herself as a professional, but that she also needed to appear Caucasian. In declaring forms of resistance, oral histories, like the debates among education officials, demonstrate the contestable character of hegemonic democratic discourse. Without these women's experiences, the process of citizenship inclusion and exclusion or the way education can negotiate between national discourses and local identities cannot be fully understood.

FEMINIST READINGS OF WOMEN TEACHERS' ORAL HISTORIES

Despite the relative accessibility of primary sources, the work of women teachers in twentieth-century Canada is greatly underresearched. Like Canadian history more generally, the history of education was initially written as a story of nationhood missing many of the people who worked for its creation. Teachers, pupils, and even parents started to garner the attention of social historians in the 1970s.[29] Feminist historians quickly became a part of this historiographical turn. In the first comprehensive collection on women teachers, covering Australia, Britain, Canada, and the United States, editors Alison Prentice and Marjorie Theobald challenged the presentation of women teachers as either victims or unwitting perpetuators of gendered school structures (i.e. young, naive, rural teachers who were being used for cheap labour).[30] This collection set out a goal which scholars have since attempted to fulfill, namely to know the various perspectives of women who taught and their contradictory positioning within patriarchal schooling.

Despite this promising start, the history of women teachers in Canada has been primarily reserved to a few scholarly articles and unpublished manuscripts. The gap can be partially attributed to the status of teachers in society. Labour historians have generally neglected teaching because it stands between the working and professional classes, and many feminist scholars have neglected teaching to examine more groundbreaking occupations.[31] Documentary histories of women teachers' professional associations in the twentieth century have garnered the primary attention of researchers.[32] There are a few exceptions. Sheila L. Cavanagh's and Cecilia Reynolds' numerous articles, and Rebecca Priegert Coulter and Helen Harper's compilation, *History is Hers*, seek the particularities of women teachers' lives in the twentieth century.[33] This latter work is particularly welcome for its extensive use of oral histories. These and other studies of women in education still mostly conform to the longstanding preference for an examination of elementary teaching within Ontario regions. This reflects the prevailing segregation of the workforce. The gap also owes something to the less accessible story of the gendering of education for secondary school women, who did not fit the maternal image as readily as their elementary counterparts. Despite comprising over one-third of most urban school staffs in the mid twentieth century, women have historically been treated as anomalies. The ability of recent work to illuminate national agendas is also limited. Jean Barman, in *Sojourning Sisters*, is one of the few historians to acknowledge that women's work as teachers had a national effect on Canada's ideals, culture, and social structures.[34]

Democracy's Angels places oral histories at the centre of understanding the localized invocations of nation-wide agendas for democracy in schools. The study is based on twenty interviews with women who taught in secondary schools, ten each from Toronto and Vancouver, for at least two years between 1945 and 1960.[35] The interviews, completed between 2002 and 2005, were secured by a word-of-mouth chain of recruitment. For the most part respondents were in their eighties, so the postwar period marked the beginning of their teaching careers. A little less than half of the women had their teaching interrupted by marriage and/or children in the 1940s and 1950s. Regardless of marital status, the majority identified as middle-class, white, and Anglo-Saxon. Only two identified with a further marginalized social group, one as a lesbian (although not out in her teaching days) and another as one of the first Chinese-Canadian women to teach in a public secondary school in British Columbia, and possibly the country. As a group, these profiles obviously do not represent the diversity of women's experiences. They do, however, represent the typical woman teacher hired to work in postwar schools.[36]

My analysis of women's oral histories joins those of an increasing number of feminist theorists who reconcile modernist questions of structural equality with poststructuralist concerns for discourse by acknowledging women's political agency within hierarchies of identification.[37] A feminist reading of oral histories, which integrates the strengths of poststructuralist and materialist feminism(s), provides productive tensions for historians to, as Marjorie Theobald describes, work *within* layers of memory, rather than beyond them.[38] There, we can discover a point at which women's narratives can expose and destabilize essentialist tropes or myths encouraged by male dominance. Throughout the book, the potential of oral history is found between these theoretical traditions, where multiple truths are located within the power dynamics of their construction, language as experience is understood in relation to material life, and the question of the self is continuously negotiated within social structures.

When considering the evidence of oral histories, poststructuralist feminists focus on knowledge production or the process through which women make sense of their lives.[39] Jacques Derrida argues that seeing life as text accentuates the notion that there is no clear window into the inner life of a person, because the view is always filtered through the glaze of language and processes of signification.[40] The role of the oral historian is not to provide the facts, even if this were possible; rather it is to analyze the way historic knowledge is created through the production of discourse as informed by experiences and subject locations. Oral history as evidence, set within a text, can lead to the re-conceptualization of the study of women's work in education or, for that matter, in some other field.[41] Historians could misread the conditions of women teachers' work as purely factory-like labour constrained by material structures, namely prescriptive curricula and authoritarian administrators. But alternative interpretations emerge from the narratives of the women interviewed in this book by looking "sideways into the picture presented ... in order to identify teachers' motivations, feelings, and reactions."[42]

The recurring echo of meaning found in these oral histories is that a quasi-hierarchical power structure in schools provided clarity of conditions that were quietly negotiable. For example, many women teachers implied that a firm pecking order gave them authority over their students and thus leeway to determine classroom content. It is the oral historian's job to explore knowledge as a linguistic representation of life which provides clues, patterns, and themes that speak to how women teachers, in relation to a multitude of conflicting truths, understood and acted upon their surroundings. This conceptual stance rejects an empiricist view of the past as objectively fixable through the scientific pursuit of facts.[43] All knowledge, including that of the women participating in research, is subject to deconstruction and skepticism.

Materialist feminist researchers provide an important note of caution. Suspicion of all truth claims is politically untenable for a feminist agenda that seeks to foster research from and for women and towards political reform. Roberta Spalter-Roth and Heidi Hartmann are critical of any feminist epistemological position that does not claim scientific credibility and generalizability.[44] Donna Haraway makes a similar argument in claiming that feminist poststructuralists fall into a dangerous territory of relativism, which is the "perfect mirror twin of totalization in the ideologies of objectivity; both deny the stakes of location, embodiment, and partial perspective; both make it impossible to see well."[45] In her research, Haraway reclaims the notion of objectivity, which she defines as the articulation of subjugated knowledges.[46] She asserts that partial perspectives, as ways of seeing, enable accessible communication among feminist researchers for change in the real world of women.[47] Considering materialist feminists' calls for a strong political agenda, the seduction for many oral historians has been to write a coherent story that privileges the seemingly transparent knowledge of women.[48] Such narratives are founded on the belief, articulated by Paul Thompson, that "transforming the 'objects' of study into 'subjects,' makes for a history which is not just richer, more vivid and heartrending, but truer."[49] Valorizing women teachers by letting them tell their story unmediated would come at the dangerous cost of depicting their narratives as another form of constrained consciousness similar to conservative rhetoric of teachers' apolitical subjectivities.

The oral historian can foreground Haraway's demands to articulate "subjugated knowledge" by acknowledging the relationship between researchers and researched. As such, materialist concern to provide a platform for political activism can be realized with post-structuralist sensitivities. Feminist fieldwork across theoretical traditions has to deal with the inherent power inequalities between the researcher and the researched, including questions of authorship, ownership of data, and use of evidence.[50] Historical knowledge produced through oral histories is, ultimately, a reported discourse created in particular contexts and analyzed within scholars' own location and research frameworks. Oral historians hope for a close fit in terms of interpretation of events between participants and researcher, avoiding distortion and co-option.

With all this in mind, the interviewees for this study were made aware that my interpretation of their narratives would take precedence. Although the interview process took place in a semi-structured format, the questions – which ranged from general biographical inquiries to specific explorations of teacher education and workload responsibilities – set parameters around the women's reminiscences. Equally influential was my subjectivity, similar to that of the interviewees themselves at the beginning of their careers, as a young, white, heterosexual, middle-class, female educator. In response, the women often took a mentorship position. They intentionally edited their stories to present happy endings, instructing me to enter teaching and thereby solidifying the value of their profession.

While awareness of contextual production of oral histories can address concerns for location, materialist feminists further caution that historians must be wary of obscuring the voices of their subjects as they make claims of their political truths.[51] This study illustrates that participants can productively disrupt the historian's agenda if the researcher is listening effectively. The interviewees repeatedly refuted my attempts to solicit stories of rebellion and radicalism. It became clear that such stories would implicate them as unsuccessful professionals and immoral women within postwar memories. Instead, as they acknowledged, much-needed public battles against discrimination would have to wait for another day. These women's remembrances therefore represent historical knowledge of how they understood and attempted to interact with their positions in education systems of a given time and place.

Feminist analysis of oral history is directly related to debates between language and materialism as sources of gender oppression. Michele Barrett notes that poststructuralism challenges materialist feminism's focus on the cause of women's oppression being rooted in economic relations.[52] We should not interpret such a challenge, however, to mean that discourse is not intimately related to material life. Materialist feminists react against the kind of work, associated with poststructuralism, which describes women's lives as floating above their contexts, rather than within them.[53] An analysis of discourse with respect to women's narratives must seek to examine the system of "controlling metaphors, notions, categories and norms which develop and delimit the subjects' conceptions and expressions of personal, work and social relations."[54] As theorist Mikhail Bakhtin argues, voices create structures through which the reality of a multitude of concrete worlds can be perceived or discussed.[55] In addition to perceiving how women construct themselves, such discussion enables the historian to better understand the ways that dominant discourses, as they relate to structural institutions, also construct women's narratives. Oral historians must read both for structure, or the experiences of the material world and the workings of it, and for culture, or the ways memories of events and experiences are organized through language.[56]

The access that women teachers in this study had to discourses of professionalism provides a case in point. Interviewees were relatively silent in conversation that associated the school with a family and their teaching with motherhood. Nurturing and caring were qualities avoided in their narratives. This silence was part of their effort to cast themselves as rational, detached professionals – personae normally given to male teachers by virtue of their sex. Alternatively, a survival metaphor dominated their oral histories. This controlling metaphor spoke to educational officials' suspicions of feminine capabilities for "democratic" knowledge. The extent of this language in each woman's narrative, however, was directly related to her status within the school hierarchy. Women with graduate degrees or who were heads of department expressed defensive language far less than other interviewees. With the removal of silences or inattentiveness to literary devices, the reader would miss how these women determined their subjectivities in relation to the structure of public institutions. Narrative studies that are founded on an analysis of discourse *or* materialism do not provide the fullest historical explanation, since the meaning of these concepts is defined in relation to each another. These women's oral histories reveal the societal imperatives by which they organized their narratives as effective teachers, as well as the ways they manipulated discourses to shape the structural parameters of their working lives. Schools did not simply impose themselves upon the identities of women teachers, nor did women teachers have full control over the shape of their teaching selves within the school environment.

Obviously the relationship between women's discursive positioning and identity formation are inextricably linked. At the centre of this relationship for feminist theorists and historians is how to express women as subjects. Given the focus of poststructuralist feminism on multiple subjectivities, the concern is that readings for material effects could create a seemingly unified "woman's discourse." Standpoint theorists provide a research method for understanding that the perspectives of marginalized individuals are distinct by virtue of their position relative to the dominant culture. Standpoint theorists, like Nancy Harstock and Dorothy Smith, contend that women as an oppressed group have a vision of the ruling apparatuses that shape their everyday worlds distinct from men that must be privileged by researchers.[57] Harstock and Smith turn to a Marxist framework as a means for escaping seemingly abstract categories of meaning that ignore the "coordering of actual activities," or the patterns of women's experiences, and changes in women's lives.[58]

Scholars have challenged this position, arguing that the desire to locate the objective "woman's" perspective continues to imply that there is a single, authentic centre of female identity, and that articulating it will lead to the liberation of the oppressed individual.[59] Chandra Mohanty argues that inferences of fixed identity may lead researchers to reproduce hegemonic discourses of non-Western women's identities and cultures as statically "Other."[60] She and other postcolonial feminists argue that it is necessary to adopt an analysis that acknowledges that women do not have a coherent self moving through history. Instead, the self is a socially constructed, unstable identity constantly created and negotiated through both dominant discourses and resistance to those conceptions. The notion of private, powerful selves separated from social selves is, as Mikhail Bakhtin notes, a myth. The self is defined in its encounter with the other; self-identity is a product of social forces.[61] Therefore a materialist or contextual analysis of oral history, informed by the feminist poststructuralist negation of the search for unity, is most helpful for the oral historian.[62]

Identity formation, as revealed through women teachers' narratives in this book, is free and structured, personal and public, as well as internally and externally shaped. These contradictions become clear when examining the interviewees' choice of physical representation within school walls. Despite awareness of a moral imperative for females in postwar society, almost all the women seemed to take for granted the importance of respectable dress. The women presented themselves as autonomous individuals, making personal choices in style. Some even spoke with frustration about the preoccupation of female students with traditional beauty. But at the same time, they made appearance central to their status as exemplary citizens within the school and community. Many participants made reference to upper-class inspiration and Christian uplift of students through garb. Such contradictions, or what feminist historians term "bad fits," highlight the very point at which the subject actively negotiates the concept of self.[63] In this case, we can see the diverse ways women teachers, in relation to gender, class, race, sexuality, and the workplace, embodied national agendas for character education while claiming gender autonomy.

Women can articulate a coherent identity but it is for the historian to explain the formation of that identity as an ideological struggle for agency within dominant institutions and discourses. Michel Foucault writes: "thinking of the mechanisms of power, I am thinking rather of its capillary form of existence, the point where power reaches into the very grain of individuals, touches their bodies and inserts itself into their actions and attitudes, their discourses, learning processes and everyday lives."[64] Identity formation needs to be deconstructed to understand the frameworks of women's differentiated experiences. What it means to be a woman and how that is defined according to the subjects' material needs and available languages should be the main points of exploration for the historian. Women's oral histories are embedded narratives to which historians need to be attuned. Oral historians need not read for a positivist rational self, but rather for identity construction in relation to others and contexts, including the interview process itself.[65]

As Joan Sangster notes, poststructural analysis helps to deconstruct the narrative form of scripts in oral histories and to acknowledge the construction of the narrative as text by both researcher and researched.[66] She further argues that feminist materialist insights are needed to force historians to examine the ways relations of power shape women's choices within social, cultural, political, and economic boundaries.[67] Although these approaches are often contested,

I agree that an integrated poststructuralist and materialist analysis provides the best framework for feminist research, particularly when dealing with oral history. This framework provides a guide for my analysis of women teachers' oral histories in twentieth-century Canada that can cross the often unstable and dichotomizing post-modern bridge. Thus *Democracy's Angels* reveals how school structures shaped women teachers' identities, while also demonstrating the ways women invoked cultural discourses to assert their authority. By openly acknowledging the complex production of oral history, historians can understand that their research priorities, such as teacher resistance, must co-exist with their subjects' own priorities, such as their daily workload. An integrated analysis also highlights that the diverse definitions of work are dependent on the discourses available for women's social status. The deconstruction of women teachers' narratives reveals the structuring paradigms and processes that have shaped their individual and collective material realities in our educational past.

Before applying this analysis to my own collection of interviews, the first chapter interrogates school officials' conceptualization of discourses and policies which women had to negotiate. Postwar educators across the political spectrum and in different regions of the country rallied behind a nationalist platform of democracy. This chapter deals with three of the most expansive areas of "democratic" reform: curriculum, character education, and administration. With specific attention to class, race, religion, and region, this chapter makes clear that reforms were based on the reaffirmation of a conservative ideal of citizenship. Subsequent chapters then provide a primarily gendered examination of how each major trend in education shaped a limiting role for women teachers within secondary schools.

Chapter 2 explores the way in which female teachers were viewed by school administrators and even their federation representatives as less professional than their male counterparts. "Womanliness," marked by sociability and irrationality, meant that they could neither embody nor teach the necessary rigorous and objective knowledge that was meant to characterize the postwar "democratic" curriculum. Unable to be men, women were accused of a lack of commitment to teaching, and thus of hindering professionalism.

While marginalized, women teachers were simultaneously praised for their potential to *reproduce* "democratic" morality. Chapter 3

examines their role as performers of traditional citizenship values –
a primary objective for the school systems' increased social services
and character education. As cultivators of the norm, they found
themselves under continuous surveillance. Those interviewed spoke
of struggling to appear "respectable" while, at times, acting out
alternative messages.

The final chapter explores women's integration as equal participants in the decentralized administration of postwar schooling. They
were given greater responsibilities in the "democratic" educational
reorganization but without a commensurate level of authority or
remuneration. As mothers of the school, women were meant to be
apolitical service providers, with the authority of the public school
remaining in the hands of male principals, inspectors, and heads
of department. Women responded by exerting control where they
could, namely in classrooms, and more specifically in the pace,
method, and lessons of instruction. Ultimately, women teachers were
quasi-citizens in the public school yet leaders in the delivery of democratic hope for the age. Their experiences question the gender-blind
inclusiveness of educational democracy for postwar Canada.

I

The Purpose
of Educational "Democracy"

To understand the position of women teachers, we must first examine the objectives that shaped their work in postwar Canadian secondary schools. This chapter outlines the ideological terrain women teachers had to negotiate before turning, in the following chapters, to their position within and reaction to the broad social shifts in education during the period.

Most Canadian educational historians, whether they focus on issues of curriculum and instruction or policy and administration, debate the extent to which progressive or traditional theories of schooling shaped education systems. Notable historians, from Henry Johnson to Robert Stamp and Neil Sutherland, have declared traditionalism the winner of this debate.[1] They argue, using Ontario or British Columbia as the typical points of reference, that Canadian education systems did not embrace progressivism in the same manner as those in the United States, and that progressivism, when included, was primarily confined to the elementary level until well past the mid-twentieth century. Robert Stamp makes the case that postwar secondary schools were marked by a back to basics, prescriptive curriculum, enforced by school inspectors, and capped by province-wide matriculation examinations to regulate student learning.[2] However other educational historians, including Paul Axelrod and Robert Gidney, recognize elements of progressivism within all levels of twentieth-century Canadian schools.[3] Gidney notes that the growing influence of psychology in the educational setting challenged traditional pedagogy and ushered in new theories of child-centered and experiential learning.[4] He also notes that the rapid growth of urbanization and consumerism demanded a new curriculum, inclusive of vocational programs, relevant to the modern world.[5]

Gidney contends in passing that the popularization of the concept of democracy in postwar Canada brought elements of progressivism into schools. Indeed most scholars have assumed that progressivism, with its promise of gentle guidance, student choice, and experiential-based learning, was the model for a democratic education. That association was not novel. John Dewey, a father of progressive pedagogy, explained: "democratic social arrangements promote better quality of human experience, one which is more widely accessible and enjoyed, than do non-democratic and anti-democratic forms of social life."[6] How could Dewey's ideal of democratic education have been a popular objective for postwar schools if traditionalism was the major influence?

Paul Axelrod has argued that such a question perpetuates the idea that postwar education was caught between two purely antagonistic modes of thought.[7] Within this binary model, progressivism produced good, democratic schools and, by contrast, traditionalism was undemocratic and bad. Such a dichotomy is especially unhelpful when exploring the popularity of democracy as an objective for postwar public secondary schools. First, "democracy" was not exclusively the preserve of the "Progressive Educator."[8] Second, most administrators and teachers did not fit these two discreet ideological categories. Except for the exceptional individual, like conservative scholar Hilda Neatby or progressive educator George Weir, most academics and commentators did not proclaim full allegiance to either dogma. Third, and most importantly, educational democracy for postwar Canada was not necessarily synonymous with egalitarian ambitions.

Most postwar educators claimed to work not in the name of progressivism or traditionalism, but in the name of democracy. While this had been a central focus for compulsory education since Confederation, it gained renewed prominence in the 1940s and 1950s as citizens sought to avoid totalitarianism in the wake of the Holocaust, ensure participatory citizenship at a time of growing civil rights and decolonization movements, and assert the superiority of Western democracies to communist regimes. Public education, along with other burgeoning social institutions and services in the areas of recreation, health, and employment, was mandated to uphold liberal democracy.[9] Secondary schools, with their special role in forming apprentice adults into citizens, were particularly important in this regard.

To that end, education officials touted the need for the best of both old (traditional) and new (progressive) theories to produce superior sites of every kind. In his much overlooked later work, Dewey makes just this case: democratic education cannot be defined by divisive "isms," the learning of skills or historical values, and teaching to the child or the subject.[10] After the Second World War, commentators used democratic maxims of unity and accord in several collections of essays on Canadian schools. In one contribution, W.H. Swift, Deputy Minister of Education in Alberta, expressed the democratic impulse for education as an era of Hegelian synthesis. Swift did not assert that progressive and traditional theories would be easily blended, "since some concepts are diametrically opposed," but insisted that "we are attempting to create the best we can by way of reconciliation ... the old and the new and, in so far as human ingenuity permits, improve on both."[11] Similarly, Sperrin N.F. Chant, Dean of Arts and Science at the University of British Columbia and author of the British Columbia Royal Commission on Education in the late 1950s, reflected on the debate between progressives' emphasis on individual needs versus traditionalists' emphasis on the requirements of the nation: "No attempt will be made here to disentangle these two basic functions of Canadian education, they are complementary and should merge harmoniously in every feature of the educational programme."[12] Swift's and Chant's conciliatory approach to programming differed little from many of their contemporaries who, also working in the name of democracy, promised schooling free of dissension and partaking of a range of the best educational methods.

The rhetoric of educational democracy, encompassing both the democratization of schools and education of citizens to uphold a democratic nation, promised individual autonomy, equality, and order in an era of seeming instability. Such guarantees reflect the often generic quality of much talk which rather vaguely publicized postwar education as everyone's business. Postwar rhetoric was not, however, simply words without consequences. As much recent scholarship reminds us, discourse "denotes statements, practices, and assumptions that share a linguistic coherence and work to identify and describe a problem or an area of concern."[13] Democratic rhetoric includes the policies, standards, and assumptions educators embraced to produce ideal postwar citizens. Canadian historians, such as Doug Owram, Shirley Tillotson, Mona Gleason, and Mary Louise Adams, have explained that definitions of citizenship, which existed under the popular banner of national egalitarianism, served to contain those qualities and practices that lay outside the desired postwar norms.[14] Educational democracy in the 1940s and '50s promised universal access, social services, and local autonomy. These offerings simultaneously reaffirmed the ideal citizens as productive individuals who would self-govern according to their positions within the social stratification of a capitalist, Judeo-Christian, and ultimately imperialist society that enshrined the nuclear family. Educational democracy, expressed through both progressive and traditional philosophies, was never primarily humanitarian. Rather, democracy was conservatively interpreted to preserve an orderly state.[15]

Despite the recognized popularity of "democratization" in the postwar agenda, few educational historians have explicitly examined how policy-makers, administrators, and other experts translated democracy on the ground. Even fewer have taken a comparative approach to determine whether this agenda was a regional phenomenon or more national. It is for this purpose that this book centres on a regional analysis of Toronto and Vancouver. The comparison, between Hogtown, with its Tory legacy, and the Pacific Gateway, with its pioneering heritage, provides a valuable opportunity to measure the relative potential of democratic pedagogy. An examination of provincial policies and local programming demonstrates that regional legacies hold true to a certain extent. British Columbia had more officials who used Deweyan rhetoric for progressive-oriented programming, such as individualized timetables and guidance/psychological services for secondary school students.[16] Ontario secondary schools were more traditionally academic in orientation, but still embraced greater local autonomy for schools and teachers than prior to the Second World War, particularly in the area of curriculum planning. Despite differences, national trends and ideology, as illustrated through senior academic and political discourses across the country, ultimately prevailed even though public education was and continued to be a provincial responsibility. English Canada's two dominant centres were in substantial agreement in the years after 1945 as they faced pressures to protect the West against godless Communism.

This chapter explores three areas in which potentially liberatory trends were evident on both a national and local level for secondary schools. The first is curriculum. Programming changes after the Second World War included increased vocational training within the diversified course offerings of comprehensive secondary schools. Enhanced equality of opportunity was compromised by policies that sorted students into academic elites and future blue-collar workers. The second area is character education. With formal guidance departments supported by psychologists and the introduction of more social studies courses, educators embraced secondary schools as a social service. The teaching of seemingly universal values, like tolerance, was matched by a simultaneous emphasis on responsible citizenship and the merits of social hierarchy. The third area is administrative reform. Educators sought to reorganize the school as a microcosm for participatory democracy, where local autonomy was honoured in decision-making processes and supervision practices. Autonomy was offered by educators within the boundaries of centralized systems and for the purpose of encouraging independence from the social welfare net. This chapter unravels the contradictory ways democratic rhetoric was invoked for learning and teaching effective citizenship.

"DEMOCRATIZING" THE CURRICULUM

In the years following the Second World War, academics and political and administrative officials spoke of a two-pronged objective for the secondary curriculum: a universal education open to all, but also aimed at producing intellectual elite. The postwar secondary school was to have a broadening, seemingly progressive purpose in developing the average citizen. In line with the inclusion of education under article 26 of the United Nations' 1948 Declaration of Human Rights, the official mandate of Canadian educators was to produce a mass population that was literate, technically trained, and knowledgeable. H.L. Campbell, Deputy Superintendent of Education for British Columbia under the Liberal-Conservative Coalition and author of well-known curriculum texts during the period, stated that "democracy, or progress based on the will of the majority, is in danger if the average citizen is ignorant."[17] Rates of attendance in high school increased rapidly. While in the 1940s only twenty-eight percent of students ages fourteen to seventeen in British Columbia were attending grade nine or higher, by 1955 that figure rose to over fifty-five percent.[18] For three to five years, the secondary school was becoming a common experience in the lives of most urban teenagers and thus an appropriate site for social reconstruction.

Vocational education, or the preparation of citizens for useful employment, was one outgrowth of the "democratization" of school curriculum. The events of the First World War encouraged educators to question education purely for the professions. The Second World War made the effective training of trades all the more urgent. The prosperity of the 1940s and '50s led to a growing urban infrastructure that included new schools to accommodate the population boom in Toronto and Vancouver. Parents sent their children to school with a fair certainty that graduates could obtain a job, at least in the expanding blue-collar sector.[19]

Politicians across Canada responded to such hopes. The federal government, led by Liberal Prime Minister William Lyon Mackenzie King, implemented the 1942 Vocational Training Coordination Act that funded vocational programs in secondary schools.[20] By the early part of the 1950s, most Toronto secondary schools were establishing new business and industrial courses. For example, Malvern Collegiate Institute created a commercial department, while Bloor Collegiate Institute increased its industrial arts and crafts courses.[21] At much the same time, the Vancouver Board of Trustees announced the renovation of industrial arts shops and home economics laboratories in more than six secondary schools.[22] When speaking at a 1956 Canadian symposium, B.F. Addy, principal of the Manitoba Technical Institute, declared that "The strength of Canada and its progress as a nation is inseparately bound with the skills and technical and scientific knowledge of its people. We must ever maintain a productive people if we are to remain free."[23]

The purely vocational or technical school, however, was unusual. Educators sought a less divisive and more egalitarian model. The most common was the "one-size-fits-all" composite or comprehensive secondary school. Such initiatives combined the technical institute and academic high school, but also provided instruction in general education for non-university bound students. The composite school meant a significant curriculum overhaul to address the individualized needs of students and to fulfill the ideal of education for "every man's child." Reflecting on this model as it swept across Canada, Winnipeg principal and assistant superintendent Ewart H. Morgan wrote: "The Canadian high school today is one of our democracy's great experiments. It adventurously undertakes to gather in the masses of our teen-age youth and to provide them a large part of the cohesive elements that bind them into a Canadian people."[24]

Implementing decisions made just prior to the war, the Vancouver board established seven new or restructured six-year composite secondary schools, to replace most separate junior high and high schools (grade seven to twelve with senior matriculation).[25] The wider range of study options in the composite school enabled the Vancouver board to introduce individual timetables as opposed to class timetables, and to experiment with the innovative use of majors for students.[26] In the Toronto area, the majority of secondary students experienced comprehensive programming within four-year collegiate institutes (grade nine to twelve with senior matriculation), retaining junior high schools for middle grades. This course of study included fewer options than in Vancouver, as more core academic subjects were necessary for graduation. However these core courses were accompanied by additional options in home economics, commercial subjects, business, typewriting, and shop.[27] Speaking of postwar trends in education, C.C. Goldring, Director of the Toronto Board of Education from 1951 to 1959, emphasized that the board needed "classes and schools that were organized differently to meet the varying needs."[28] For example, in 1952 alone North Toronto Collegiate Institute (C.I.), Harbord C.I., Humberside C.I., Jarvis C.I., Oakwood C.I., and Riverdale C.I. experimented with remedial programs in most of their academic subjects.[29] Although based on differing strategies, Vancouver and Toronto boards signaled that secondary schools were focal points for ensuring a breadth of moral, physical, and labour force competence.

Attempts to increase and diversify programs to include all types of students did not necessarily result in equality within the system. Although the average girl or boy was attending school for longer than ever, the majority of those who entered high school failed to graduate. Figures show that only one quarter of high school students across Canada graduated in 1956.[30] Retention rates in urban centres were typically higher than in rural areas, but only one-quarter to one-third of students were completing grade twelve in Toronto.[31] Statistics were significantly higher for British Columbia, and specifically Vancouver: approximately fifty percent of children were completing grade twelve in the early to mid-1950s.[32] Statistical variation could reflect a number of factors from the lure of employment opportunities and the socioeconomic demographics of the school population to the different types of postwar comprehensive schools.

The seemingly more academic bias of Toronto's programming may have been a tacit acknowledgement of the unrealistic promise for equality of vocational and academic programs. This point was made explicit by Ralph Tyler, University of Chicago professor of education and renowned curriculum theorist, who wrote in the 1953 issue of the British Columbia Teachers' Federation (BCTF) newsletter, *The B.C. Teacher*: "We have been doing something about getting more and more of our youth population into the school, but all too often we have failed to realize that equal opportunity is not thus assured. Many children, because of their limited background, are not receiving in the school the opportunity ... to live as intelligent citizens in a free society."[33] Tyler's remarks accurately describe the postwar secondary school in which general education was offered to one and all, yet students were still not positioned to reap its benefits equally. A survey conducted in 1957 by the Vancouver School Board showed that only thirty-one percent of grade twelve students had chosen the general program. From 1945 to 1961, only approximately twenty-seven percent of the total secondary school population in Toronto was participating in non-academic programs.[34] Even with a poor graduate rate, it is likely students remained in university entrance programs because employers, parents, and educators continued to believe in its prestige and feared the stigma attached to general and vocational streams in schools.[35]

While some have seen the development of vocational education as a moral commitment to equal opportunity, others, like American sociologist Aaron Benavot or Canadian historian Harry Smaller, have observed it as "a natural outcome of expanding democratic societies bent on integrating and socializing new citizens."[36] Smaller supports this observation by pointing out that in Ontario, most purely vocational and technical institutes were situated in working-class, immigrant, and industrial urban communities. Ron Hansen's work on composite schools explains that their growth can be attributed, in part, to the hope that the public would have confidence in a new school concept that embraced expanding notions of egalitarianism. At the same time, he argues, the concept flourished in postwar Canada when policy-makers needed to create the perception of comprehensiveness in order to temper potential public unrest over class differentials, including class-based schools.[37] It is not difficult to see how the inclusive and flexible postwar curriculum could also be viewed as a giant sorting system to funnel students along predetermined channels.

Many public commentators were not subtle in communicating their belief that general and/or vocational education was a suitable dumping ground for "unsuitable" students, namely newly arrived immigrants, working-class youth, or even the intellectually limited, who might become semi-educated workers to meet the demands of industry in an expanding capitalist society. In 1957, Dorothy Thompson, a columnist for the *Globe and Mail*, described general education as "utilitarianism at the expense of precise knowledge, and apparently assumes the average American (Canadian) child is half-moron."[38] These sentiments were echoed by education officials. George M. Weir, self-proclaimed progressive, head of the Department of Education at the University of British Columbia, and later minister of education, described the early stages of vocational training in the following manner: "There are jobs for the fit, and we are trying to fit the unfit for jobs. That is the whole purpose of our vocational training."[39]

For these educators, the paramount problem was not how to educate the masses or accommodate children of limited capacities, it was what to do about the gifted child. Educators were anxious that the intellectual elite, seen as the future leaders of the nation, not be overlooked. Discovering and developing untapped human ability was considered one of the greatest weapons in the intelligence race of the period; a race that reached its peak with Russia's Sputnik in 1957. School promoters used Soviet technological and scientific advancements as a reason to focus on developing intellectual leaders. In 1957 Dr Samuel R. Laycock, renowned educational psychologist and professor at the University of Saskatchewan, warned Toronto audiences that his latest study showed: "The gifted child in Russia is getting every opportunity to develop his talents ... Long before the end of high school [in Canada], gifted boys and girls meet a distaste for academic work. They are made to travel the pace of the average child."[40]

To focus on the intellectual elite, many educators argued, was not undemocratic. Indeed, ignoring the gifted simply for the principle of universalism was portrayed by many as unjust and dangerous. Historian Jacques Barzun from Columbia University wrote for the *University of Toronto Quarterly*: "We cannot afford to waste talent and keep ourselves at the common level of amiable dullness when

every 'people's democracy' manufactures as many *elites* as it does
classes of fighter planes."[41] Hilda Neatby, University of Saskatchewan
history professor and outspoken education critic, asserted that the
country's democracy could only be assured with the re-intellectual-
ization of schools. She believed that non-university bound students
were genetically inferior burdens on an overcrowded secondary system. In one of Neatby's many popular texts, *A Temperate Dispute*,
she cited statistics that identified seventy percent of children as inca-
pable of intellectual development past age twelve or fourteen. As a
result, educators should properly focus resources on the more promising thirty percent.[42] She argued that if this did not occur, "we
will be looking for a master race to organize us."[43] Neatby led the
Canadian campaign against progressivism. Although she did not
reject the principle of universal access to education, Neatby insisted
that education should set a high academic standard for all students
so that the fittest would survive to lead a democratic nation.[44]

Her assertion that the best kind of universalism should mean
access for all to a traditional, academically oriented education was
representative, albeit in a more tempered form, of postwar provincial policies. In the 1950s, British Columbia and Ontario appointed
royal commissions to investigate education: both invoked the principle of universality, while highlighting the need for every student to
be intellectually challenged. The 1950 Ontario Commission on
Education, chaired by Justice John A. Hope, took a moderate position somewhere between progressive and conservative ideas.[45] Leslie
Frost's Tory government primarily supported the report's traditional
elements, namely, the commissioners' lengthy declaration that:
"mastery of subject matter is the best present measure of effort and
the most promising source of satisfaction in achievement. We are not
unduly concerned that a proportion of school tasks should be hard
and unpalatable, because much of life is equally so."[46] Although
vocational programs continued to retain students, William Dunlop,
minister of education in the 1950s, concentrated his efforts on rein-
stating history and geography as separate subjects in place of the
progressive favourite of social studies, curtailing course options in
high schools, and limiting grants for extracurricular activities.[47]

As the space race intensified, so too did the focus on intellectual
leaders in British Columbia. In 1958 its Royal Commission on
Education, led by Sperrin N.F. Chant, concluded that the general
aim of the public school system should be "that of promoting the

intellectual development of the pupils."[48] Towards this goal, the
commission recommended the reclassification of school subjects so
that more time would be devoted to the "central" subjects of English
and math and less time "wasted" on art and home economics. It also
recommended that teaching techniques, like the project method,
should only supplement external examinations and competition in
the classroom.[49] Almost all the Chant recommendations were implemented in some form or another by the minister of education, Leslie
Peterson, in the early 1960s.[50]

Most educational authorities were faithful to a conservative conception of democracy – the promise of universality, but limited by
the necessity for intellectual elite. The concept of a democratic curriculum was for most prominent postwar critics of education based
on equality of access and not equality of opportunity.[51] Secondary
schools represented an investment in human capital that promised
successful competition in the volatile postwar world. The effects of
economics on school objectives were highly visible. Population
increases and a teacher shortage put resources at a premium.[52] As
Goldring noted in a 1959 *Globe and Mail* article, educators faced
with "overcrowding schools and all types of abilities" had to focus
on the idea of the "same opportunity rather than equality of opportunity in terms of ability or need."[53] A more academic curriculum
could promise equality at more affordable costs while in fact favour-
ing those pupils who were intellectually and otherwise gifted by reason of class, gender, and ethnicity.

"DEMOCRATIC" VALUES

In addition to curriculum reconstruction, the development of character was a critical postwar educational objective. The comprehensive secondary school would expand professedly progressive services
and courses that would provide social, physical, and emotional guidance for the "whole child." The character-building function was
intended both to assist students' personal development and to teach
them responsible civic choices. Instruction of democratic values
promised personal and national freedom. For that reason, school
officials placed the objective of character education on par with
intellectual stimulation in their agenda for educational democracy.

This was the message of William F. Russell, the president of
Columbia University Teachers' College, in an address to the Toronto

chapter of the Ontario Secondary School Teachers' Federation
(OSSTF) in 1950. He started by arguing that freedom was "not only
confronted by hostile armed forces," but in seemingly peaceful times
"by that sly enemy within and without – Communism."[54] In Russell's
opinion, protection of democracy began with educators' eliminating
the "great gap between knowledge and conduct."[55] Familiarizing students with the knowledge of their rights and responsibilities as citizens within a democracy was not enough. Students had to learn how
to perform their citizenship duties according to the nation's culture.
The patriotic imperative for teaching democratic values informed the
1951 article written by Paul R. Hanna, Professor of Education at
Stanford University and a specialist in the area of social studies, for
The B.C. Teacher. As he explained: "In a divided world, where the
totalitarian governments are effectively using education to indoctrinate for authoritarian values and to immunize against democratic
values, the democracies have no alternative except to do a fundamentally better job of preserving and improving our way of life."[56]

Guidance programs were a specific manifestation of efforts to provide morally grounded and productive curriculum and life choices.
Such services had been for the most part an incidental and nebulous
part of school life for almost two decades prior to 1945.[57] Not until
the postwar period did school officials formally organize guidance
departments and services in secondary schools across the country.
These programs were intended to address public concern that youth
were rejecting traditional values. Public expressions of fear escalated
over a supposed rise in juvenile delinquency due to inferior wartime
mothering, an increasingly consumer-oriented culture, and exposure
to communist sentiments.[58] Guidance counselling was therefore central to a postwar reconstruction agenda to restore order and a sense
of normality. There was no better time or place to indoctrinate
"proper" character than sites where almost all teens spent a number
of their formative years. Dr Jack Griffin, first president of the
Canadian Mental Heath Association, explained that the "child is in
a relatively controlled environment for several hours each day and
the possibilities of building in him sound emotional habits and attitudes as well as good social relationships are unexcelled."[59] Offering
services ranging from individual counselling to aptitude studies, the
secondary school began assuming the functions of other social institutions in order to help students function better in society.[60]

By the early 1950s, guidance services were implemented in the comprehensive Toronto secondary schools through Attendance Departments, complemented by Child Adjustment Services and Child Guidance Clinics. The Attendance Department assisted 5,943 children and parents in 1951, up by twenty-two percent from the previous year.[61] According to Edward Davidson, the chairman of the Toronto Board of Education, secondary schools had fully implemented guidance services by the end of the decade. He outlined the mounting work of the Attendance Department, including visits to truants' homes to "improve trouble which may be financial, psychological, physical and environmental" and contributing to a clothing centre for students who lacked "adequate attire."[62] Guidance programs were expanded to address reports of growing absenteeism, parental neglect, juvenile employment, delinquent behaviour, and health problems.[63] British Columbia started formally addressing these same issues with the inception in 1944 of the Division of Educational and Vocational Guidance within the Department of Education. This division in the 1948–49 school year alone approved thirty-four counselling schemes for the province.[64] Support for counselling included the distribution of guidance materials, bursaries for secondary school in-service training, and studies on pupils' employment aptitudes. Additionally, under its own initiative in 1955, the Vancouver board co-ordinated with the Department of National Health and Welfare and local secondary schools to establish training programs for "special counsellors" who would assist teachers with designated problem pupils.[65]

Such social services were imbued with the pro-active, scientific "expertise" of psychologists. Psychologists' claims to specialized knowledge of children's development guaranteed them a primary place in character training.[66] The "scientific" methods of psychologists, rather than the subjectivity of teacher observation, were incorporated into postwar schools as a progressive and democratic method to enable fair and accurate measure of student maturity. Longstanding faith in science's ability to measure and control human behaviour soared in the postwar search for guarantees in an age of uncertainty. The resurgence of scientific testing came despite increased post-Holocaust public skepticism to claims to a hereditary basis of character and intelligence. Toronto board officials certainly considered the mental health community to be their partners in producing proper

citizens. The board took over Child Adjustment Services from the
Department of Public Health in 1951, and consequently began to
establish permanent psychological services for secondary pupils.[67]
By 1954, the board reported regular visits by psychologists to service
"problem children" and train teachers to administer group intelligence tests.[68] By the end of the 1950s, Dr Stogdill, a psychologist
working with the Toronto board, reported to a newspaper that the
heavier load on the child adjustment services staff necessitated hiring
more mental health specialists for secondary schools.[69]

Psychologists flourished in Vancouver secondary schools. Mental
testing had an exceptionally strong presence in British Columbia's
schools, and was established as early as progressives Harold Putnam
and George Weir's 1925 *Survey of the School System*. That report
recommended that a Bureau of Measurements be set up to conduct
some of the first standardized intelligence testing in Canada. By year
ten of the Division of Tests, Standards, and Research, which replaced
the Bureau, over 500,000 achievement tests and aptitude tests had
been conducted.[70] While tests were explicitly designed to differentiate the bright from the slow, supporters believed they also served to
give reliable guidance to moral worth. Weir asserted that: "dullness
and moral worth are related almost as closely as twin brothers."[71]
Weir made regular pronouncements, in line with progressive educator and American eugenicist Edward L. Thorndike, that intelligence,
nationality, and socioeconomic background correlated positively. He
concluded that the most intelligent and moral were from middle-
class families of British ancestry. While psychologists presented testing as an instrument to demystify the developmental needs of each
student, those needs were set within the bounds of race, culture,
and class. Mona Gleason cites, by way of example, poor scores on
Stanford intelligence tests given to interned Japanese students of
British Columbia as legitimating educators' insistence on assimila-
tion through the use of English.[72] Gleason further notes that the
emphasis of psychologists "on the satisfaction of children's needs for
affection, belonging, independence, social approval," instead of providing justification for diversity and self-expression, lent itself to the
demands of social authorities for the production of an "obedient,
industrious, and happy" citizenry.[73]

The affirmation of traditional racial, class, and gender boundaries
was a clear part of the character-education agenda of Toronto and
Vancouver secondary schools. Educators expressed concern that in

the mass secondary-school age, students would neither learn nor accept their appropriate social position. Middle-class youth, particularly males, symbolized hope and prosperity because of their potential for scholastic achievements and professional careers.[74] By contrast, working-class adolescents, and especially ethnic minorities coming from seemingly culturally impoverished homes, conjured up the specter of delinquency and required a moral discipline rather different than their class and racial superiors.[75] Part of citizenship training in schools, therefore, was teaching all students "responsible" behaviour that varied according to their appropriate positions in society. H.L. Campbell revealed this philosophy in a 1952 lecture. He indicated that without training "responsible citizens who seek the common welfare rather than selfish goals," modern universal education may reach a point in which all are educated for white-collar work and "no youth are willing to do necessary physical work of the world."[76] Fundamental values of integrity and service to others needed to be taught to guarantee class and gender as well: "will young women with high school education be content to marry and raise families on a farm?"[77] To address these concerns, Toronto and Vancouver educators complemented greater social services with more formal and informal classes in the lessons of normative citizenship.

Like discussions of the aims of guidance in schools, talk of instilling "democratic" values in Canadian youth through revised course offerings was most often steeped in vague language of liberation. Both the Toronto and Vancouver school boards increased their social studies course options to include subjects from history and geography to law, economics, and political science. The importance of such courses is indicated by the fact that the number of social studies credits required for graduation, notwithstanding electives, was equal to mathematics in both school systems. The overall purpose of social studies courses in Toronto and Vancouver was similar and not surprisingly, explicitly intended to invoke patriotism, skepticism regarding left-wing propaganda, a sense of brotherhood within the country and the world, respect for law, and acquisition of such personal habits as courtesy and neatness.

One innovative course for Vancouver secondary schools provides some insight into the specific agenda for postwar reconstruction of "normality." In the early 1950s, British Columbia created a new course entitled *Effective Living* that was implemented for grades ten to twelve. In support of its goal of open minds, the course encouraged question and answer and discussion and personal reflection, rather than traditional memorization or recitation. All course units, including Personality, Family, and Community Health, underscored "developing a stable heterosexual pattern," "developing habits of constancy and loyalty," and "adjusting to accepted customs and conventions."[78] The course guide offered such leading questions as "Why is wearing the right dress a mark of maturity?"; "I spend every cent I can. Society won't let me starve. Is this a mature attitude?"; "What is the importance of religion to happiness in life and in marriage?"[79] Toronto schools would not offer a similar course until the 1960s, but did address these units within their 1942 social studies curriculum revisions, particularly in Physical Education and Health.[80] From establishing the nuclear family to becoming a mature worker, social studies courses clearly differentiated proper and improper citizenship.

Educational historians have particularly noted lessons in implicit racial superiority within social studies courses. Timothy Stanley argues that by 1925, school textbooks had contributed toward British Columbia becoming a white supremacist society. He demonstrates that geography and history texts transmitted imperialist and racist ideas of a province born out of white man's progress over the morally depraved Asian and First Nations "Others."[81] José Igartua has undertaken a similar study for Ontario, but specifically addressing the 1940s and '50s. Approved history texts, namely George W. Brown's *Building a Canadian Nation* (1942) and Arthur Lower's *Canada: A Nation and How It Came to Be* (1948), detail how a hierarchy of the races was a basic component of secondary school texts. Igartua argues that these texts represent the British as the authors of freedom and democracy, fighting off threats to the birth of Canada, namely Aboriginal and French peoples.[82] Social studies courses, like the new social services of the postwar secondary school, thus served disciplining, limiting, and sorting functions.

While social studies is most often given the greatest attention by citizenship scholars, character education pervaded informal activities. For example, lessons in the reaffirmation of the nuclear family were central to the secondary school environment in both cities. Joy Parr concludes that authorities considered the disruption of the nuclear family to be a cause for unrest and it thus garnered a great deal of attention in the postwar years. She argues that legal heterosexual coupling, with the middle-class father as breadwinner, was a national metaphor for a strong consumer economy, cohesive and peaceful relations, and thus a defense against Communism.[83] Societal trends fed fears of social breakdown. Particularly worrying were veterans coming back mentally scarred from fighting, mothers entering paid labour in greater numbers than any previous peacetime period, increasing numbers of urban immigrant and working-class families, and divorce rates steadily rising from 88.9 per 100,000 married persons ages fifteen or older in 1951 to 124.3 in 1968.[84] No wonder the moral backbones of Canadian youth needed stiffening.

According to A.D. Flowers, a principal in British Columbia writing in a Vancouver newspaper, children needed to learn "more than just reading, writing and arithmetic. Boys had to learn how to be boys, and girls had to be taught how to be ladies."[85] Vancouver school reports made special mention of their ladies' fashion shows to exhibit the great work of home economics, the strength of their future nurses' and teachers' clubs that would direct unmarried girls into admirable professions, as well as mother-daughter and father-son evenings to solidify gender identification. Toronto school board reports highlighted night classes in homemaking, domestic arts classes for immigrant women, and more coeducational sports, like square dancing and badminton.[86] This latter program was part of a wider array of secondary school offerings in both cities, including marital classes, which were intended to foster nuclear families. William Blatz, the director of the Institute for Child Study at the University of Toronto, made this point when he recommended that teenagers mingle more so they "can sublimate their sex appetite into directions which will aid them to maintain the ideals of chastity and faithfulness which our social culture considers to be essential."[87]

Christian ideals underpinned educators' encouragement of students towards middle-class, domestic goals.[88] These goals provided a bulwark against godlessness, symbolized by the potentially harmful influences of a burgeoning popular culture, including homoerotic crime comics and salacious movies starring James Dean and Marilyn Monroe.[89] While materialism encouraged the growth of capitalism, and its offerings of the middle-class life, social authorities worried that youth would become self-indulgent or unproductive without Christian discipline. A survey conducted by the Canadian Youth Commission in the mid-1940s indicated that most young women and men were aware of and even shared educators' concerns. They agreed that while schools taught them important subjects and developed thinking abilities, they were less convinced that they had

suitable learning in citizenship, specifically, sufficient preparation for
the wise use of their leisure time.[90]

J.G. Althouse, acting in his role as Chief Director of Education for
Toronto schools, appealed to board members, early in 1950, to
address the proper use of youth's leisure time. He noted that prior to
depression and wars the West had been lulled "into a false sense of
security" based on the "assumption that knowledge meant wis-
dom."[91] With the threat to democracy, he asserted, children understood that freedom was not a natural state. Youth's years should be
spent in practicing self-discipline, greater human understanding, and
religion.[92] Althouse was reaffirming a policy for religious instruction
that had been implemented in elementary schools since 1944. At
that time, Ontario Premier George Drew's Conservative government
introduced the "Drew Regulation," which legislated two half-hour
periods of religious instruction per week in public schools. This
instruction was under consideration for secondary schools upon recommendation by the Hope Commission in 1950. During the postwar period, religious exercises, inclusive of a scripture reading,
repetition of the Ten Commandments at least once a week and the
Lord's Prayer daily, and memorization of selected Bible passages,
opened each secondary school day.[93]

Spirituality, as a replacement for worshipping material progress,
would also be a central lesson for Vancouver secondary students. An
early call for religious instruction was again progressives Weir and
Putnam. Their *Survey of the School System* proposed the option of
Bible study in public schools to compensate for insufficient character
training in other social institutions.[94] After sectarian compromise,
Bible study was approved as an extramural course in 1941 for grade
nine to twelve students.[95] The course rationale stressed personal
enlightenment motivating students towards social obligations of
harmonious living. By 1942, the British Columbia School Trustees
Association persuaded the education minister H.G.T. Perry to have
schools post the Ten Commandments in "prominent locations."[96]
Two years later he would pass legislation to open the school day
with Bible readings followed by recitation of the Lord's Prayer.[97]
Christianity was emphasized as being part of good citizenship. The
centrality of mainstream Christianity was certainly the message for
minority students, including Doukhobor and Aboriginal youth, who
were being integrated in the British Columbia school system in the
postwar period.[98] For all youth, the central tenets of "democratic"

citizenship were clear: students were to adhere to Christian ethics, uplift traditional family values, and realize the potential contribution of their social status.

The difference between those educators who would claim progressive or traditional alliances was not so much the substance of these values but rather the method of their transmission. For the healthy psychological and social development of students, progressive adherents supported the introduction of social studies courses, albeit emphasizing methods of discussion, rather than rote learning. They saw school as a critical part of the increasingly wide social safety net, inclusive of healthcare initiatives and unemployment provisions, which came to characterize Canada in the postwar period. It was this extra responsibility that concerned conservative educators. Hilda Neatby acknowledged that citizenship training was admirable in so far as it did not detract from academic goals.[99] This was the tone of a series of editorials in local and national newspapers in the postwar period. In 1958, for example, Philip Deane of the *Globe and Mail* extensively critiqued secondary schools in the United States in an article entitled "Character, Not Missiles, Is the Challenge." Citing the work of American historian Arthur Bestor, well-known education critique and author of the *Educational Wastelands: The Retreat from Learning in Our Public Schools* (1953), Deane blamed schools offering girls courses in "marital adjustment" for creating ignorant students.[100]

Most educators did not assert an either/or choice between education for life adjustment or knowledge of traditional subjects. Political moderates may have agreed that schools were becoming burdened with new responsibilities, yet approved of helping children to develop wholesome human relationships.[101] While Toronto and Vancouver schools embraced direct methods of character education, a focus was also placed on indirect, less costly methods, including dress codes, extracurricular activities, Home and School or Parent Teacher organizations, student involvement with volunteer organizations and industry, and, most importantly, exposure to teachers of good character.[102] Character training, regardless of method, encompassed professedly progressive aims for personal development and contribution towards a broadening social safety net. Yet, at a time when transgressions of normality were believed to threaten democracy, these aims were firmly and conservatively rooted in pre-war patterns of gender, class, and racial hierarchies.

ORGANIZING FOR "DEMOCRACY"

Autocratic pedantry was out of fashion in the postwar years. Educators rationalized the trend towards decentralized decision-making powers as both a progressive step towards equality and a necessary lesson in self-sufficiency. Students need not become dependent on a welfare nation. In keeping with that rationale, most postwar educators agreed that the secondary education system needed to be reorganized as a laboratory for participatory democracy. School officials needed to redistribute power so that school communities, teachers, students, parents, and administrators from the rural and urban regions could meaningfully contribute to educational and national betterment.

Such sentiments were international in scope, according to the editors of The B.C. Teacher and its sister newsletter of the OSSTF, The Bulletin. Both extensively covered British conferences and reports on the role of education in the making of national democracy. A February 1951 issue of The Bulletin that detailed a British report on the best forms of school organization was typical.[103] The authors presented three potential structures for the secondary school. The first was factory-like, a place in which students processed facts like widgets before being spit mechanically into the work world. This model treated students as automatons and disregarded their need to cultivate personal relationships. The second model, the happy family, focused on the pursuit of happiness for all school members. While the authors agreed that personal fulfillment is a positive goal, they argued that true democracy could not exist unless citizens are motivated by a broader purpose. The third model, the democratic school, focused on members taking individual responsibility to enrich the entire community. In such an ideal school, relationships among staff and students, and staff and administrators, and administrators and political officials were to be marked by consultation and mutual respect. The environment was not authoritarian, but rather enabled choice, individuality, and teamwork. The authors concluded that: "Only experience of life in a democratic school community can give young people the values they need and the understanding upon which to build full and happy personal lives."[104]

If the ideals of democratic partnership were to be realized, one of the first issues for Canadian educators was regional equality. This was one premise behind the postwar trend toward larger school districts. Consolidation promised more adequate funding and facilities to outlying areas.[105] Popular demand for equitable distribution of resources had swept Canada for years prior to the war as better roads, proliferation of motorized cars, the mechanization of farm work, and increased technical education lessened the rural and urban divide. Provincial authorities intervened to centralize education funding so that taxes would be collected and redistributed more evenly, based on the needs of districts. By the mid-1950s, provincial grants across Canada started to climb as some 780 larger boards amalgamated 16,000 smaller boards.[106] According to the Superintendent of Education in British Columbia, J.F.K. English, the greatest advantage of consolidation was "the contribution of the larger unit to social living. Because of the facilities offered by the larger unit for secondary education, rural and urban children mix readily, and social barriers are broken down."[107]

Change came quickly and broadly in 1944 British Columbia, when the provincial government appointed Dr Maxwell A. Cameron, an education professor at the University of British Columbia, to be a one-man commission of inquiry on financial and administrative reform.[108] Cameron recommended the creation of seventy-four large districts out of an original 650.[109] The new entities would be financed by a basic district rate of taxation, with provincial grants to cover a share of total costs that "would always be well over half."[110] Grants that seemed generous in 1945, however, quickly became inadequate when inflation, birthrates, and capital expenditure costs all rose. After an investigation by H.L. Campbell in 1955, a revised formula increased school districts to eighty-two and, more importantly, replaced Cameron's fixed grants with a diversified plan that addressed local needs for capital building costs and transportation expenses.[111]

Ontario's school consolidation plans were more haphazard and slower than British Columbia's. During the 1943 election, Conservative leader George Drew, in an attempt to stave off a left-wing Co-operative Commonwealth Federation (CCF) victory, guaranteed the provincial assumption of fifty percent of school taxes.[112] Again postwar inflation, a population boom, and an increase in capital projects meant that provincial grants would slip to below thirty percent of total costs for some school areas.[113] Larger school districts were the answer to spiraling costs. Not until a Hope Commission recommendation in 1950, however, did some 536 large regional boards voluntarily replace 3,465 local administrative units.[114]

Some educators and communities resisted centralization schemes, arguing that they abolished local authority and identities while not necessarily erasing financial disparities.[115] To justify consolidation, provincial authorities advocated strong local controls. For example, Cameron advocated that local residents elect their own school trustees, who would work directly with the province through district superintendents to determine allocation of resources, staffing decisions, and priorities for programming.[116] The British Columbia Teachers' Federation supported this revised structure in a 1959 brief to the Royal Commission on Education: "As school boards assume policy-making responsibility and cease to be primarily executors of policy made in [the provincial capital of] Victoria, they may be expected to attract to their membership outstanding, community-minded citizens."[117] Similarly, the Hope Commission argued that amalgamated boards should assume more decision-making powers over standards of teaching, school management routines, and selection of curriculum materials.[118] J.G. Althouse spoke of the delicate, yet critical, relationship between local and central authorities when implementing new reforms: "Forward steps in Ontario education are taken when a number of communities become interested in new phases of educational service ... Our reforms march forward on a ragged front ... [but] they march forward with the informed understanding and active support of the people who maintain and patronize the schools."[119]

One major initiative to produce a smoother and clearly democratic partnership between local and central authorities was a postwar change in the conception of supervision. In particular, inspectors in Toronto and Vancouver shifted from the older arm's-length critical assessors to locally employed collegial assistants. As new, less qualified teachers were responding to the demand for their services, inspectors could not provide the necessary personalized assistance. Ideal supervision was re-conceptualized as democratic, decentralized, and collaborative. In 1956, G.E. Flower, the Director of the Canadian Education Association's Kellogg Project in Educational Leadership, described the transformation. Under the old system the provincial government would send out inspectors to ensure that local boards were using grant money properly, following all school regulations, such as attendance laws, and following the prescribed course of studies, particularly judging the competence of teachers.[120] With the creation of larger school districts, inspectors in those areas no longer skipped from board to board auditing standards. Rather, larger districts like Toronto and Vancouver were granted permission by the province to employ their own inspectors.[121] In theory, these new inspectors, being locally appointed, would be able to better address community needs while ensuring provincial standards. J.F.K. English of British Columbia described the inspectors, whose title in that province was changed to district superintendents of schools in 1958, as working "in a closer relationship with school boards ... [with] more administrative work in addition to their special responsibility, which is the supervision of instruction in the schools."[122] While inspectors/superintendents worked in an executive capacity, typically with due respect from trustees and teachers, they were no longer the locus of provincial power. Instead, according to the Public School Acts of Ontario (1954) and British Columbia (1958), the city boards of Toronto and Vancouver would use inspectors/superintendents in their new administrative capacity: to evaluate and record the organizational and instructional quality of a school district and, where necessary, provide recommendations for change to maintain provincial standards.[123]

Given the extra duties of administration for the local inspector, there was less time remaining for instructional supervision.[124] Inspectors required the growing support of assistant supervisors, grade consultants, and directors of instruction. Vancouver appointed four teachers in 1955 to the newly created position of "teacher-consultant." Teacher-consultants, who became province-wide with the Public Schools Act of 1958, were meant to assist teachers, particularly those at the probationary stage, with their instructional methods.[125] For Ontario, according to the Supervision and Inspection Committee of the OSSTF, it was the school staff, and particularly the heads of departments, who took on the duty of regular peer supervision.[126] School officials in both provinces looked to the principal for internal school supervision. In an article entitled "The New Principal," G.E. Flower explained that postwar Canadian officials had borrowed from the British model of the principal as headmaster.[127] As a master-teacher in close daily contact with other teachers, pupils, and the community, the principal was ideally suited to be an instructional leader rather than an administrative coordinator. Local principals' associations developed, and university summer courses on principalship thrived, in efforts to address the previously overlooked role of the principal on the supervisory team.[128]

Whether principal, department head, teacher consultant, inspector, or superintendent, the expected form of supervision in the postwar secondary school had changed from judgment and enforcement to a more democratic process of collaborative review for improved instruction. C.W. Booth, Deputy Minister of Education for Ontario, spoke to the revised aims in supervision at a national level in the September 1959 issue of *Canadian Education*. Booth argued that supervision had changed from "cold, critical analysis imposed from above to the present friendly, sympathetic, co-operative appraisal of daily work by supervisor and teacher for the benefit of teacher and pupils alike."[129] The prime purpose, he insisted, was to prompt professional self-study and regulation. He concluded that: "Supervision at its best is a co-operative project, involving pupils, teachers, department heads, principals, superintendents, and inspectors – all working together and giving their best for the school, the community, and the nation."[130] But while the rhetoric of the period often managed to frame supervision as democracy in process, stories of supervision were not always that innocuous. Boards and teachers spoke of inspectors who remained over-authoritarian, especially in rural areas where they had more power, trustees who blacklisted teachers from certain districts, and principals who withheld teachers' increment pay with overly critical written reports.[131] Educators treated these issues as scandalous when they found their way to newspapers, because excessive supervision disregarded one principle of participatory democracy; a sense of autonomy. As British educator Sir Arthur Binns stated at a Principals' Conference held at the University of British Columbia in 1958, "You can never make professional people out of men and women who merely or even mainly carry out the orders of other people."[132]

The need for autonomy in a substantive educational democracy carried over from the re-conception of supervision to curriculum reforms. The postwar years saw growth in the participation of teachers, and even lay groups, in the development of curriculum. If teachers were required to transmit an increasingly complex program of study, and take responsibility for making this knowledge fit each student, then they needed to be trained participants in curriculum development. It no longer sufficed for one or two "experts" who were removed from the classroom to dictate materials for teachers to follow.[133] While both the initial writing of course studies and their final approval remained in the hands of provincial experts,

Departments of Education across the country were increasingly willing to consider the desirability of teacher and lay representation on general curriculum policy and procedure committees, and to a greater extent on subject committees to revise or prepare courses of study and materials.[134]

Faith in democratic procedures for curriculum-building found some room in the policies of Ontario. In 1949, the newly appointed Tory minister of education, Dana Porter, announced the "Porter Plan."[135] Porter was assisted by the head of the Ministry of Education's curriculum branch, Stanley Watson, a rare self-proclaimed progressive in Ontario political circles.[136] A significant component of the plan was a relatively wide divestment of power to school communities. The Department of Education, through coordinating committees, provided suggested courses of study to local committees who could disregard them and create their own.[137] Furthermore, province-mandated departmental examinations, except for Senior Matriculation, were abolished, which freed school staff to determine their own course assessments.[138] The process for curriculum development also underwent reconstruction. In addition to the standard input of superintendents, principals, and teacher-training personnel, curriculum committees would have official representation from Home and School Associations and the Ontario Teachers' Federation (OTF).[139] The OTF had a uniquely co-operative relationship for a teachers' federation with provincial authorities in this period, which provided for strong leadership from teachers in curriculum design. Over 5,000 teachers on 139 local curriculum development committees revised more than 1,400 courses in 129 areas.[140] The Department of Education encouraged teachers' participation: "the acceptance of the responsibility for curriculum revision provides teachers with an opportunity to reach their true professional status ... group participation will give teachers practice in those democratic techniques and procedures ... It will afford the opportunity for the development of democratic leadership."[141]

Within a year of this statement, Porter left his position with the Ministry to pursue leadership of the provincial Tory party. His replacement, W.J. Dunlop, did not see curriculum reforms as a priority. By the end of the decade, only twelve committees remained and only eighteen percent of teachers participated.[142] Education leaders in British Columbia shared Dunlop's underlying skepticism about the program. While school officials in the province sought curriculum feedback from teachers and lay groups, they did not call for the same widespread consultation and local powers. According to H.L. Campbell, the British Columbia government believed that new teachers with lower professional qualifications lacked the ability to decide independently on courses of study.[143] Undeterred by rebuffs, the BCTF wanted direct representation on the province's Central Curriculum Committee in 1948.[144] Despite being guaranteed only consideration of representation, the federation and its teachers continued to participate in some curriculum committees, albeit in relatively low numbers compared to Ontario. Approximately 125 teachers worked on various standing and advisory curriculum committees in 1958.[145] In 1961 the Department of Education formally recognized the value of their contributions and granted the federation three places on newly established secondary and elementary Professional Curriculum Committees.[146]

Although central authority, expressed through prescribed content and inspections, would continue to characterize the postwar secondary school, officials supported a shift in policy that encouraged participation by an increasing number in the education community. Movement toward democratic reorganization, or at least the rhetoric of democratic administration, resembled for some educators, such as Stanley Watson of Ontario and G.E. Flower of British Columbia, a Deweyan model: educators' co-ordination of experiences to stimulate change by and in the best interest of those whom the changes affected. Flower supported the creation of an environment "to stimulate, to encourage, to assist, to guide, and even to direct teachers so that they will experience the maximum professional development and hence make available to their pupils the richest possible learning experiences."[147] Most school officials who supported such reform did not speak directly of progressive influences. Instead, they made the case for system-wide democratic procedures based on their cost-efficiency and productivity. After all, the consolidation of schools was a money-saver, as was the extracurricular, voluntary participation of teachers in curriculum-planning. Some academics and political officials proffered an even more conservative ideological justification: practices in participatory democracy, which offered elements of local autonomy and space for individual voices in administrative matters, rightly discouraged citizens from dependence on the state. They warned that without democratic reforms, the secondary school might produce citizens who were reliant on the welfare of government-supported education and this might lead to a welfare nation.

This conservative message was the foundation of Frank MacKinnon's widely read texts on education, history, and governance in Canada. At the time principal of Prince of Wales College (later the University of Prince Edward Island), he was well known within political and administrative arenas of education. In *The Politics of Education*, MacKinnon wrote that "democracy itself is on trial" because the state was simply telling schools how to educate, and doing so according to fads.[148] He argued that the refusal of political authorities to grant teachers and administrators enough control over education resembled a totalitarian regime.[149] He asserted that there would be greater efficiency if teachers were not forced to adopt the duties of administrators or "play politics," but simply had the "freedom to teach."[150] MacKinnon was not arguing for each person to have decision-making powers within the school. Rather, each member of the school should concentrate on their specific function in the system. MacKinnon wanted teachers to be free from interruptions by inspectors and bureaucratic duties like heavy paperwork, so that they could focus on the academic training of young people. If not, he argued, the state would continue to dominate; teachers and students would get into the habit of receiving rather than getting, and expecting rather than doing.[151]

Peoples' dependency on the state, according to MacKinnon, was sparked by undemocratic school organization and was hazardous to teachers and students. It was, thus, the teachers' responsibility to not only protect their rights within the school, but to ensure democratic rights in their classrooms. Teachers could only teach effectively if they inspired self-discipline. Such arguments in favour of autonomy influenced instructional methods in postwar secondary schools. The Toronto board experimented with the implementation of language labs for French courses, to allow girls and boys to follow their own pace of study along with dictation cassettes.[152] The Vancouver board proudly announced that their straps were locked away and discipline through "man-to-man" talks was the modern approach that got results from teenagers.[153] Secondary schools in both cities used workshop techniques and debating in social studies classes to encourage students to form their own political opinions. In addition, towards the end of the period, Vancouver and Toronto schools experimented with television programming, provided by the

Canadian Broadcasting Company, to motivate students to develop their own interpretation of the content provided in the classroom.[154] According to postwar psychologists, healthy adolescents could only develop within a democratic setting that enabled them to practice inner discipline; they needed to have freedom in school to make their own choices and mistakes. George Roberts, a Durham Board principal and past president of the OSSTF and OTF, explained to secondary teachers in the 1959 issue of *The Bulletin* that flexibility could result in wrong decisions by students, but that: "This, we are told, is a lesson in responsibility for democratic choice, and a risk that must be taken."[155]

School officials' desire for individuality within educational democracy fit snugly with a conservative vision of a productive citizenry that served, rather than burdened, the state. Roberts warned: "'joyriders' are perhaps the greatest obstacle in the way of one of the teacher's major objectives: the nurturing of the individualist in the age of conformity."[156] It was not simply the health of the student but rather the health of the democratic nation that concerned Roberts and many other educators. Roberts worried that Canadian schools were following the trend of the United States where "having created a welfare state of the body, they are now trying to create a welfare state of the mind."[157] Roberts and other conservative critics, including MacKinnon, who referred to education as the new "social service," were also concerned with the government's social security initiatives during the postwar period, such as health insurance, unemployment insurance, and workmen's compensation. While more broadly based welfarism could be interpreted as protective measures for labour, the state provided only those concessions that would thwart socialist activities and secure a labour force fundamental to the Fordist regime of accumulation.[158] As this chapter has suggested, schools were to ensure that each person made the right choices to contribute as good citizens to the "democratic" nation.

Educational officials worked to produce secondary schools in the name of democracy, a term that embodied diverse values. In the fear-ridden postwar years, few rejected the values that the term conjured up in the minds of the public: freedom, equality, autonomy, and order. But what did "democracy" really offer for the postwar educational agenda? Democratic objectives, from national to more localized political and administrative discourses, and inclusive of both progressive and traditional theories of learning, produced an educational agenda that solidified, more than it disrupted, pre-war patterns of normality. The ideal citizen was reaffirmed through postwar secondary schooling as white, middle-class, and heterosexual. The conservative invocation of citizenship was often masked in the fluidity and multiplicity of language for democratic values, relations, and practices in secondary education. A closer examination of the assumptions and practices that underlay such discussions reveals that potentially democratic visions were rife with hierarchical, bureaucratic, and autocratic methods designed to "lead and direct an adequately socialized majority."[159] Universally accessible education was envisioned as providing equality of access but not of opportunity. Moral stability through character education provided for personal growth but always within the bounds of traditional values. The secondary school was a laboratory for practical democracy which provided for individuality and autonomy; it was intended to teach students an inner discipline that was to guarantee social stability. This critical examination of educational democracy illustrates that the concept itself is at once identifiable and clear, but also unstable, contradictory, and at times, elusive.

The next chapters will suggest what the conflicted message of educational democracy meant in classrooms. In particular, they will explore what the gendered implications were for the agents of its implementation. What did freedom, morality, and autonomy actually offer to women teachers in the postwar secondary schools of Toronto and Vancouver?

"Democratic" Knowledge, Teacher Professionalism, and the Female "Weak Link"

The professional standards set for postwar teachers implied that any committed and properly trained individual could further democracy. The growing body of feminist research has refuted such easy assumptions, arguing that liberal discourse, such as that in postwar education circles, marginalizes egalitarian principles of professionalism.[1] Political theorist Diana Coole explains that reason is the idealized crux of liberal thought. It endows the holder with power to participate in Western democracy. In European philosophical tradition and political theory, only man can possess reason. Western thought, Coole argues, continues to assert gendered hierarchies of knowledge and citizenship, "mind over body, culture over nature, reason over emotion, order over chaos," within which the feminine is a metaphor for the lesser terms.[2] The knowledge-bearing, rational, and autonomous subject is conflated with dominant notions of masculinity, and the feminine "Other" conflated with subjectivity and emotionality. Women are, as Lorenne M.G. Clark suggests, in the "ontological basement" of political life.[3] Carole Pateman's work on the "fraternal pact" in the public sphere stresses that liberal discourse positions woman far from the disembodied and reasonable citizen, symbolized through the freedom-fighter male soldier. Ironically enough, given assumptions regarding woman's lesser capacity for violence, she is conceptualized as a threat to social order.[4] Within this essentialist binary, only men can transcend personal interests to legitimately participate in and uphold orderly public politics.

At least in theoretical terms, the ability to reproduce or teach curriculum productive of democratic citizens is predicated upon this gender dualism. This is Jo-Anne Dillabough's primary point as she explores how Enlightenment concepts have re-emerged in the modern narratives of teachers, and diminished the view of women as professionals.[5] She argues that contemporary British educational discourses present "neutral" representations of teachers in which women are free and equal to men in their capacity for independent educational practice within a liberal democracy. Simultaneously, however, governing authorities deem seemingly feminine characteristics of personal reflexivity, authenticity, and sociability as ineffectual. A "good" teacher becomes a technician of state-determined standardized outputs, not a socially engaged critical reformer. Dominant masculinist models of autonomous and politically detached subjects denote success. Drawing on the work of Valerie Walkerdine and Helen Lucey, Dillabough notes, "it is still the bourgeois male teacher or student who is honoured with the title of 'rational being' in the purest sense ... women teachers and female students cannot possess knowledge in their own right because they are viewed as moral vessels through which liberal democracy and the rational society are cultivated."[6] The structure of both teaching and professionalism has located women teachers as symbolic of the private sphere, unable to fulfill the rational ideal for liberal democratic citizenship. At the same time, women teachers, positioned as mothers in the school and as guardians of the nation, must support the very democratic principles that underlie their inferiority to men teachers.[7] This, Dillabough suggests, "leads to women's exclusion from the formal language of teacher professionalism, yet simultaneously defines their inclusion on the basis of female subordination."[8]

Feminist scholars of women teachers' identity formation have examined the relationship between knowledge production and gender social construction through a contemporary lens. With the notable exception of Walkerdine and Lucey, few have explored the historical evolution of this relationship. The contractions between the ideals of knowledge production and the gendered codes of professionalism can readily be detected in postwar Toronto and Vancouver. Canada required instructors who gained and transmitted expert knowledge to technical, vocational, and academically streamed students. Teachers were to be instrumental actors for "democratic" state goals. As outlined in the last chapter, this meant producing technologically literate workers for capitalist accumulation and citizens with higher-order rationality for Western supremacy. This orientation came at the expense of a broader democratic purpose for developing students' unique strengths. It also disadvantaged socially engaged, reflexive teachers.

This chapter demonstrates how women teachers, like students who were sorted in the new "democratic" curriculum that devalued non-academic streams, were classified as gendered in their capacity for academic/rational knowledge. Most educators did not correlate secondary teachers' competency with "feminine" capabilities such as an effective connection with children or appreciation of learning theories. Rather, in the era of the space race and faith in scientific expertise, teachers were evaluated according to technical functionalism, measurable student achievement, and objective standards of practice that took masculinist advantage for granted.[9] Women teachers in Toronto and Vancouver were confronted by education officials, from politicians to federation representatives, who affirmed that men were natural scholars and thus more committed to academic qualifications as professionals. Women teachers, who flooded schools in response to postwar staff shortages, were routinely counted as less qualified, less capable, and less committed.[10] Women, with their assumed primary obligation to the home, could not fulfill the intellectual and technical ideal for "democratic" citizenship. Yet, ironically enough, they were to be its handmaidens in ushering in the new postwar world.

This chapter moves significantly beyond those feminist political and social theorists who concentrate on women's exclusion from democratic life. It examines the responses of women themselves to their contradictory inclusion as professionals in schools. How did they define their identity given the gender dualism? Did they embrace their perceived private sphere capability despite its weak status, or take up forms of competence usually reserved for dominant masculinity?[11] Do their narratives even question these distinctions? Without the experiential understandings of the women teachers themselves, the gender dualism of teacher professionalism within liberal democratic discourse remains at best abstract and, at worst, universal. Their oral histories reveal that the majority of women attempted to cast their teaching selves as rational, knowledge-bearing professionals. The following section demonstrates the ways women's grip on such an identity was made tenuous by education administrators and their own social locations.

A DISEMBODIED RATIONAL IDENTITY

In the course of interviews, teachers revealed that they understood they worked during a period in which there was increased public faith, and corresponding government actions, for schools to contribute to the progress of the West. With burgeoning ambitions but limited resources, postwar citizens relied upon teachers to meet the challenge of the nuclear age. School officials needed instructors who could act on these hopes, but worried about their capacity to take on the task of modern democracy. Hilda Neatby voiced this dilemma when posing the question: "Is Teaching a Learned Profession?"[12] A teacher-training manual used in Ontario during the latter part of the postwar period, written by W.T. Newnham and A.S. Nease, similarly asked "Is Teaching a Profession?"[13] Although these two administrators answered in the affirmative, reduction in the qualifications needed for teaching to address a labour shortage, even as teachers' responsibilities grew, was greeted with uneasiness.[14]

Teachers' federations across the country supplied thorough in-depth analyses of what it meant to be a good teacher for educational democracy. Commentators writing in the BCTF and OSSTF newsletters agreed that classroom instructors had to defend democracy by nourishing intelligence in youth, thereby preparing them for employment. Teachers were not to instruct *the subject or the child,* the typical paradigm for progressive and traditional learning theories, but were to know their subject in sufficient depth to translate specialized knowledge, and instill a desire for intellectual development in youth.[15] This commonplace consensus was revealed in a 1959 article on the definition of the professional teacher. J.L. Ord, Superintendent of Schools for Ontario's Windsor District, in *The Bulletin's* "The Qualities of a Good Teacher," pointed to a person's feeling for teaching, their interest in understanding children, and serving students' educational needs. Equally important was sound scholarship and a thorough knowledge of subjects.[16] These two qualities were echoed by a prominent British Columbian educator, Edgar Dale, that same year in *The B.C. Teacher.* He presented the professional teacher as an "an efficient learner" who had "mastered the subject matter of his own field."[17] He further insisted: "Our democratic tradition of universal education was fought for by public-minded citizens ... he [the teacher] must see himself as a person in the public service, dedicated to helping others build a freely communicating, inclusive society."[18] While debates continued regarding the best methods for achieving these ends, namely a progressive emphasis on experience-based learning or traditional teacher-directed instruction, substantial agreement existed about the qualities that made for a good teacher.

Professionalism was, in fact, commonly presented as relatively apolitical. Specific qualifications for professionalism often sounded innocuous. Newnham and Nease assumed that teaching was a typical profession in requiring university education, professional training, and recognition by the public.[19] Conservative Neatby pointed similarly to public recognition, an ethical code of moral integrity, and skills in teaching practice.[20] The implication was that potential teachers, like their students, had every chance to obtain the knowledge necessary for proficiency. Underlying these seemingly gender-neutral concepts of competency, however, was a hierarchy of knowledge that subordinated the caring, communicative teacher to those deemed intellectual craftsmen.

The intellectual part of teaching was continuously stressed by postwar commentators. Neville Scarfe, Dean of the University of British Columbia's Faculty of Education and self-proclaimed progressive, actually warned that affective teaching could create gullible and undiscerning citizens. In "The Aims of Education in a Free Society," for the Second Canadian Conference on Education in 1962, Scarfe compared learning to scientific research, within which the teacher's job was to mentally train students for clear logical thinking, thereby decreasing students' "susceptibility to *emotional persuasion* and subtle propaganda."[21] For Scarfe, a teacher's ability was judged first and foremost by the development of rational powers in his or her students. Of course, in democratic fashion, he was not simply reserving rationality for university-bound students: "Thinking is in no sense restricted to academic subject-matter ... Music and vocational subjects may engage the rational powers of pupils equally so."[22] Ken Argue, Scarfe's more traditional colleague in educational philosophy, was cruder in his prioritization of a teacher's personal aptitude for working with youth. In the March 1953 issue of *Maclean's* Argue stated: "Many people think that as long as you love children you can teach ... Dogs love children."[23] These educators signaled that intellectualism, rather than a natural connection with children and youth, was the prized talent for teachers. This priority fitted well with a renewed emphasis in secondary schools on streaming students based on intelligence testing with faith in science-based "experts."

The narratives of the women in both cities reflected this conception of professionalism. When referring to their colleagues or role models, the majority of women plainly referred to them as good teachers. It was difficult to tease out a more precise definition, as it seemed self-evident to them. When asked what exactly a good teacher *was* during the late 1940s and '50s, Donna Weber, who taught in Vancouver secondary schools, answered: "Someone who knew the subject ... who could put it across in a way that the student could enjoy it and take it in, learn something, change their behaviour."[24] Donna's general, third person response was typical. She and the other teachers were acknowledging the basic dual function for them of knowledge expertise and communication with students that was established by teacher representatives and political officials. At the same time, however, the women recognized the different values accorded to professional scholarship and supposedly natural sympathies. Catharine Darby, also of Vancouver, argued that a good teacher was one who was "interested in kids," but she summed up the best teachers as "all scholars."[25] Catharine asserted that "anyone who didn't fit into that category [scholar] soon drifted away – they went elsewhere." Phoebe McKenzie of Toronto echoed these sentiments. Much like school officials of the period, she contended that caring was when "there was order in a classroom and there was going to be respect ... the big thing was to get your [students'] schoolwork done and get them to university."[26] These women recognized that professional authority was predicated upon rational expertise; a quality that could garner respect by setting teachers apart from parents, critics, and even many political administrators.

When the women were asked if or how they perceived themselves as good teachers, their rapport with youth seemed secondary in their own evaluation. Most of the interviewees called upon dominant masculinist conceptions of teacher professionalism, portraying themselves as disengaged scholars and technicians for student achievement, to define their successful careers. For women with university backgrounds, which accounted for seventeen of the twenty interviewees, their liberal arts background was central to teaching. They often discounted the significance of their teacher training as "how to" and "boring."[27] In contrast, they provided detailed and energized accounts of the undergraduate and/or graduate courses in which they learned their subject areas. Compared to the easily passed year at the Ontario College of Education (OCE), Karen Phillips, a teacher in Toronto, recalled her undergraduate degree in languages during the 1940s as difficult, but referred to her professors as "inspiring, brilliant, and famous." Despite her unusual qualification of a doctorate in English, Karen's heavy emphasis on academic work versus professional training was far from unique.

Women without graduate degrees, and in less traditional academic subjects, still asserted the centrality of their university training. Vancouver's Catharine Darby recounted her effectiveness in teaching home economics in the late 1930s and early '40s as being related to her triumph in science, involving quite a few courses in conjunction with the medical school, still an uncommon practice for women at the time. Her scientific knowledge lay at the heart of her effectiveness: "When you get into dyes there is a tremendous amount of chemistry involved. When you get into baking a cake ... there is physics involved ... it's no wonder it is a science field." Other women did not dwell upon academic backgrounds, despite their university training, but they nevertheless asserted expertise in their teaching area. This was particularly the case for the physical education teachers, most of whom taught for the Vancouver School Board. Sophie Canning spoke extensively about her background in the 1940s playing for championship sports teams and, in fact, working as a professional athlete to pay for university, as the basis of her teaching proficiency. Obtaining her first job had nothing to do with her teacher training or her ability to interact with youth generally. Rather, she stated: "I started at fourteen on a senior women's team so I was on a championship team and so they wanted a good athlete – that's how I got the job."[28]

Demonstrating expert knowledge, regardless of teaching experience, seemed essential for urban employment. Many women in the study, particularly those in Vancouver, had to start careers in quite isolated regions of their province. Rural schools, with their smaller budgets and attendance problems, were almost always less desirable.[29] The interviewees, like the broader education community, credited city situations with superior standards, greater possibilities for promotion, and higher salaries. Teaching in centres such as Toronto and Vancouver was deemed a privilege reserved for the strongest "experts" in each field. June West, who taught English and physical education, affirmed this in observing, "It was very difficult to get jobs, particularly in the city, so most of my classmates had to get jobs out of town ... Barrie, Alliston, you name it. But with higher grades I got a job at [a Toronto school] just starting."[30] Cecilia Reynolds' study of becoming a teacher during this period supports June's memory. Reynolds shows that hiring practices in the 1940s, often based on personal connections, meant that women were placed in multi-grade, rural schools in which they were the junior staff member with a male manager.[31] In contrast, men were more readily placed in urban schools, and if they gained experience in rural areas, they were typically given their smaller school to teach and manage alone.[32]

The women asserted that it was their superior knowledge that eventually got them not only a job in the city, but employment in the best academic schools, promotions to teach senior grades, and even appointments to typically male positions like heads of departments.[33] Sadie Chow stated that she did not get a position in the city initially because "first of all I am Oriental."[34] Chow, the only visible minority woman in the study and among the first Chinese women to teach at public secondary schools in the country, argued that she forced school officials to see her ethnicity as a non-issue by proving she was an expert in home economics. As a result, she believed that she obtained a position at one of the best schools in Vancouver and later became a department head at a different secondary school. In Toronto, Muriel Fraser acknowledged that it was critical for her to have attended the University of Sorbonne to study French in the late 1940s in order to access the "serious French students" and become head of the languages department. These women implied that they needed to go above and beyond what was expected of their male peers, which at that point was a university degree plus one year of training at a College of Education. These requirements were often waived to find enough teachers, especially for rural areas, but formal teacher preparation and higher credentials were increasingly expected.[35]

Despite numerous interviewees being educational pioneers in their own families and communities, the women teachers portrayed their accomplishments as part of a seemingly normal process of building credentials and climbing the professional ladder. They constructed narratives as typical professionals working within the bureaucratic system; technical experts for standardized outputs. Perhaps Phoebe's earlier reference is most telling. She defined teacher competency as control and discipline for high examination results

and the production of university-bound students. British Columbia's
women teachers made a similar case. Their oral histories were characterized by language of efficiency and productivity as they explained
how they got observable, concrete results for their work as experts.
Alma Erickson, a teacher in math and science, claimed that her
school had a reputation for good teachers because the staff was a
disciplined cadre of professionals. She defined discipline in this way:
"Well you taught the material and you got good results from your
students and later in the year when they wanted a good course and
they were going on to university, they wanted to enroll in your
classes."[36] These results were not just expected from the traditionally academic courses that Alma taught. Donna Weber expressed
similar expectations of her physical education students. She stated:
"I was considered to be a good teacher. I didn't have any discipline
problems ... I also just followed the system that was there ... It was
a very academic school."

Stories of successful secondary-school graduates supplied the
dominant theme in women's narratives. While discussing her pedagogy in teaching French, Beth Merle noted: "I have a former student
who is a PhD in French and has developed this programme ... she
can get them [students] used to hearing different voices for the language."[37] For Beth, this former pupil's accomplishments confirmed
the professionalism of her mentorship. Similarly, Muriel Fraser
focused the interview on her successful graduates that used French
and German in their careers: "One needed it [bilingualism] ... ended
up at one point being the president of York University." Through
stories of their former pupils, women teachers demonstrated that
they had, in fact, produced leaders for their communities. Despite
teaching in vocational and general as well as academic streams, few
spoke of any students other than the university-bound. Furthermore,
the interviewees rarely discussed classes as a whole, or students that
they had personally helped from "slipping through the cracks" of
the system. The women did not discuss failures in their classes, even
when directly questioned. It was almost as if their memories of the
most successful students ultimately kept the women from "slipping
through the cracks" of educational "democracy" themselves. If their
interviews are a reliable guide to their feelings, their relationship to
star graduates was what made these teachers feel successful.

The interviewees expressed their professional competency, even as
they acknowledged women's precarious standing by describing their

careers within a survival theme. The women repeatedly used defensive language to suggest a lack of respect by educational officials. Phoebe McKenzie, a teacher in one of Toronto's collegiate institutes, repeatedly returned to this theme: "There was strain on me. I knew I had to prove myself again." In Phoebe's case, the strain to prove she was a good teacher was directly related to her marriage. She had many interruptions in her career in the late 1940s and '50s as a result of getting married and having children. She typically deferred to her husband's "very successful" teaching career. Although not dealing with the tensions of marriage and motherhood, like Phoebe, Muriel Fraser described her career as "managing to survive." At the same time, she noted being passed over for promotion to head of the French department because a male colleague wanted the position and he was a "family man" who had served in the war.

In the postwar years, women – as mothers, nurturers and social creatures – were viewed by the school community as less capable than men of acquiring and transmitting "rational" knowledge. The secondary status of those seemingly "natural" characteristics attributed to them, like sociability, reflexivity, and subjectivity, is troubling in itself. Of particular concern is how school officials positioned women in association with these allegedly inferior qualities, and thus as second-class professionals. Women were presented with the dilemma of balancing their "feminine" subjectivities, constructed as inappropriate for the profession, and emulating "masculine" attributes, considered unacceptable for women at that time.[38] Not surprisingly, most of the women constructed their oral histories through stories of emotional detachment, noted by Emma Rich in her study as "a utilitarian approach to teaching, with less emphasis on responding to students' needs or the processes of learning, and more emphasis on learning outcomes and control."[39] Such a picture of the professional self was a seemingly irrefutable defense against any accusation that women were not capable of setting aside their tendency towards emotionality and sociability to work at producing rational citizens for the strength of the nation.

This defense was ultimately quite fragile, given the resistance of most contemporary educational authorities to the possibility that women could grasp the knowledge necessary for professionalism. Nonetheless, these proud narratives of teaching expertise challenge liberal democratic rhetoric that conveys women's personal inadequacies, rather than their social positioning, as the "weak link" for

postwar professionalism. The women interviewed fashioned an
identity out of their educational accomplishments and their scholarly expertise, and defied prevailing gender codes that dictated that
teacher professionalism was a male prerogative.

WOMEN TEACHERS' PROFESSIONALISM AS PROBLEMATIC

Despite faith in their academic prowess, women teachers had to con-
front the common distinction educators of the era made between
teacher training for the secondary level, dominated by men, and at
the elementary level, dominated by women. Superior occupational
status was denoted for the secondary level because of its focus on the
academic stream of university-bound students. This status was most
often constructed by postwar school officials as simply an issue of
higher credentials, with secondary teachers holding university
degrees. A closer reading of teacher educators' perceptions of the
qualities of female-dominated elementary teaching, however, reveals
that such distinctions were based on the pervasive conception of a
gendered rationality; women teachers in secondary schools had to
deny guilt by association with female elementary teachers. In both
Toronto and Vancouver, women accounted for approximately thirty
percent of secondary teachers and eighty percent of elementary
teachers.[40] Educators implemented a change to the structure of
teacher training to bring elementary and secondary teacher candidates within one setting, that being the university. While this move
created an appearance of improved opportunity for all teacher candidates, like students who were brought together in comprehensive
schools, the result was sustained differentiation of the offerings and
assessment of programs.

Milton LaZerte was a leading proponent of the establishment of
Faculties of Education across Canada that would encompass all
levels of teaching-training under one roof. LaZerte was Dean of
Education at the University of Winnipeg, and the expert to whom
most educators turned when discussing the criteria for teacher professionalism. He stood out among many educators of the period
who insisted that the lower qualifications for elementary training,
and thus for mostly female teachers, needed to be addressed to
increase the public's waning trust in the knowledge of its educators.
Most notable was his 1949 report for the Canadian Education
Association (CEA) on ways to improve the status of teaching,

thoughts he extrapolated upon in his 1950 Quance lectures, *Teacher Education in Canada*, at the University of Saskatchewan.[41] He argued that teachers needed adequate university-based training to provide them with a body of technical knowledge so that they could act as scientific researchers in their fields. Using the language of economic efficiency, LaZerte fought for mandatory degree requirements for both secondary and primary instructors. Those without university training – notably, of course, women in the elementary sector who qualified through Normal Schools – lowered professional standards, since: "The public judges a profession by the lowest not by the highest qualifications."[42]

LaZerte saw his demands partially fulfilled in 1956, when the Faculty of Education at the University of British Columbia opened with Neville V. Scarfe as Dean.[43] The Normal School, the Summer School of Education, and the School of Education at the University were subsumed into this new faculty. British Columbia, in conjunction with Alberta, was seen as a leader in raising the standards and status of teachers generally and of elementary teachers in particular.[44] Elementary teachers could receive a Bachelor of Arts or Education degree after four years, but were permitted to teach after achieving only one year of university credits. The same year in Ontario, "Normal Schools" were renamed "Teachers' Colleges" in an effort to raise the prestige of the elementary level. It was not until 1974, however, just before these colleges were absorbed by university faculties of education, that elementary training obtained degree-granting privileges.[45] Teachers' colleges continued to distinguish elementary and secondary training programs, however, with few cross-over course options or instructors. They remained much the same as before reorganization, with the universities gaining little control over teacher certification. This stayed in the hands of each province's department of education.

The continuity of distinct elementary and secondary programs, and the devaluation of the former, is conveyed in the description by George A. Hickman, Dean of the Faculty of Education at Memorial University in Newfoundland. The new teacher programs were separated by grade levels, which he categorized as general and professional streams.[46] Professional education, according to Hickman, was specialized training that embraced preparation in academic areas. Here he speaks of a teacher's expertise, clarity, and logic to become "a reasonably intelligent member of a staff which concerns itself with the reconstruction and administration of the curriculum of the school; an understanding of the principles governing classroom organization, management and control."[47] Hickman made clear that it was the secondary level, dominated by male teachers, to which specialization applied, "for it is obvious that a broad general education is better for the elementary school teacher."[48] The general education in Canadian teacher-training centres included, according to Hickman, the development of knowledge and skills that should be the common possession of everyone in a democratic society, such as personal growth and responsible citizenship. As he outlined it, general education prepared elementary teachers to cultivate the social, not public and professional, elements of education. His words evoke the image of a housewife for the nation: "They [general educators/ elementary teachers] are concerned with the natural world in which man makes his home, with the social world of which he is a responsible part, and with the personal world within which man discovers himself. They contribute to the student's capacity to function well ... as a member of a family."[49] Hickman's language makes clear that secondary teachers were functional and public actors for intelligent citizenship, whereas elementary teachers were preparing to be nurturing mothers.

LaZerte and Hickman represented not simply the common perception of the lower credentials needed to teach at the elementary level, but also a general assessment of women's teaching abilities as inferior and unskilled. The stigmatizing effects of this point of view were evident in the oral histories of the women in this study, especially for those who were trained, and often held their first positions in, the elementary division. For some, elementary training happened within Normal Schools, prior to consolidation, but again this differed little from later university-based programs. Normal School or the shorter elementary training at university was a far more affordable option, especially for women, who earned less than men, and whose families were less likely to consider them life-long wage-earners. It was also considered by the public and educational administrators to be a more "natural" fit for their motherly qualities. Of the twenty women in this sample, four attended Normal School; three were without a university degree before teacher training. These women taught in Vancouver. The regional difference may simply be the sample of this study. One survey of the era suggested British Columbia secondary schools had a higher percentage of degree-bearing teachers than any other province, but credited this fact to also having the highest proportion of men teachers.[50] The regional difference may lie with the more academic bias of Toronto collegiate institutes. For a secondary school to obtain the title of collegiate institute, it had to have more than five members on staff with specialist certification that could not be obtained without a university degree.[51]

Not unexpectedly, the Vancouver women who had trained for elementary schooling recognized that they were regarded as less professional by colleagues and administrators. Claire Anderson, a physical education instructor, did not identify herself nor speak in the first person when discussing the admirable qualities of teachers during the postwar period. She asserted that almost all of the people in her schools were professionals, "except me, they had their degrees."[52] Claire described her own ability, which she explained as not justifying an assessment as professional, as her love of children: "I just wanted each kid to have an experience of happiness with one another and sharing." Claire was among the many women who acknowledged the differential values accorded to academic and caring professionalism. Sophie Canning, who had received a Bachelor of Physical Education from the University of British Columbia but also trained at Normal School, offered a similar reflection. She stopped a line of questioning about her education and said: "I want to say two things. I was never smart but I was always energetic." Throughout the interview, she described herself as unconcerned with her professional status. What really mattered most to her was the respect she earned as a disciplinarian, and as someone who cared enough to find out about her students. She was one of the few to speak at length about a student's personal needs, recounting a story in which she replaced shoes stolen from one of her students. Sophie actually credited her elementary training for this response, "because the high school [teachers] were a cold sort ... become pompous I guess."

Such a caricature appeared not to trouble those women purely trained for high school employment. They often perpetuated the association of elementary teaching with mothering, firmly disassociating themselves from such a role, while identifying themselves as stalwart professionals. Their focus on students' scholastic achievement matched the primary purpose of the secondary school. Beth Merle of Toronto explained that her choice between elementary and secondary teaching was easy: "I didn't want a class of little kids in front of me. If I was going to do French it had to be secondary." Fran

Thompson, a specialist in English, said: "all high school teachers probably had the same thing; they loved their subject ... never occurred to them that they had to know anything about their students."[53] Fran and Beth's university credentials and location within traditional academic areas afforded them a better chance to disassociate themselves from female stereotypes. While at times they expressed enjoyment about interactions with students, they purposefully set their mastery of subject matter in direct opposition to the values of nurturing youth that were allied with female elementary instructors. Some were self-conscious about the distinction they drew. Grace Logan, a Latin teacher in British Columbia, recalled the well-known stigma when she described being "horrified" when an inspector came to watch one of her lessons during a mandatory one-week elementary practicum: "he said to me had you ever thought of continuing in elementary education and I thought, he doesn't think I can do secondary ... I was really, really quite disappointed ... I never considered elementary."[54]

The necessity for these women to differentiate themselves from elementary school teachers had much less to do with elementary training per se than with perceptions of the female teacher in the postwar period. Even female staff in secondary schools were viewed as less professionally competent and more under-qualified than their male counterparts. In particular, educators leveled suspicion at women who entered the profession to address vacancies left by servicemen during the Second World War, and to make up for the growing teacher shortage in the late 1940s and '50s. According to a February 1946 survey by the Canada and Newfoundland Education Association, predecessor to the CEA, there were over 4,000 too few qualified teachers.[55] In 1952 the total shortage was estimated at 6,556, with increases to the decade's end. Teacher supply represented a national emergency, declared F.S. Rivers, Superintendent of Professional Training in Ontario, and R.W.B. Jackson, Professor at the OCE, in their report for the journal of the CEA. In Ontario the situation was most acute in rural areas and at the elementary level, but urban secondary schools also needed 200 more teachers annually within the decade than universities were expected to produce.[56] F. Henry Johnson, coordinator for teacher education for the British Columbia Department of Education at the time, told local newspapers that the province would be short 750 secondary school teachers by 1956.[57] Rivers and Jackson concluded that population change caused the shortfall. They predicted a near doubling of enrolment for all levels of schooling across the country from 1945 to 1960.[58] The postwar baby boom occupied elementary classes, while secondary school increases were spurred by immigration and a general demand for higher education.

Most provinces, including Ontario and British Columbia, adopted emergency measures to address the shortage. Many continued wartime policies that were still in place when the women interviewed obtained their first teaching positions. Responses included the consolidation of schools and renaming teachers' colleges. More ambivalent initiatives included lowering entrance requirements for higher education and shortening teacher training. The Ontario and British Columbia Departments of Education resorted to issuing a large number of temporary certificates or Letters of Permission, requiring only one year of training after grade thirteen and two short summer courses for those planning to teach elementary school, and similar crash summer courses and reduced practice teaching after a baccalaureate for secondary candidates.[59] In 1947, British Columbia officials reported over 129 teachers in the junior/high school level had temporary certificates.[60] In Ontario, one in thirteen secondary teachers enrolled in summer courses when they were first offered at the OCE in 1954–55.[61]

Provinces also initiated recruitment campaigns by way of radio broadcasts, newspaper columns, booklets, and posters. While new candidates were sought, palliative measures were advertised to encourage the return of trained and experienced teachers who had retired or left teaching for other reasons, notably marriage or motherhood.[62] According to William Dunlop, Minister of Education for Ontario, these strategies were effective. In 1952, he spread the good news that "by emergency measures, it has been possible to prepare, during the year, a sufficient number of teachers to ensure that no school was closed for lack of a teacher."[63] While the situation was not quite as rosy for British Columbia, particularly in the interior regions where schools were closed due to staff shortages, in 1947 the Vancouver board announced that temporary certification and teachers coming from eastern Canada had solved the problem.[64]

Women answered officials' calls for more teachers. Their rates of participation, especially for older women who were married, grew during the Second World War as they filled in for absent men. At the peak, women accounted for over seventy percent of the teaching force. While their rates of employment dropped to pre-war levels at the end of the Second World War, the shortage of teachers allowed women's employment to reach near war-time rates by the mid-1950s.[65] Toronto Board of Education *Year Book* statistics in 1954 show that 271 of the 754 secondary school teachers were women, and 51 of them were married.[66] Vancouver produced similar statistics: 246 of 755 secondary teachers, 68 married.[67] Given the numerous and incommensurate levels of certification for the two provinces during this period, it is difficult to ascertain the numbers who held temporary or under-qualified certification for the secondary level. One BCTF study of the specific qualifications of married women teachers conducted early in the period concluded that approximately forty percent possessed "second-rate" qualifications and were teaching only until necessity no longer dictated.[68]

School officials nevertheless relied upon women's flexible labour and supported policy shifts and specific programs to entice them into the workforce. For example, in 1954, British Columbia's Department of Education began Future Teachers' Clubs in high schools.[69] Although policy did not allocate these clubs by gender, Vancouver secondary schools' yearbooks show all-female clubs.[70] Departments in both provinces embarked on teacher recruitment drives overseas, typically hiring women for pre-specified boards and under an assisted immigration scheme, who would otherwise be unable to afford such travel. Lastly, both Toronto and Vancouver boards recruited women who had left the profession due to marriage. Toronto officials used the newspapers to recruit married teachers throughout the 1950s. Z.S. Phimister, Superintendent and Chief Inspector of Schools, reported to the *Globe and Mail* that the Toronto board would even lessen mandatory maternity leave for those "young women teachers supporting their husbands who are attending medical school or theological college."[71] Officials in British Columbia extolled the virtues of married women by announcing in their newsletter that without bringing them "back to the profession, even though they have been absent of years ... there is no doubt that chaos would have existed."[72] Sheila L. Cavanagh argues that policies enticing married women into the profession cannot be seen purely as a triumph against gender discrimination.[73] Instead, women perceived to be of the marrying variety or who were already married were hired as symbols of society's heteronormativity; a point explored in depth in the following chapter.

Broader policies supported recruitment endeavours for women teachers, and specifically those who were perceived as the marrying kind. In 1944, Vancouver women who married after placement in a school gained security of tenure, and for Toronto women, an official bar to married women was lifted in 1946,[74] although women were often still expected to leave their jobs once they became pregnant. Furthermore, in 1951 the Ontario Teachers' Federation created a single salary schedule to base pay on qualifications, not gender. This policy was enacted in conjunction with the province's 1952 Female Employees' Fair Remuneration Act. Due to the leadership of Hilda Cryderman and Mollie Cunningham in its executive, the BCTF adopted this policy in 1954: one year after it was enacted by the newly elected W.A.C. Bennett Social Credit government.[75] The BCTF had encouraged boards as early as the mid-1940s to remove overt sex differences, and most complied, with Vancouver reported as one of the last to hold out.[76] Wage discrimination would continue as the majority of women teachers could not secure higher paying administrative positions in these cities.[77] British Columbia statistics show that women's pay was approximately fifty-six percent of men's in 1945. Although the disparity would drop, a twenty-three percent differential remained in 1954–55.[78]

Postwar inducements enticed back four married interviewees who taught in Vancouver. Abigail Sears remembered that originally, after getting married "you knew you were out." She continued teaching because of "an order in council in Victoria for me to be permitted to teach because I was married ... the principal went to bat for me."[79] Abigail only stayed six more months until she was pregnant with her first child. While most women did not refer to explicit policies such as permits, they did remember pressure-filled requests to return to the teaching force from influential local administrators. Sadie Chow was adamant that after the birth of each child she was not going back to teaching. Each time, however, she recalled a "phone campaign" from the Vancouver board's home economics coordinator insisting that she come back to school. Sadie was convinced by this coordinator who stated: "with your mind, you'd just sit home and vegetate ... you know your children don't have the quantity of time with you, but I am sure they have the quality because you always take them everywhere." Sadie's recollection indicates that while the barrier to married women working may have lessened, mothers still needed to justify their presence. In explaining her decision, Sadie insisted she was a reluctant participant, always found good child-care, and did not seek out the position.

Her desire to justify returning to work is understandable, given that five of the seven teachers in this study with offspring described confrontations with male colleagues. Abigail, for example, submitted a teaching application after she had left a position to have her fourth child. After a long time without a response, Abigail followed up by telephone with a male friend and colleague. The male friend informed her at that point that a "mother of children should not be working; they should be in the home." Alma Erickson recounted with some laughter that after she returned to teaching, male teachers assumed she was inexperienced and treated her like a beginner. She described one man, a novice himself, having the nerve to tell her she should not be teaching since she was married with children. Although teachers' federation representatives, political officials, and educational administrators in both Toronto and Vancouver encouraged women's participation in the public system, the women's stories indicate that they still encountered intense scrutiny, even opposition, from their male colleagues.

Political representatives claimed that the emergency programs they established, and to which women responded, produced minimally acceptable teachers for Canadian education. Herbert Edgar Smith, Dean of the Faculty of Education at the University of Alberta until 1955 and frequent contributor to professional journals, stated: "By hopeful definition they are temporary measures, devious in detail, and all to be deplored ... but Departments of Education have to face an electoral demand that classrooms be kept open and at least some kind of teacher provided for them."[80] Smith was correct that the measures were temporary. When the shortage abated in the mid-1960s, British Columbia and Ontario Departments of Education scaled back teaching permits and elevated requirements for teacher-training.[81] The problem for school officials was that emergency programs supplied recruits but did not relieve public concerns about professional standards. Temporary measures were viewed by many educators, particularly federation representatives, as exacerbating an ongoing problem that afflicted the profession. Researchers asserted that a shortage was not simply the result of an increased student population. The problem resided with individuals, particularly men, choosing either not to enter or to leave teaching. Many researchers and political officials stressed that the male shortage was due to the profession's lack of prestige.[82] By implication, those teachers, primarily women, who were obtaining positions at the secondary level in increasingly larger numbers during the period, were second best.

Given this context, some women's stories were marked by moments of embarrassment. Such emotion was poignant for Marion Hayes, a Toronto collegiate institute teacher in history and English. Despite having a degree in hand, she reluctantly, and in hushed tones, admitted that she did not take the regular one-year OCE course, but was one of the teachers who worked while taking two summer sessions. She whispered: "I'm actually one of the few people and not many of my friends know about this ... I'm one who did it in the summer. They needed more teachers and there was a twelve-week course and then about five weeks to follow it up."[83] Marion may have been unusual among the Hogtown group. Three Vancouver women disclosed either taking crash summer courses or receiving temporary certification prior to formal training. They described themselves as being at the mercy of administrators, who sent them to remote locations with extremely bad working conditions. Moreover their positions were not secure, and their certification was nonrenewable without the personal recommendation of their local board or inspectors. When speaking of her first teaching post in a mining town in 1949, British Columbia's Sadie Chow explained that she was "granted an elementary temporary teaching certificate for one year ... it was the lowest form ... if you looked at the conditions, you wouldn't want to renew it." She went on to say that she wished for a husband to take her away from that job. Claire Anderson painted a much happier picture of her early rural positions. At the same time, she noted that a top male administrator at her Normal School simply told her where she was needed and she went. The result was two rather isolated schools, and then a technical school outside of Vancouver, all of which were described as being problem locations and at which she was not initially given her subject area to teach. Although these women were filling positions at a time when the "democratization" of schooling relied on their labour, they did not count on appropriate praise or compensation.

These stories reveal that women's inferior status was not simply a matter of them having lower qualifications but reflected women's position as flexible reserve labour. Many male administrators questioned the motives of female careerists, claiming that their natural inclination was, and should be, marriage and full-time motherhood. J.D. Aikenhead, professor of education at the University of Alberta in Calgary and a specialist in school administration, undertook research on why individuals entered or returned to the profession. He argued that opportunities were open for women to improve the learning of children and youth in their communities. Aikenhead acknowledged that "more women than men had returned" to teaching.[84] He asserted that this was simply a public extension of women's propensity for nurturing. They entered the system, he contended, not for a steady wage, but due to their "fondness for children, a liking for colleagues, and a desire to serve society."[85] Aikenhead reassured public officials that women were not planning to become a permanent presence in secondary schools: they did not view teaching as a career providing a living wage in the same way as men did. His incorrect assumption, based on the middle-class, nuclear family ideal of the period, was that all women desired to be supported by their husbands.

However, over half of the women interviewed in this study did not marry and many provided financial support to parents. Of those who did marry, some spoke of the financial necessity to continue or resume working due to their husbands' illness or loss of employment.[86] Regardless of economic necessity, many women simply viewed teaching as one of the only avenues of work in which they could apply their own education. When asked if she knew before entering university that she wanted to be a teacher, Beverley Hurst stated: "Education was important. I was good at languages and there weren't that many things you could do in that day and age. I wasn't going to be a nurse and I didn't think I wanted to be a secretary particularly ... teaching was a good thing to do with my courses."[87] Others spoke of teaching as a long-term career option, because they could continue to work while married. Melanie Kilburn explained that she pursued teaching, instead of medicine in which she was most interested, knowing that her long years of undergraduate school would not go to waste when she married. She explained: "It was either you had a career that would fit in with marriage and children or if you were going to go through this long training then you would always be full time. Now how did that fit in?" Most officials ignored women's desires for a family life as well as long term service and remuneration.

The recruitment of men, however, was viewed more realistically. Aikenhead, for example, argued that men were not becoming teachers because of a lack of prestige, "slow promotions, few well-paid top positions, and low salaries."[88] Freelance journalist Max Braithwaite voiced his opinion that "the really alarming fact is that the average male teacher stays in the profession only eight years."[89] Improved salaries were perhaps the most common recruitment measure. Percy Muir, secretary of the Ontario School Trustees Council, told the Canadian School Trustees' Association: "We get a large number of capable women teachers but we are not getting the men. An appro-. priate salary for a single girl is not adequate for a man and family. But there's not much we can do about it. The law says we must pay an equal salary to women."[90] Salaries did steadily increase after the war. Pay for secondary school teachers in Ontario doubled from 1945 to 1960, and had improved substantially in western provinces.[91] George Roberts, past president of the OSSTF and OTF, argued that salaries were getting so much better that teaching was competing for men's employment with the field of engineering. He optimistically stated: "In 1958 Toronto hired some 40 university engineering graduates, gave them summer courses in pedagogy and sent them into high schools."[92] In this instance, crash courses in teacher training were not problematic. This different assessment occurred for the same reason that the Toronto branch of the OSSTF campaigned against a uniform salary payment for elementary and secondary teachers, regardless of sex; men as breadwinners were priorities in the public institution of the school and thus had a right to a higher salary.[93] The male president of the Toronto branch was cited in the 25 September 1952 issue of the Telegram as objecting because secondary school teachers were losing their right to bargain independently of the less prestigious women-dominated elementary affiliates.[94] While the same kind of campaign would not be made by the BCTF, perhaps as a result of a strong female presence on their executive, that province's male administrators made similar comments about the preference and rightful place of men in secondary schools.

Women acknowledged that they were expected to step aside in deference to men. Alma Erickson of Vancouver got her first job teaching because of the war; she then lost it when servicemen returned. She said: "they [school officials] figured they [women] should be released to let men have the jobs so that's that." Alma

explained that she worked happily for years as a substitute secondary teacher until her husband became seriously ill and she had to
support their family. Alma, like many women, accepted men's priority as a moral imperative given their status as soldiers and breadwinners. This was certainly the rationale for Muriel Fraser of Toronto
who passed on a promotion so that a married man would receive
advancement. Muriel recounted: "there was a chance to go to [a
Toronto secondary school] and again I turned it down because there
was a fellow in the French department who was married with a family and I knew that if I didn't take it, he would get it." Muriel's narrative is particularly revealing because she saw no contradiction in
her belief that married men were entitled to career advancements,
while both her parents were financially dependent on her throughout much of the 1950s. Nonetheless, her story expressed what was
rarely openly spoken by the interviewees; men fulfilled the ideal of
the good teacher automatically, while women had to prove they
were up to it.

Of course, few officials during this era of popular egalitarianism
openly declared that men were preferred for secondary schools,
regardless of their credentials. In a rare, revealing statement, Charles
Ovans, general secretary for the BCTF in the 1950s, admitted: "Given
a choice in anything above primary grades, a school will take a man
to a woman."[95] Most school officials simply asserted that men were
more attractive because they obtained more advanced degrees, especially in the allegedly more intellectually rigorous subjects of mathematics and science that were in high demand during the period
of the space race. Men, therefore, could provide rationally sound
instruction for youth, ensuring there would be leaders for the nation's
secure and prosperous democratic future, in which science would be
critical. Women, in contrast, were framed by educational discourse
as being unable to fulfill this primary "democratic" objective. As a
result, they were vulnerable to accusations of undermining teacher
professionalism and, with it, the public's faith in education. Officials
feared, or perhaps hoped, that female propensities for home and
motherhood would reduce their commitment to the noble vocation
of teaching. This is particularly evident in information available
from British Columbia and Ontario teachers' federations. Federation
representatives expressed concerns to their membership and the
public through newspaper columns that women were "unethical,"
"unfair," and "unprofessional"; comments that struck at the heart of

an occupation that was valued for its fulfillment of educational democracy.

The OTF, created by The Teaching Profession Act of 1944 that amalgamated all existing associations as a means of raising the status of the profession, feared the influence of female recruits.[96] Although policies, like short summer courses, the lack of unified contracts, and low salaries, were implicated in lowering the prestige of teachers, it was women, single and working before marriage, married, and mothers, who were regularly identified as the weak link in the quest for professional recognition.[97] Such beliefs were not restricted to male members of the OSSTF. Eileen Gladman, female Chairman [sic] of the OTF's Relations and Discipline Committee, pinpointed the problem as women's inability to separate personal and public interests. In an article published in the May 1959 issue of *The Bulletin*, she explained: "Many times, too, a woman teacher accepts without question the idea that family responsibilities of any kind come before the fulfillment of the contract she has entered into as a teacher. Whatever may be the motive let us stress the ethical and professional importance."[98] Historian Sandra Gaskell provides the most extensive examination of women's supposed offences. Women were incriminated as undedicated because of the general belief that teaching was not a career for them, but, rather, a short job between school and marriage.[99] They were simply working for luxuries, unlike male teachers who were considered family breadwinners. Regarded as transient workers, women teachers were accused of willingness to accept positions outside of union contracts and, most abhorrently, of underbidding men for positions by accepting reduced money or benefits.[100] With such allegations on hand, many men in the federation readily dismissed their female colleagues, with little interest in obtaining greater pensions or administrative positions.[101]

Throughout the late 1940s and '50s the BCTF made similar complaints. In a February 1955 column entitled "Some Ethical Considerations," appearing that same month in the local paper, the editor of *The B.C. Teacher* appealed on behalf of the federation to "all married women teachers, and to single teachers about to be married, to be considerate and fair."[102] The article began by extolling the democratic changes to the education system since the Depression regarding married women, to the point that school boards admit married women are among their very best teachers. The editor noted that despite demonstrating a professional outlook comparable to single women, these same school boards now had complaints. In particular, school boards were "fed up" with women abusing leaves of absence to be married in the middle of term and accepting positions knowing they were pregnant and would have to be replaced.[103] He was not alone in his reservations. According to Vancouver School Board committee reports and other regular newsletter columns on the subject of the woman teacher, male inspectors, superintendents, and principals were appalled that women might teach to earn pocket money until marriage, take time off for *unsanctioned* domestic reasons, and shirk their extracurricular duties and other special assignments for work at home.[104] The marrying teacher, who had been only recently accepted, was now under surveillance for not being able to let go of her domesticity. The editorial warned that unless women dealt with these issues fairly "they will not only be acting unprofessionally as individuals but they will be creating a condition which will tempt school boards to return to policies against the employment of married women teachers."[105] Another column was even more stern, warning about the federation's position: without written consent from administrators before taking leave for marriage, women were in breach of the code of ethics and would be brought before the executive to be "severely dealt with."[106] While few women faced dismissal as a result of these indictments, it is clear that federations in both provinces defined women themselves, and not society's sexist view of women or women's limited opportunities within education, as retarding the status of the profession.

Not surprisingly, no interviewee acknowledged accusations of unethical professional practice on her part or on the part of her female colleagues. A number insisted, instead, that women were often more ethical than their male counterparts. They even referred to men as "cheaters" when they attained superior results to women teachers from their students. Donna Weber, who taught physical education in Vancouver, noted that men were successful coaches at her school because the "boys were taught to cheat" in basketball by committing fouls in order to win the game. Her philosophy was that "if you couldn't stop them [the opposing players] properly, without breaking the rules, then you didn't deserve to win the game." Alma Erickson, also of Vancouver, repeatedly spoke of men who were determined to do better and cheated by "practically teaching the exam." She said that the male head of her department would often set the exam so that his students got the best results. Knowing that her own students were equally bright, she insisted that the examinations be set for all classes. While these stories target male teachers' unethical actions, they also attest to these women's ethical competency as teachers in this era.

Women's relative silence, as noted previously, on most discussions of their association with "feminine" attributes such as motherhood, nurturing, and emotionality, may also signal their defense against accusations that they could not put personal interests aside for their work. On the rare occasion that interviewees did voluntarily and directly speak to the issue of caregiving for their students, the women actually spoke of such actions as being inappropriate or even unethical. When asked if she had performed a counselling role for her students, Jessie Russell responded: "no I didn't, but some teachers did … I didn't get into that because it's wrong … I was the teacher, they're the student. I'm not your counsellor or your mother that you're gonna come to and talk to me about your boyfriend."[107] Jessie mentioned a fellow teacher who often had students in her office to talk, a practice which she found objectionable. Grace Logan of Vancouver, at one point in her interview, suggested that her classroom worked "beautifully" because "when you came into my room, it's like you're coming into my home." When following up on her metaphor of a home, Grace immediately retracted her previous description and stated that the school was not a family environment and she was not nurturing of the students. Rather, she asserted, this type of environment was "proper … a great disciplinary feature."

For Sophie Canning, the gendered sanctions associated with "feminine" attributes such as an emotional attachment to students had a more ominous implication. Sophie is a lesbian who was not out during this period in her life. She states: "I would not tolerate it; [homosexuality] was a terrible word." If her sexuality had been revealed, she would have been fired from her job teaching physical education to girls. She recounted a story, at length, regarding a female student who "idolized" her and invited her to come with her family for an outing one weekend. Sophie refused the girl's offer and explained to her that she was only her teacher Monday to Friday. She recalled: "her [the student's] face fell but that … you know, it was times like that I was lucky that I was able to keep it that way and you know what I mean … you had to watch that nothing got affectionate." Sophie's oral history demonstrates another reason why it could be important for women to call upon a masculinist professional image:

in her case, to keep a safe distance from students. For Sophie, it was a necessity for her very livelihood. Still more than the other teachers interviewed here, she felt confined by codes of heterosexuality that emphasized difference and women's problematic professionalism. Her narrative, similar to the other women's, was rife with examples of potential problems resulting from assumptions regarding her "naturally" nurturing femininity and illogical capabilities for knowledge production.

The response of these women to inferior positioning within postwar educational democracy demonstrates that there were no ready, simple solutions. As Emma Rich reflects from her work on women in England's teacher-training programs for physical education: "there is no simple materiality, no correct behaviour which these women can unequivocally achieve."[108] She remarks: "Their inclusion in their profession is contradictory, by mere virtue of the fact that as women they remain subordinates in a dominant Gender Order which underpins the dominant educational discourses."[109] Illuminating the struggles of women teachers in postwar education, therefore, is not to suggest that women could not attain the attributes of the "good" teacher. Rather their narratives illustrate the discursive and practical means by which they made sense of their teaching selves. Caught in an essentialist double bind of professionalism equating to dominant masculinity, the women's narratives marked the apprehensions they experienced in fulfilling postwar objectives emulating and producing the rational "democratic" citizen. Throughout the interviews the women spoke of their need to prove they had a place within the public secondary school system as professionals: a status allotted more easily to men by virtue of their sex. Their identity as teachers was less tenuous, according to the women, if they presented themselves as detached, knowledgeable scholars who could produce intellectual leaders of the nation. Given these women's various educational backgrounds, teaching subjects, and social locations, their narratives do not reify an essentialist binary of professionalism. Rather, they were positioned both by themselves and by school officials across uncomfortable gender differences. The image of teacher as subject expert and thus rational citizen was much easier to construct for women who were single, with advanced university degrees, and who taught in academic-oriented subjects and regions. For others, the grip on a scholarly identity and professional recognition was even more tenuous, as they acknowledged holding inferior positions due to such factors as motherhood and elementary rather than secondary school training.

While the women's narratives demonstrate that they were unable to completely resist or alter masculinist conceptions of the modern teacher, they nonetheless asserted their ability to embody professionalism. Each maintained that a great teacher could be a woman of sound scholarship. The women admitted their struggles, however, in gaining recognition as "good" teachers: they were handicapped by the competing and multiple frameworks that identified them personally, socially, and occupationally as less professional than their male counterparts. Their narratives support the contention of feminist theorists that liberal democratic discourse offers professional autonomy in seemingly androgynous form while perpetuating a gender dualism that restricts women's access to and capability for professional knowledge. Yet if women were precluded from equality with men, they might offer something different. The following chapter addresses the role for women teachers as moral vessels for a democratic order, rather than knowledge-bearers for democratic citizenship.

3

Moral "Democracy" and the Woman Teacher's Citizenship Performance

The woman teacher of postwar secondary schools was situated as the moral gatekeeper for democratic citizenship. Feminist theorists argue that within liberal discourse, women are collectively celebrated as daughters of the state, guardians of the nation, and cultivators of citizenship.[1] In theory, women are reproductive, benevolent actors or virtuous beings.[2] Although there is an explicit conflict between "democratic" knowledge and women's "natural" abilities, no such tension arises for their role as cultural benefactors. Instead, as Madeleine Arnot and Jo-Anne Dillabough describe, women are the keepers, cultivators, and symbols of democracy.[3]

Without claims to rationality, and thus formal political agency, women serve to uphold democratic citizenship and the state itself. While women are critical to the enterprise, nationalist rhetoric privileges male hierarchies and suppresses awareness of gender located on the margins. Valerie Walkerdine and Helen Lucey argue that this discourse, in Foucauldian terms, is a non-coercive but deeply conservative strategy because "women of all classes have been placed as guardians of an order which is too difficult to escape."[4] Women teachers in particular, they explain, are given the awesome responsibility of nurturing the democratic ideals of citizenship: free will, equal opportunities, and choice. Their actions are set, however, within educational parameters that constrict their authority in terms of "correct" and "incorrect" mothering, and serve to reconstitute the legitimacy of a masculine version of the "right" citizen.[5] Nira Yuval-Davis summarizes this position as follows: "Girls did not need to act; they had to become the national embodiment."[6] As adult women, teachers had to embody the national ideal while disavowing the authority, resting on rationality and coercion, properly owed to male citizens.

This was the tightrope women teachers walked in Toronto and Vancouver. In the context of postwar reconstruction, progressive and traditional educators alike mandated objectives for students to gain an appreciation of the values of democracy and the ability to express those values in gender roles, family patterns, and work habits. Teachers were responsible for implementing new social services and guidance courses to instruct youth about their freedoms and rights as citizens. Attempting to recover from wartime instability and fears of social deviance in the atomic age, officials defined rights, and thus the work of teachers, within a normative structure. This definition of the nation's values was best expressed in the white, Judeo-Christian, middle-class, nuclear family. Women teachers were expected to shore up this ideal. As such, women needed to embrace their "womanliness." At the same time, they were cautioned against unbridled femininity, with its emotional and sexual wiles, because it might threaten "masculine" rationality.[7] In other words, women teachers were responsible for perpetuating normative femininity, while simultaneously accountable for preserving masculine ideals of conduct. Sheila L. Cavanagh argues in her study of women elementary teachers in the first half of twentieth-century Ontario that the education community demanded that "women adhere to more rigid standards or social propriety and moral deportment to demonstrate their professional enculturation."[8] Citing the work of Penina M. Glazer and Miriam Slater, Cavanagh explains: "Women had to be sensitive to an ever present scrutiny of their performance, personal style and presentation of self."[9] Women teachers' oral histories demonstrate an embodied, daily, and active negotiation of prevailing definitions of feminine respectability. They regularly spoke of struggling with physical performances to represent both their gender role and occupational duties.

Judith Butler's theoretical framework of gender as performative is helpful for understanding women teachers' discussions of their physicality in schools as both symbolic and negotiable sites of nationalist rhetoric. Butler argues that gender roles are not signifiers of a core gender identity, but social roles developed within specific historical contexts and learned through the "stylized repetition of acts": "the gendered body acts its part in culturally restricted corporeal spaces and enacts interpretations within the confines of already existing derivative."[10] Restrictions within cultural, social, and even occupational codes do not, however, mean that women cannot take ownership of their identities. Gender roles are socially sanctioned creations that are, as Butler states, "put on, invariably, under constraint, daily and incessantly, with anxiety and pleasure."[11]

In recent decades, feminist historians in Canada have explored women's embodied performances of professional and national identities. Notably, Kathryn McPherson applies Butler's framework in *Bedside Matters: The Transformation of Canadian Nursing, 1900–1990*, which explores the relationship between performance and women's social and occupational identities. She argues that nurses learned to play their part "not only in terms of the occupationally specific skills and responsibilities they took on, but also in terms of the behaviour and attitudes they had to exhibit."[12] Listening to nurses' own articulation of their presentation, McPherson demonstrates that public expression shifted over the century in response to modifications in the definition of femininity and in the political economy and legal and social norms established by nursing leaders, administrators, and educators.[13] While she is particularly attentive to linking the social conditions inscribed on the nurses' bodies, McPherson, like many other Canadian feminist historians, references women's historical body within the world of medicine, biology, and physical health.[14] However that preoccupation does not capture the full picture. As Butler demonstrates, women's historical body is enacted daily in diverse contexts and social locations. Teaching ultimately provides as good an example as nursing. The teaching body is worthy of particular exploration given its instructive value and representation for the nation's future citizens.

This chapter explores women teachers' embodied performances of "democratic" values within postwar Toronto and Vancouver public secondary schools. How did they negotiate a liberal democratic order that romanticized women as sentinels and thus active participants for the restoration of postwar normality, while also positioning them as passive conductors of predetermined patriarchal morals? Playing the role of cultural guardians was problematic, especially given that the traits of "proper" postwar citizenship were not emblematic of the women's lives. Women teachers' narratives illustrate their attempts to embody their prescribed roles while at the same time negotiating space in which to exercise options, performing those citizenship qualities they deemed most effective for their gender and occupational identities. The first section of this chapter outlines the roles assigned to women teachers as the cultivators of students' "democratic" morality. The following section explores the ways interviewees both embraced and struggled to perform normative values expressive of the respectable woman, notably via heterosexuality and the nuclear family.

EMBODYING "DEMOCRATIC" VALUES

One postwar slogan, "The character of a people determines the character of its democracy," set the moral terrain for educators.[15] Schools were to be in the forefront of establishing the appropriate intellectual, as well as moral, standards of "the people." Secondary schools, as the first chapter detailed, taught democratic values through increased "progressive" social services, including guidance programs and school psychologists, as well as the more traditional means of social studies courses, which conveyed the legal and historical development of Canadian citizenship. Scholars have typically placed progressive and traditional means at odds with each other, with the former supplying a liberating influence, offering contemporary values so students can freely analyze the world's problems, while the latter seeks acceptance of revered values and customs of the past.[16] Ralph Tyler, whose curriculum theory work was often quoted during this period in Canada, called this one of the "eternal" conflicts in education.[17] For the majority of educators in the postwar context, however, the liberation or conformity conflict had little meaning in the day-to-day world. They employed both progressive and traditional programming for character education. Liberation was the goal for all educators who revered the democratic promise of freedom, security, and opportunity. It would be delivered, however, through conformity to normative values that heralded past customs, but were also deemed by social authorities as critical for contemporary issues and a secure future. Specifically, social studies courses and guidance services focused on Christian ethics to combat the period's supposed rampant materialism and godless popular culture. Similarly, school curriculum and psychologists reaffirmed the white, middle-class, nuclear family as the primary basis of a consumer economy and a defense against Communism.[18] Adherence to these fundamental values, educators asserted, taught students how to protect their freedoms as Canadian citizens.

Such views certainly informed the Royal Commission on Education in Ontario, which saw autonomy and obedience as equally important to citizenship since "intelligence alone had not prevented citizens of other countries from choosing nefarious political systems."[19] Frank Wilson, a trustee for Chilliwack, British Columbia, and a regular contributor to The B.C. Teacher, similarly explained that civilized living required reconciling freedom with a necessary adherence to rules: "[the] free man actively supports and maintains the order and the harmony of the society ... the servile man is kept in order. The foundation of a free society, therefore, is a body of citizens who keep order and who positively understand and support the rules and standards which are essential to that order."[20]

For educators across the political spectrum, teachers played the central role of ensuring "liberating" citizenship through lessons in conformity. After all, teachers, second to parents, had the greatest contact with youth in their formative years. An article for The Bulletin in 1951, "In Praise of Teachers," vividly described the teacher's responsibility as a patriotic duty. The author described each school, with masculine imagery, as a "miniature nation, where the young citizens are forming habits, acquiring attitudes towards the world they live in and towards their fellow-citizens ... The teachers – it is almost too awful a responsibility to put down in black and white – are the statesmen in those miniature nations."[21] It was teachers' classroom personalities and appearances, more than their style of instruction, which was credited with forming attitudes and habits. In 1953, traditionalist Sidney Katz wrote in Maclean's, "Moral behaviour can't be taught as a subject like reading ... the greatest influence for good is what the teacher is and how he acts."[22] Progressive educator Neville Scarfe likewise remarked, "what is best learned in the school is acquired incidentally, as if by infection, rather than by direct instruction. Children are very imitative and they need, therefore, to have examples of high quality persons in the classroom."[23] Although progressives believed that teachers' indirect influence enabled students to discover the moral compass for citizenship and traditionalists argued that teachers provided a cost-efficient means of inculcating values, they agreed that the personal qualities embodied in a teacher were of the utmost importance for the development of students and thereby citizenship.

What exactly these qualities were tended to be rather vague. The B.C. Teacher contained several articles trying to define them. One was a reprint by Sidney Hook, professor at New York University and author of *Education for Modern Man*, which first appeared in the December 1953 issue of the *New York Times Magazine*. Hook maintained that teachers were the unacknowledged legislators of the free world, because the "teacher by his manner and practice serves as a living example to his students."[24] He listed teaching's seven deadly sins: "discourtesy, indifference, courting, popularity, bluffing, superficiality, bullying, and dogmatism."[25] In an address to student-teachers at Hamilton Teachers' College in 1954, Ontario educator J.G. Althouse provided his own list of professional qualities, including a sense of humour, authority, affection, firmness, and courtesy.[26] He reminded candidates for the vocation that their ability to affect students' behaviour and learning "depends on your own temperament, your own intelligence, your sensitivity and your attitude towards life."[27]

A closer examination of school officials' list of ideal qualities for a teacher's character reveals a gendered necessity. While some of the attributes such as indifference and courtesy recommended by Althouse, Hook, and others invoked a nonspecific figure, most shone an intense spotlight on women's moral bearings. In one of many articles published by the OSSTF on this issue, Norman McLeod, past president of the federation, insisted that teachers generally had to emulate community standards. He wrote: "Any teacher who feels secure and satisfied in the complete privacy of his own class-room and his own home is living in a strange paradise."[28] It becomes clear that McLeod is directing his comments to women teachers when he goes on to specify that it is mandatory for a good and happy teacher to have a soft voice, use elegant language, and "avoid nagging."[29] *The B.C. Teacher* published similar moral imperatives. In a 1946 issue, the editors reprinted a report by Toronto principals which they argued was equally applicable to men and women teachers.[30] This assertion is highly suspect, considering the content of the article and the authors' use of the feminine pronoun (unusual for the period). Like McLeod, the authors made explicit references to "feminine" attributes, such as a pleasant voice, not fussing too much, and a love of children.[31] The authors referred in detail to housewife-like duties as critical, silent influences on the character of students. In this description, each teacher reproduces, rather than produces, a constructive learning environment by "dressing modestly and tastefully; keeping her desk and the window-sills neat; having a few good large pictures, if possible, and having them well placed; and arranging displays of work in an artistic manner."[32] Such BCTF and OSSTF missives made it clear women teachers not only shouldered responsibility for the moral development of their students, but were themselves susceptible to behaviour that compromised their ability to do so.

The ethical scrutiny women teachers endured in the course of their federations' public relations campaigns, as touched upon in the previous chapter, is one of the strongest signs of their obligation to character education. Other authorities similarly took for granted women's special role in education. Feminist historians have noted that women teachers have long been specific targets for surveillance by the public. North American studies have examined nineteenth-century lady teachers who, placed on a pedestal as moral guardians, Republican mothers, and Protestant missionaries, were scrutinized for private and public behaviour that did not fit within the bounds of femininity.[33] Sandra Gaskell argues that surveillance of their personal life continued into the postwar era. Women who taught in rural communities, she notes, lacked anonymity and were often subject to ad hoc employment contracts and conditions.[34] In a number of cases, elementary teachers complained to their federation about losing their jobs because male trustees and ratepayers claimed they failed to respect community values.[35] For postwar, urban, secondary school teachers, on the other hand, psychologists assumed the role of community overseers. Their dictates pushed women teachers to reproduce citizenship's highly gendered discourses.

Psychologists assumed an unprecedented place in postwar secondary schools, and focused on women teachers, assuming that they carry gendered roles from the home into classrooms. They urged teachers, as they did mothers, to temper their authority over children, warning against their tendencies to smother children with their domineering inclinations. Samuel Laycock was particularly influential in this regard. In a survey of classrooms across Canadian provinces, Laycock charged the "dithery" and "tense" teacher, "who sees all her Johnnies as individuals whom she can boss or dominate," with thwarting children's psychological fulfillment.[36] In one contribution for *The B.C. Teacher*, he was emphatic about his gendered perceptions of mental health and stability. Poor mental health in teachers revealed itself with "emotional problems," "malicious gossip," "over-sensitive" personalities, and "nagging."[37] To overcome these problems, Laycock encouraged teachers to consult the burgeoning field of educational psychology. While he associated women teachers with moral stability for students and the nation, Laycock identified male authorities as the determinants of female capacity. Psychologists affirmed that women's embodied selves were sites for the differentiation and medicalization of what was normal or abnormal, right or wrong gender behaviour in class-rooms, as elsewhere.[38]

Laycock's assertions on the national scene permeated administra-tive and academic discourses in both British Columbia and Ontario. Dr C.G. Stogdill, who worked with the Toronto board, affirmed Laycock's statements about the Canadian home in a 1952 *Telegram* article: "watch for over-solicitous mother ... parents should avoid any hard-and-fast set of rules in bringing up their children."[39] In Toronto, Althouse's address to inspectors and student teachers advised them to search for the "danger of over-teaching," which he characterized as teachers who "talk too much."[40] Vancouver school board officials responded directly, claiming that "talking too much" was a problem for their new teachers (who were primarily women) and was being addressed.[41] A contributor to *The B.C. Teacher* noted that psychologists' allegations against women were circulating across North America. She wrote: "Some recent studies have found teachers as a group, more neurotic than other groups of women."[42] While the author disagreed, she cited social authorities who "think we tend to be an emotionally immature group."[43] Psychologists provided scientific justification for educational authorities as they sought preferred behaviours from their female staff.

Evidence from the women interviewed suggests that they were conscious of their unique position as role models for "democratic" citizenship in Canadian secondary schools. Explicit acknowledge-ment informed many Vancouver narratives. Unlike their Toronto counterparts in the collegiate institutes, whose oral histories empha-sized the importance of scholarship to their careers – a mark of the women, as a group, having different training, levels of certification, and subject specialties – the Pacific Rim professionals were more likely to focus on their moral duties. For example, Catharine Darby explained that her job involved training students in the best values. Asserting her perspective as a detached, objective professional, she rejected the idea that such training was a form of mothering but had to admit "teachers were role models for them [students]." Grace Logan described doing the best she could "to be a role model" for students, creating an atmosphere "conducive to learning [with] good manners to decent speech." She later concluded that the school and her discipline "was sort of forming of good character."

The persistence of this theme reveals the extent to which all the women understood themselves to be positioned as symbolic of moral citizenship. A few interviewees openly recognized that educational authorities considered women, more than men, to be the primary caregivers when it came to infusing "proper" citizenship. Donna Weber recounted community "expectations of teachers' behaviour, especially women." As she pointed out, "teachers were the ones we learned things from ... [we] couldn't raise a ruckus, we couldn't be rude, we couldn't be impolite." In her mind, female teachers had a particular moral duty because "women were always considered to be natural teachers ... there were certain things men did well and certain things women did well." Interviewees also expanded upon reflections of men "cheating," referring to some men as "immature" or engaging in immoral practices; women were regularly thereby positioned as more ethical practitioners. Ellen Stewart recounted numerous incidents from this perspective. In one, a male colleague complained to students that she was far too strict. In her subsequent rebuttal, Ellen asserted that she was a fair disciplinarian whose students, unlike those of her fellow teacher, learned "formal organization," "boundaries," and "a security in which they can act."[44] Her indictment of her colleague was a particularly strong accusation given the code of ethics championed by both federations that warned against talking about other teachers.[45] The regularity with which women were accused of ethical violations and gossiping suggests that the code targeted women – the sex perceived as less rational.[46] In this case, Ellen provides an example of resistance with her acerbic comments regarding her colleague, affirming the moral shortcoming for which her sex was much more likely to be held culpable.

While some interviewees referred to specific lessons they taught, like school officials of the era, they believed that role-modeling had a greater effect than lecturing students about morality. Ellen Stewart and Sadie Chow were among the few women who told stories about giving ethical instruction. As a coach, Ellen emphasized orchestrating games so that her students would learn sportsmanship above all else. The rules of the game helped produce "beautifully, socially well-trained young ladies, and they loved to play." Sadie Chow argued that her instruction went beyond making a dress in home economics; her pupils were encouraged to dress for economic productivity.

In her grade twelve classes, "the kids would bring something we would wear on a first job interview and we would critique one another and see you know, the effectiveness of it ... this allows you to get into the world." Even these narratives of direct instruction, however, convey the centrality of *representing* or mimicking democratic citizenship through gendered embodiment rather than *producing* democratic citizenship. Sadie was especially representative of this perspective, in part due to her specialty. This home economist stated quite matter-of-factly that "appearance is your first key to your whole personality." She described a dressing scheme designed to make her the "epitome" of students' aspirations: "every week I wore a different colour and the object of the game was to teach kids how to colour co-ordinate and to accessorize." As the only racialized teacher in the group interviewed, such observations may also reflect her own need to camouflage herself in the face of potential critics, as well as a hard-won consciousness of becoming successful by literally clothing herself in respectability.

Toronto women also spoke to their function as moral benefactors. While not as direct as Vancouverites, they regularly engaged in metaphorical discussions of the school as a kind of show. They described their teaching lives as the performance of a myriad of expected appearances. Beverley Hurst of Toronto described teaching as being "in our own show pretty well." Phoebe McKenzie recalled advice from other teachers not to "get emotionally involved, just put on a show." She responded: "So I put on a big show." Women in the study portrayed themselves as well-trained actresses, stepping on stage in front of classrooms and quickly becoming appropriate in language, dress, and personality.

Few women identified the educational structures that insisted on such performances. Specifically, few spoke of the imposing presence of their federation or psychologists during their careers. This may be because they still followed the profession's code of ethics that warned against "airing their dirty laundry in public" or because they regarded themselves as free agents. In any case, at least in their days of retirement, these women had their revenge on male experts who had sought to constitute themselves as pedagogical authorities. Their comments reflect the very tensions officials exploited either in condemnation or praise, namely, that women teachers were upheld publicly as moral guardians and then expected to surrender their ability to make judgments of students to male scientists external to the education system.[47] Karen Phillips recalled opposing as superfluous many of the prescribed rules of the guidance department. She said, "All my career, if some of these rules were not very smart you opposed them. It took me ages to turn in the reports they demanded on attendance. I couldn't see the purpose of the information that took so much time so I didn't do it." Other women indicated that they ignored circulated warnings against over-mothering. Claiming to be strict disciplinarians, they denied the relevance of such admonitions. Phoebe McKenzie of Toronto even apprehensively admitted that she "had the misfortune of slapping the face of a girl whose parents were both PhDs in Psychology." She recalled the girl as previously very insolent and subsequently her "devoted servant." When Sophie Canning taught in Vancouver, she enforced physical punishment. After witnessing a boy step on a girl's foot, she remembered: "I went right over to him and I stepped damn hard on his foot ... I could see my name in headlines, teacher breaks child's foot." She emphasized that she "had no time for psychology." While psychologists, federation officials, and even politicians may have been social forces in the public profiling of women teachers, most interviewees asserted that such external voices had little to do with the day-to-day realities of their classrooms.

Women in both Ontario and British Columbia did cite teacher training as a source of influence. Melanie Kilburn stated that she learned the expectations of "looking and acting like a teacher" during her time at the OCE in 1951 to 1952: "you had white running shoes ... your posture had to be just right and your uniform had to be just so. Most of the people in Phys. Ed. ended up looking like Phys. Ed. teachers ... We needed that to get into the schools." Donna Weber identified a University of British Columbia professor who told her two weeks before graduation that she was not going to succeed as a physical education teacher. The reasons, Donna explained, were "because I had poor posture, I smoked, and my running shoes weren't clean." Proper posture and abstinence from smoking had long been associated with healthy, feminine behaviour. Mary Louise Adams notes that the high school curriculum in the postwar period for girls' physical education included calisthenics for the improvement of posture and gracefulness for much the same reasons.[48] A clean and crisp uniform, which the interviewees identified as important, symbolized scientific hygiene and military order, both offering potential salvation for delinquent youth. Such purity and order invoked themes that infused "democratic" values of the age. Melanie's and Donna's memories of learning orderliness and reproductive health from their teacher-training years were understandable. Teacher-training manuals of the period such as *Teaching in the Modern Secondary School* (1952) advised readers that service to the community depended on a positive answer to the following questions: "Am I neat and clean in personal appearance? Do I insist upon my right to live a normal life in the community, yet recognize those social behaviours that are unacceptable to the community? Do I keep myself physically clean and attractive?"[49] Early in their careers, teachers learned that performance of citizenship duties required that their exterior image reflect hegemonic societal ideals.

This lesson carried into the workplace. For the most part, the women commented that interactions with administrators in the schools where they worked ingrained the importance of women's physical presence in the classroom. For example, on the west coast Grace Logan commented that she had a school board inspector speak to her after one class and "he had just one complaint, that my voice was too loud." She said, "I wasn't aware it was loud, I tried to lower the tone of my voice." Similarly, in Ontario, Karen Phillips recalled an incident in which an inspector "told the French teacher that she hadn't powdered her nose, her nose was shiny. She should pay more attention to her appearance." Although Karen did not imply that this incident taught her to powder her nose before teaching, the memory clearly lingered because it summed up school boards' efforts to discipline their female staff.

While Beth Merle's narrative also involved an administrator, in this case the principal, she emphasized her own role in shaping the presentation of her female apprentices. She recalled setting some of the boundaries of dress for younger, student teachers in the later part of the postwar period. When a neophyte wore a short skirt, the principal reacted by asking: "Are you going to speak to that young woman, or am I?" Beth took up the task. She suggested further that it was important not to wear dresses with busy patterns because students were readily distracted. Beth stressed that she shared with younger women a desire to be attractive, but within appropriate classroom boundaries. She proudly commented on wearing a navy dress with red inverted pleats that she "heard a lot about" from students. Such recollections reveal that merely stepping into the classroom did not make the teacher. Experience had, after all, taught Beth the nature of appropriate garb. Those in training had yet to learn that lesson.

Phoebe McKenzie also noted the appearance of her student teachers. She asserted, however, that their look, which was different from hers, was positive because it caught the students' attention: "You know it is very refreshing every week or two to have somebody young and attractive to come in to teach [laughter]." Unlike Beth, Phoebe found the new styles of dress in the 1950s to be liberating. Like the recollections of Beth and Phoebe, many women's stories addressed other women's ability to present as teachers. A positive sense of self sometimes related to the negative images of other women. In such distinctions, the women interviewed signaled their understanding of and their commitment to ideals that identified them as respectable members of their profession.

THE VIRTUES OF "DEMOCRATIC" APPEARANCES

Women teachers had to negotiate respectable feminine appearances that wedded them to patriarchal values. Respectability was largely synonymous with restoring those lifestyle norms that had been shaken by the war. The paramount image teachers were expected to convey was that of a happy participant in the nuclear family. Interviews illustrate that women understood the imperative of this idealized model. When asked about their regular workday routines, many began by referring to dress. Detailed in their descriptions, they were most adamant about their distinct personas in the mixed-sex environment of the secondary school. Beth Merle of Toronto forcefully explained that she always wore "a skirt or blouse. Certainly not pants. You didn't wear pants then." Vancouverite Abigail Sears was equally clear: "No pants!" She claimed to have been the first woman in her secondary school to wear pants in the mid-1960s, an act which sparked a whispering campaign against her. Melanie Kilburn explained her early experience in a Toronto collegiate institute taught her the importance of shifting from gym tunic to classroom skirt: "I had a wrap-around skirt and as I whizzed down the hall, I would be wrapping it around ... so that it would cover the bare legs." Melanie strove to hide any hint of the unladylike glimpse of bare legs and shorts after she left the gym. These interviewees were ensuring that as working women they were not perceived as taking on masculine appearances or positions.

Such memories convey public trepidation surrounding the ever increasing number of women in the male-dominated public sphere, in this case the secondary school. In her research on women's Second World War work in the military, Ruth Roach Pierson argues that public fear over the destruction of femininity rose as women joined the "masculine" workforce. [50] Such fears were exacerbated in the postwar period as women's employment rose again. When "abandoning" the family home under any pretext, women faced scrutiny, and were at times accused of working only for material luxuries or taking the rightful positions of men, both viewed as fundamentally immoral. Kathryn McPherson asserts that a visual advocacy of heterosexual values was especially critical for women undertaking professional lives during this time. She demonstrates that healthcare administrators, who believed a more youthfully feminine figure would increase the attractiveness of nursing and deter entry into other employment options, encouraged an exaggerated feminine figure. [51] Administrators invoked the heterosocial youth culture of the age by persuading women to attend residence dances, wear more tailored uniforms, and to use a smoking area in hospitals. [52] Nurses' uniform signified their official subservience to male doctors and created a more normative connection between the profession and heterosexuality than in the past.

Although teachers did not have to wear a uniform, school officials did provide edicts for women's dress that signified both their heterosexuality and their respectability. This is evident in the regular controversies that emerged in British Columbia newspapers regarding female attire. For example, a principal reportedly suspended three girls for wearing slacks, with Stan Evans, the assistant secretary of the BCTF, affirming the legal right of schools to ensure that "skirts really make ladies." [53] At the same time, women were encouraged not to take femininity too far, emulating the modern woman by wearing tight sweaters (which were "disturbing for male students trying to focus on their work") and sheer nylon blouses. The latter were actually banned for female employees. [54] Women could protect their position in the workplace by exhibiting a proper feminine appearance: one that asserted gender differences. Clear distinctions solidified the differential levels of authority between male and female teachers. The dress and deportment of women teachers also served to reproduce the nuclear family, with men being promoted as the legitimate breadwinners in the school – a central character lesson in the educational agenda of postwar "democratic" citizenship.

Sheila L. Cavanagh argues that the nuclear family model was as much about compulsory heterosexuality as fears of growing lesbianism. Permission for married women to teach provided an opportunity to condemn homosexuality.[55] Teaching afforded white, middle-class, educated women a socially acceptable means to transcend traditional family structures. With a shift in tolerance for married women, who became a necessary part of the system, came a heightened intolerance of independent women living outside marital relationships. Where once such women had been the admired backbone of Canadian education, they were increasingly suspect, being dismissed as inadequate spinsters. Although married women still faced accusations of unprofessional behaviour, Cavanagh asserts that single women were more often chastised for not being of a marrying mind. Women's greater access to higher education and paid labour provided new opportunities to opt out of heterosexual relationships, leading to societal anxiety that lesbianism would result. Single women teachers who "refused to organize their private lives and sexuality around a man," were treading on dangerous ground, potentially understood as "emotionally maladjusted, sexually inverted, celibate and/or queer."[56] Madiha Didi Khayatt, in her work on lesbian teachers, supports this point by exploring the ways sexologists and psychologists of the period imposed a medicalized model of sexuality that connected the lack of a stable nuclear family background with spinsterhood, mental illness, and subsequently lesbianism.[57]

Fears and accusations of instability were particularly pronounced for young, fertile women who chose independence. As during the industrial revolution, these independent spirits were finding careers in expanding city centres that offered less supervision and more leisure.[58] Many single teachers of this period, including those interviewed for this study, fit that mold. They were not old spinsters but rather young, urban, single women. Cavanagh suggests that postwar discussion of the unmarried teacher assumed a eugenics cast. She quotes an excerpt from an article entitled "Better Teachers, Biologically Speaking" published in *Education Digest*, a popular education magazine: "the married are, on the whole, biologically superior to the unmarried (… longevity, keeping out of jail, and freedom from mental disease) so are the fertile superior to the sterile. It is desirable not merely that teachers should marry, but also that they should have children."[59] When young, eligible, white women refused to marry, they appeared to challenge their obligations as future mothers and reproducers of democratic citizenship.[60] As professionals, they also failed to communicate the nature of proper citizenship.

Ontario and British Columbia school officials, more subtly than their counterparts in *Education Digest,* glorified the marriageable woman in their schools. For example, at the beginning of the 1952 school year in Toronto, C.C. Goldring seemed proud of the shortage of women teachers due to high marriage rates. He reported to the *Globe and Mail* that "men like the motherly qualities of the kindergarten teacher, the rim lines of the physical education teachers, and the home economics teachers' skill with the skillet."[61] Similarly, Vancouver newspapers regularly put sexually attractive women teachers on display. One such picture, "Pretty, New Teachers," was accompanied by the caption claiming that these teachers were "enough to send dad to school with junior."[62]

Educational authorities simultaneously alluded to fears of independent women when discussing the image of female teachers inside school walls. Cartoons in the papers used the spinster image to police teachers and celebrate in contrast young, attractive, marrying women. The threat of the spinster teacher loomed large. She was characterized by a spindly body covered by an oversized skirt and jacket, glasses hanging from her sharp nose, and hair tightly pulled back in a bun: a far from attractive vessel for reproduction. One cartoon that advertised "Education Week," an annual campaign across Canada that encouraged communities to learn more about their schools, depicted such a figure surrounded by dead plants, bored children, and falling pictures of apples (in other situations a recognizable sign of students' affections for their teacher).[63] School officials viewed the spinster, with her apparent rejection of or inability to fulfill the role of wife and mother, as an unacceptable ambassador to the public.

The promotion of this view could very well have been a public relations exercise to swell the ranks of women teachers. In 1955, the report of the west coast conference of the Canadian Education Association noted that: "It was hoped that some mass medium process could be devised to parallel 'Medic' for the medical profession, and 'Dragnet' and 'Mr. D.A.' for the police departments. At present, all we have is 'Our Miss Brooks,' which is worse than useless."[64] Our Miss Brooks may have been "useless," albeit a successful radio and television personality in the late 1940s and '50s, because she was yet another spinster teacher. Even her obvious attractiveness could not counterbalance her sharp wit, tough talk, and failure to win Mr Boynton, the school's biology teacher. We can only speculate whether the CEA would have referred to Miss Brooks as no credit to the profession when she finally married Mr Boynton and lived happily, we suppose, after the show was cancelled in 1956.

Women teachers were awkwardly positioned between the deviant spinster, who rejected her "natural" purpose, and the single, sexy "it" girl, who had motherhood potential if she contained her feminine wiles. An article in *The B.C. Teacher* acknowledged the contradictions. The author encouraged readers to see women teachers as more "normal people." Instead, "the public lamented because we dressed dowdily, until it was presently discovered that we spent too much on our clothes. About the same time we were found to be using too much lipstick, although it was admitted that some of us would be easier on the eye if we used it."[65] The women's oral histories were shaped by both images, although for most, neither seemed a fit, as they were conscious of the dilemmas of each. This conundrum is evident in both the narratives of single and married women in the study.

Fran Thompson's memories of her teaching days as a single woman are representative of many of the women's narratives. When she began teaching in a Toronto school, Fran asserted, she did not want to emulate the social character of her mentors. She stated: "I had a rather prejudiced opinion myself. I bought the stereotype that these unmarried women would be old spinsters ... she dressed in long black skirts, thick stockings, and funny looking coats." By contrast, she characterized her own appearance when she began teaching in the 1950s as having been "well dressed ... always a skirt or something like that." This vague description did not fully separate her from the spinster teacher. Fran additionally distinguished herself from her predecessors by referring to the kinds of topics she discussed with her students. She specifically referred to debates over sex education: "conservative people saying, 'You mean unmarried teachers could stand up and talk about birth control and in a school.' I was laughing because I knew that was already going on." Throughout her narrative, Fran represented her self as "with it" because of her well-dressed appearance and liberated message of womanhood and sexuality. She was nevertheless also cautious. Due to condemnation by critics of the "new woman" of the postwar era,

Fran did not wear corset-cinched waistlines or tight sweaters over perky breasts. Furthermore, big crinolines, hats, and high heels were impractical in the school setting. In the end, Fran found solace by performing the appearance of traditional and respectable femininity while simultaneously acting out alternative visions of womanhood to her students.

Phoebe McKenzie, married with children during her teaching days in Toronto, similarly asserted her need to negotiate complicated terrain. Like other wives, she never specifically invoked the image of the spinster. Instead, Phoebe cheerfully mentioned her daughter's joke that she was "one of the first modern women." She defined "modern" as having the ability to be married, raise children, and have a career. Without further questioning on the subject, Phoebe felt the need to add: "but I had a very good reputation as a teacher before I got married ... we were very moral." Her comments reflect the fears that surrounded the modern woman, especially postwar experts' accusations of women's sexual wiles. Physical education teacher Jessie Russell of Vancouver, who was also married, referred to skepticism about her basic femininity due to her subject area. She alluded to societal misgivings about potential associations with a muscular physique and stereotypical butch lesbian exterior. She remembered a university professor bringing students to watch her teach a physical education class for the explicit reason that: "you keep looking feminine, you're not a jock, you dress nicely and you, you know you're careful about your appearance and you do a good job at the lesson." Jessie conveyed her own comfort by highlighting her ability to be an effective teacher while simultaneously exhibiting her womanliness. She went on to describe her work in the gym as having a profound influence on the presentation of her students' sense of self. Jessie explained that she "just wanted to look like a nice P.E. teacher, I didn't want to look sloppy ... like my hair was always in a ponytail ... I met one [student] at a reunion and she said every morning she would try and do her hair the way I had it." She, like most of the women interviewed, made concerted efforts to steer through the pitfalls for women's embodiment of postwar norms.

Sophie Canning, a square dancer and caller in her off time, also claimed to have dressed the part demanded by the times. As a lesbian, however, she depicted her dress less in terms of expressing a non-spinster identity than in covering up her demonized sexuality. For Sophie, this was not primarily workplace imagery. Her teaching attire provided a protective second skin, as she had to always live her life in the closet. Unlike the other women interviewed, she insisted that she only wore pants, never a tunic: "long blue pants, fairly tight, and one time I had to do something and I was dressed up and this person came up [to me and said], 'My god your legs aren't blue!'" Sophie concluded: "see, I had a dress problem." Unlike the other women interviewed, her "problem," as she defined it, was not the result of admonishment from school officials or even inability to convey the appearance of respectable femininity. Rather, Sophie recognized the need to play a part, not revealing herself too much, at the same time as she rejected the binary of the postwar model for femininity. For example, when asked why officials took issue with women wearing pants, as she did, Sophie reacted with surprise. She took a moment to recount a story in which it was liberating to ignore the rules. Sophie recalled teaching a dance program to a mixed class of boys and girls: "God it was fun and I started them out exactly – get with whoever you want ... and they can dance with whoever they want and they were so at ease that they [the boys] didn't have to pick a girl you know and then away we went." Sophie was refusing to impose the same hetero-social programming for her students that she felt urged to portray.

Sophie was perhaps most explicit concerning her resistance to postwar edicts when she followed questions about dress with her own inquiry: "Are you Christian?" She proceeded to explain that she had renounced organized religion in her life due to the hypocrisy. Sophie was referring to the historical pathologization of homosexuality through the imposition of Judeo-Christian morality.[66] Christian ethics, as Mary Louise Adams argues, underpinned the ideals of middle-class domesticity during the postwar period.[67] Ewart H. Morgan, Assistant Superintendent in Winnipeg, suggested the increasing role of the school in church duties with his contribution to a national symposium on Canadian education in the late 1950s. He argued that the secondary school "finds that life is unitary, that the cultivation of the intellect cannot be separated from the cultivation of the spirit, and that mind and body and spirit must be 'educated' together."[68] It was not any spiritual belief that was proffered by educators. Instead, the postwar secondary curriculum took for granted that democracy depended on Anglo-Saxon political traditions and Christian heritage. The belief that "all men are brothers and the children of God, the belief that there is a spark of the divine in every man ... these are beliefs which distinguish our Western world from all previous civilizations and which give to it its characteristics virtues."[69] The duty of the educational system was to ensure that teachers "have truly grasped and taken possession of the spiritual heritage of our civilization."[70] Karen Phillips remembered that the school board members' first question at her job interview was "What church do you belong to?" Like earlier generations of women teachers, Karen and others here understood themselves as a contemporary expression of the traditional "angel in the schoolhouse."

The interviewees reflected on lessons in Christianity provided in the context of social studies, bible-reading courses, and in opening exercises. Such lessons were considered the basis for democratic values and a protection against both the seeming godlessness of the country's communist enemies and their potential influence on impressionable youth. Toronto teacher Phoebe McKenzie stated: "I insisted on excellent manners ... we had opening exercises. First thing was 'God Save the Queen' on the P.A. Some wouldn't stand up, so I insisted they stay out in the hall. I probably shouldn't have done that. If I were reading the eighth Psalm I would point something out. I would probably get fired for doing that today." While Phoebe did not explain further, we could reasonably assume that her non-Christian students were resisting the imposition of these religious teachings; an action that she would not tolerate. On the west coast, Grace Logan recounted using biblical readings to teach her female students the etiquette that was expected of them in the community. After recounting a story in which she was embarrassed for not knowing proper dining manners, Grace said: "I used to read then the little bit from the Bible about a woman ... what the values there are to be expected in a woman, because I thought many of them you know were now going to be out into the wider world than their school ... of course we used to read the Bible to them in the morning." In her mind, proper behavior derived from Christian ethics. Most of the women wanted to ensure students were aware of such ethical implications for their lives, as the teachers were for themselves.

Many of the women described teaching not simply as a job, but as a vocation or a higher calling, making them pillars of their community. Alma Erickson, typical of those interviewed, explained her choice of profession as fate. She forced her two-and-a-half-year-old brother to participate in home school lessons as she played teacher before her own school years. Jessie Russell called herself a "born teacher," obviously still a badge of honour as, when I visited her, a refrigerator magnet read "Teachers are born not made." For many, their work to ensure effective citizenship transcended the boundaries of the school walls. June West tied citizenship training to her own sense of obligation. Her philosophy was that students would become "very community-minded" in their own lives if they "knew I cared about them and the community." For her part, June noted that she contributed to Red Cross projects and chose to teach with the National Defense overseas. Melanie Kilburn stated simply that "The school was the community and vice versa." When discussing her volunteer work outside of the school, as well as her leadership of extracurricular activities within it, Melanie explained: "I'm sure that was just the CGIT training [Canadian Girls in Training] ... you just did something if it was needed." Phoebe McKenzie remembered working for many charitable causes through her affiliation with a women's missionary society during her teaching years. For such enthusiasts, their role in the community was intimately connected to their religious commitment to service to others.

Such service had a history predating professional associations' desires that their members actively demonstrate their value to the wider public. Women invoked older, turn- of-the-twentieth-century notions of "municipal housekeeping."[71] In an effort for social betterment and the institutionalization of public welfare, middle-class, primarily white Christian reformers, many of whom were women teachers, based their demands to the government on the ideal of caring for the community as they did the home.[72] The postwar re-emphasis on the family and welfare allowed female teachers to reclaim a central role in the functioning of the state. Most interviewees believed that religious observance and service to the community were directly related to loyalty to the country. As Christian women, they supplied respectable role models for the country's future citizens. The women specifically expressed a desire to uplift students they perceived to be economically, racially, and socially disadvantaged. In addition to Christianity and heterosexuality, women teachers' whiteness and middle-class backgrounds were implicit in their affirmation of normative citizenship. Although they acknowledged femininity's fraught character, few women directly or even indirectly referred to their own class or race. Their silence reflected the dominant demographics of the teaching profession, which was comprised

of Anglo-Saxon, middle-class exemplars of citizenship.[73] It also
speaks to them taking for granted such dominance.

Franca Iacovetta argues that while Canada's exclusionary immigration and refugee policies visibly defined desirable citizens by race
and class, efforts to remake those immigrants who were eventually
welcomed into the land of opportunity have been often overlooked.[74]
Women immigrants were encouraged by social workers and health
experts to abandon traditional homemaking traditions and adopt
allegedly more healthy and moral ways of shopping, cooking and
child-rearing. Iacovetta argues that campaigns to "Canadianize"
working-class, immigrant women's domestic lives were a strategy
in "domestic containment." She defines domestic containment as
"state-sanctioned and volunteer efforts within Western countries to
police not only the political but also the social, personal, moral and
sexual lives of its citizens – a process, which, ironically, involved
the repression in liberal Western democracies of individual rights
and freedoms in the name of demographic rights and freedoms."[75]
In Canada's case, the dominance of the Anglo-Celtic nuclear family
stabilized increasingly pluralist values.[76] Iacovetta notes that night
classes and cooking courses provided by the Toronto Board of
Education were a large part of attempts to morally uplift newcomer
mothers. As the first chapter outlined, these same efforts were also a
large part of the Vancouver board's diversified programming. While
those interviewed did not directly address such specific campaigns or
their participation in them, they were matter-of-fact about the relationship between their domestic appearance, embodied through
their whiteness and socioeconomic status, and their power to guide
poor and racialized minority students.

One of Karen Phillips' recollections of a Toronto woman colleague
in the 1950s communicates such assumptions: "There was one other
woman for a while in the English department. She came from a
wealthy family and used to dress up in all her finery, evening dress
with jewelry, for the class, so that these poor working-class children
would know what it was like to see something like that." While her
example clearly exceeded the limits of the ordinary with its picture
of flamboyant entitlement, it nevertheless embodied relations of
power that were for the most part demonstrated less eccentrically.
For many Vancouver interviewees, issues of racial diversity in their
schools, even greater than class issues for the Toronto women,

marked their performances. Alma Erickson described the pressure of keeping up with her middle-class female students, who came to school "in their cashmere sweaters, one hundred and some dollars." "Looking neat and smart" was important, Alma explained with some hesitation, because the kids who came down from "south Van, from the Indian reserve and those people down there didn't have that much money and some of them would come to school in running shoes, girls would come, um, poorly dressed." The women's narratives often took on the commonplace ethnocentrism that drew on some national rhetoric of the period. Catharine Darby spoke of "a lot of Chinese, real scholars among them [and] a lot of immigrants coming in, there were quite a few Italian people – it was postwar ... they wanted to do better for their children when they came to Canada." Her part, as she described next, was to show students from these families techniques in home economics that were "as useful as possible, so it meant that we didn't do ethnic stuff, it would have been too narrow ... the clothing we made was Western." Catharine took for granted the duty to transform such new Canadians into proper citizens. Others interviewed deemed such work as "civilizing" or teaching etiquette to students who were "savages." Catharine's narrative, as with most claiming racial and class privilege, suggests that while some women struggled with normative values, many accepted conventional notions of dominant femininity.

That the struggle or ease by which women performed dominant citizenship was based on their social locations is particularly apparent from the narrative of Vancouver's Sadie Chow, a second-generation Chinese woman whose family was working class. Sadie, a home economics teacher, identified herself as struggling to look Caucasian in order to garner respect from students and the school community. She described early attempts to "white"' her life in cooking and dress as a necessity for her teaching, and offered one extensive story in illustration: "I was teaching a lesson on less tender cuts of meat ... all of a sudden I heard a chair snap and this girl stood up ... she said, 'I'm not gonna take anything from a goddamn Chinaman anymore!' and she got up and banged out the door." After explaining that the student eventually apologized for her remarks, Sadie said that until that point "I had lived my life not realizing I was really Oriental because my look was Caucasian like, you know, like the banana – white on the inside, yellow on the outside." She explained that after the war all those people who had the appearance of the enemy, whether Japanese, Italian, or German, "fell into a syndrome, you know, hide what you really are." Sadie commented that throughout her early professional life, "I was so busy turning myself into a Caucasian that I really didn't give my own heritage a whole lot of thought until the last thirty years ... now, you see I have all kinds of Oriental motifs in the house." Her remarks reveal most starkly the social sanctions that accompanied a woman's failure to successfully symbolize postwar normativity. Although racism marked her teaching identity, she still asserted her ability to dress in a finer way than most, and to teach her female students how to present themselves effectively in the world. Her account also indicates that women, even as they tried to embody moral standards for Western democracy, produced varied performances of the ethical, professional, and attractive feminine teacher. Almost as an aside to these memories, Sadie noted that some of her Chinese students would come to her for advice about their social lives. Specifically, she recalled "some students once, who I think were dating someone Caucasian, and we started to talk and they said, 'what do you think of mixed marriages ... what do you think is acceptable?'" Sadie did not disclose her advice, yet her comments were a powerful illustration of her contradictory role as a racial minority in producing students' value systems. She faced and largely accepted the commonplace imperative to reproduce the nationalist, "democratic" values of the period, but her body betrayed other histories and possibilities.

Women teachers negotiated their performance by juggling personal lives, public personae (including gender respectability), their definitions of professional identities, their functioning in the workplace, and the necessities of their students' lives. These women's awareness of the social sanctions that shaped their presentation of self speaks to the body as a powerful, contextually specific, and daily signifier for nation, gender, and professionalism. Their stories also suggest that women were part and parcel of postwar social regulation. They often constructed stories in which they were obviously acting out domestic virtues. The ability to exhibit these values, many of which the women shared or could easily display, garnered them a measure of power and respectability within their schools and community. Melanie Kilburn's description of running down the hallway from the gym to the classroom in her wrap-around skirt demonstrated accommodation even as it admitted that gender display took different forms. In fact, Melanie was one of many women who maintained a critical view of society's expectations of female students. She recalled being greatly disgruntled by a young girl's preoccupation with appearance: "One of my really good kids got the ball and was in the perfect place for a lay-up shot and she dropped the ball and said, 'Oh, I broke my nail.'" She told the student: "How could you give a darn about your fingernail?" With resignation, Melanie stated: "They didn't want to mess their hair ... appearances were everything." Despite such advice, teachers' narratives illustrate that transgression was problematic because of the paradoxical position of women teachers in the unfolding of educational democracy. Women understood that they were empowered and scrutinized, upheld as the epitome of virtue and morality because of their maternal qualities, and suspected of potentially dangerous, irrational behaviour.

The appearance of the "respectable" woman teacher therefore was not straightforward or easy to produce, but rather a complex web of performing appearances and identities. This chapter illustrates some of the ways those appearances, particularly normative notions of femininity, sexuality, and family, were both upheld and rejected in women's lives and teaching. For some interviewees, this meant negotiating the conflicting images of the old spinster and the modern woman. Others largely conformed to the appearance of traditional womanhood while acting out alternative visions of gender and family roles, which were considered pragmatic and necessary for effective teaching. Their narratives expose the false essentialism of gendered "democratic" values, as the non-essentialist character of women's reproduction of national rhetoric is revealed through their postwar performances.

If women's function for educational democracy was reduced to moral benefactor and exemplar of patriarchal values, how was it possible for contemporary school officials to define women as appropriate agents for participatory democracy? In exploring this question, the following chapter examines the gendered responsibilities and authoritative structures of the newly decentralized secondary schools of Toronto and Vancouver.

4

More Responsibility, Less Power:
Gendered Participatory "Democracy" for Schools

Without the participation of citizens, liberal democracy is not genuine: this principle informed the postwar secondary school system.[1] Key to ensuring engaged citizenship is the state's ability to afford each person equal representation within the public realm. The democratic ideal requires individuals to have the autonomy to articulate and contribute a political consciousness to the nation.[2] Public schooling is meant to provide the opportunity for each student to attain the knowledge and values necessary to achieve political capital. The modern public school as an institution celebrates the ideals of equal and autonomous participation in the democratic order. Such celebration has masked the exact nature of citizen participation, and particularly the issue of gender.

As the two previous chapters have demonstrated, democratic discourse did not grant woman the role of legitimate political agent. Political philosopher Jane Roland Martin argues that by positioning women as virtuous and benevolent actors for liberal democracy, the state actually designates womanhood an apolitical status.[3] Further, Carole Pateman attests that women, portrayed as psychologically unbalanced, tied to the private sphere, and a source of disorder in the public realm, are socially constructed as unable to articulate a political consciousness.[4] Women are thus historically and discursively positioned as apolitical, despite their formal inclusion by the Western state as participatory citizens.

In the 1940s and '50s, the Toronto and Vancouver education systems set out to create a microcosm of liberal participatory democracy. The democratic school model focused on students, teachers, and administrators each assuming the right and responsibility to enrich the community. The days when teachers received curriculum from above and students had little flexibility in the courses required for graduation were disappearing. Inspection procedures were similarly revised to encourage community and personalized supervision of teachers. Collegial supervision was intended to complement external inspection and be a source not so much of clinical analysis as of warm encouragement. More importantly, teachers and their federations secured greater legal and decision-making powers. During this period, teachers were granted the right to hold public office and federations achieved compulsory membership and the right to certify members' credentials. Canadian secondary schools were organized as laboratories for society's "democratic" relations: places where students learned to value and practice their right to individual autonomy as responsible citizens. Both progressive and traditional educators supported such reforms as symbols of the contrasts between democratic nations and the authoritarian regimes of the country's communist enemies.

The democratic appearance of schools did not necessarily result in democratic practice. For female teachers, unlike their male colleagues, formal commitments did not afford opportunities for greater political influence. They faced a critical contradiction: how could they lead if they were assigned an apolitical status? The answer was twofold. First, they assumed new responsibilities for participating in educational democracy, even while they were still second-class service providers and disqualified from the official powers of administration. Second, women teachers emerged as political actors, but in a redefined sense. Avenues of conventional political participation may have been closed, but they used everyday means to resist masculine monopolization of active citizenship.

This chapter explores how women, as teachers, occupied a contradictory position as leaders within a patriarchal institution that questioned their authority. This position was the result of educational policies that formally espoused an egalitarian environment, yet refused the majority of women administrative positions and political organization to control their work environments. In the past two decades, feminist scholars have demonstrated that women's educational labour is regularly exploited in this manner.[5] Political theorist Iris Marion Young contends that an examination of women's collective resistance provides a vantage point beyond the view of liberal individualism to the systematic and institutional processes that define political agency.[6] Through this lens, the machinations of state institutions that exclude women's full political participation become clear. At the same time, women should not be assumed to be simply victims. Women educators, while typically overloaded with caregiving duties, and labouring with limited security and without access to the highest paying, most powerful administrative positions, nevertheless found their own freedom to teach within the postwar secondary school.

The first section in this chapter provides an overview of the systemic discrepancy between women's responsibility and authority in the school systems of Toronto and Vancouver. The next two sections consider women teachers' narratives, which tell stories of secondary schools that remained highly patriarchal, centralized, and hierarchical. At the same time, these sections examine women's negotiations of the discrepancy between responsibility and authority with reference to two areas: curriculum redevelopment and inspection reforms. Women's adaptation, resistance, or accommodation varied not so much according to region as by their subject areas and promotional status within secondary schools.

THE FREEDOM TO TEACH

The physical rearrangement of the school was itself symbolic of the education institution as a laboratory for egalitarian relations. Administrators refurbished postwar classrooms to reflect a co-operative social environment: open spaces and movable desks allowed for flexible lesson plans and group work; equipment for teaching included the new use of radio and motion pictures to address diverse learning styles; and expansion projects provided larger gymnasia, libraries, and industrial workshops for a growing school population.[7] These changes, for all the financial strain they represented, required new practitioners. No longer was "the old-fashioned bully and half-trained teacher" sufficient, deemed Morrison Watts, Director of Curriculum for the Department of Education in Alberta.[8] Instead, Watts asserted, "co-operative action and self-discipline are far superior to imposed authority, [and] are characteristics of modern teaching."[9] The school emerged as a place reflecting Canada's commitment to democratic life, where all members belonged and where each individual contributed to the social order.

Individual freedom is a recognizable dictum for progressivism. Adherents to this philosophy asserted that secondary school officials were lagging in efforts to eliminate forces that deprived teachers and students of the freedom to do better. Educators from Neville Scarfe to Samuel Laycock suggested that the "impersonal, highly conservative and authoritarian system" would only change if administrators addressed issues ranging from the large size of classes to the excessive focus on examinations.[10] On the other hand, traditionalists such as Hilda Neatby and Frank MacKinnon worried that the adoption by teachers and schools of a "free" philosophy would mean wholesale acceptance of "open area activities, voluntary attendance, pupil control of curriculum, inquiry methods, abandonment of competitive tests and grades (marks)."[11] As John Dewey later observed, "inchoate curriculum, excessive individualism ... is a deceptive index of freedom."[12] Ultimately ultra-progressivism, like ultra-traditionalism, was dictatorial in its pedagogical demands.

James M. Paton, a professor of English at Macdonald College (which later became the Faculty of Education at McGill University) and a prolific writer on education, argued that such extremes held little validity for education theorists and classroom teachers of the period. Paton's conclusions were ultimately pragmatic: "Whether these ways are likely to be labeled traditional or progressive, student-controlled or teacher-dominated, is of very little importance, provided the young people actually learn and enjoy the experience enough to want to go on learning by themselves."[13] His conclusions were in keeping with dominant trends that held dogma of any stripe out of fashion. Instead, teaching autonomy, complemented by the expectations of self-discipline and co-operation, was paramount. While progressive educators identified this as sound pedagogical practice, traditionalists urged national necessity. As the first chapter explained, many authorities worried that without autonomy, citizens would fall into dependency on and demand too much of government. If students and teachers were simply told what to do and had no political voice, how would they become productive citizens? Civic responsibility was the key lesson and independence had to be taught within a practical living situation that included knowledgeable and moral guides.[14] Few educators espoused dichotomous solutions for political citizenship: at the system level, complete autonomy for local staffs *or* standardized governing procedures, and at the classroom level, self-discovery lessons *or* systematic readings.[15] The majority of theorists and administrators asserted the need to "have faith in the goodness of our fellow man, our teachers, and our children."[16] Schools aimed for environments in which members worked and learned together for their mutual benefit and individual development.

Educators across the philosophical spectrum asserted that school reorganization should trust teachers to carry out the demands of educational democracy. Conservative Hilda Neatby asserted that teachers "should have the freedom to speak their minds on education matters."[17] Progressive Neville Scarfe similarly argued that "because of the known restrictions, many great minds of the nation do not even attempt to enter the teaching profession."[18] Referring to general criticism of teaching, Scarfe reasoned: "People become trustworthy only by being trusted. They learn self-discipline only by *not* being disciplined from outside."[19] Such influential commentators firmly believed that teachers required freedom of practice to instill a sense of initiative and co-operation in students. Furthermore, to be respected as professional partners in the community, they needed autonomy to make decisions. Changes to curriculum and inspection procedures had the most immediate effect on the teachers interviewed for this study and will be examined later in the chapter when addressing women's resistance to the gender hierarchy of the system. School authorities also favoured initiatives directed at disseminating political authority to teachers through the vehicle of their federations.

One of the most significant changes in Ontario came in 1944 with the passage of the Teaching Profession Act. Agitated for by the province's five existing teacher organizations, and supported by George Drew's Conservative government, the act created the umbrella organization of the Ontario Teachers' Federation.[20] A clause in the legislation provided for compulsory membership for all teachers in government-funded schools. With the solidarity and financial support of a large membership, the OTF was able to campaign for better remuneration, control over certification, and rights to negotiation.[21] Not until 1975 did the federations win the right to strike or mandatory collective bargaining.[22] Nonetheless, the OTF's broad-based authority provided teachers with more bargaining power with boards. For example, in the mid-1950s it became a statutory requirement for boards to use a contract that outlined in writing salary, holidays, vacation and sick days, and reasons for discontinuing employment.[23] Furthermore, the OSSTF created the "pink letter" (also referred to as "grey listing") to warn teachers not to apply to boards negotiating in bad faith.[24] These measures provided a certain

degree of power to control working conditions and wages. Salaries
increased steadily throughout the period, and the OTF's adoption of
a single salary schedule, despite continued gendered differences,
undermined boards' ability to institute ad hoc financial agreements.[25]
The 1953–54 decision by the OSSTF, the Ontario Public School
Men Teachers' Federation (OPSMTF), and the Federation of Women
Teachers' Associations in Ontario (FWTAO) to accept the principle of
licensing their members was also significant.[26] While the Department
of Education still granted certification, licensing signified the federations' new role in deciding who would be teachers. Licensing was a
form of internal regulation which the federations believed would
raise the status of the profession by giving teachers the power to
decide their own code of ethics and training qualifications.[27]

West coast teachers gained similar rights during the postwar years.
The British Columbia Teachers' Federation, since 1917 composed of
autonomous local associations, was the primary organization for
teachers. Prior to 1945, the BCTF changed its constitution to ensure
compatibility among the bylaws of its associations: thereby ensuring
boards recognized the federation as the official collective bargaining
agent for teachers.[28] With broad-based support secured, the postwar
years would be the BCTF's "coming of age."[29] Legislation passed in
1947 made membership compulsory for all teachers, achieved in
part by a tacit agreement with the government not to strike.[30]
Furthermore, the federation made steady gains in salaries, with the
average wage rising by eighteen percent between 1943 and 1945
alone.[31] Government pension plans were also strengthened. In 1950,
the federation secured a six percent government pension contribution; 1958 amendments to the Teacher's Pension Act increased service pensions. The BCTF also won some control of training and
certification.[32] By 1961, the BCTF adopted an official membership
categorization plan to assess basic competencies.[33] As in Ontario,
this plan would not usurp the certification powers of the Department
of Education, but was a critical step in giving a voice in educational
qualifications. The demand for professional authority extended
beyond the education system. As early as 1944, the federation sought
an amendment to the Municipal Act to eliminate the restriction on
teachers holding public office.[34] After great public dispute between
the BCTF and the Union of British Columbia Municipalities, teachers gained this right in 1958.[35]

The freedoms obtained by the teachers' federations in Ontario and British Columbia during the 1940s and '50s represented a hard-fought extension of full citizenship to all members of the school community as the democratic state harmonized its principles with its practices. The Education Week slogan of the period that "education is everyone's business" invoked the other commonplace phrase of the day, "politics in these days is every man's business."[36] A contributor to *The B.C. Teacher* resolutely made this point when referring to teachers' rights to public office and effective organization in federations: "No group has been more directly charged with the responsibility of inculcating democratic principles in the future adult citizens than teachers ... Can we then justifiably expect teachers whole-heartedly to attempt to achieve this aim and still openly deny them their own democratic rights?"[37] While such statements could be interpreted as a genuine rationale for professional self-control, some scholars, such as Jenny Ozga, Martin Lawn, Bob Bessant, and Andrew Spaull, argue that state concepts of professionalism can suppress more radical demands for improved working conditions.[38] In other words, teacher groups sometimes reproduce the status quo. In this process, Michael Apple argues, teachers actually become increasingly proletarianized. Rather than gaining additional autonomy, they face intensified work.[39] Bryan Palmer notes that the government's general approach to labour during postwar capitalist accumulation included initiatives, such as health insurance, unemployment insurance, and workmen's compensation, that ensured a stable and secure workforce.[40] But he too argues that while these programs could be interpreted as protective, they also acted to thwart alternatives to mainstream liberalism. In fact, as Palmer suggests, the gap between classes widened during this era because "the state made more effective use of the carrot than it did of the stick."[41] Winning the freedom to teach could be seen as the counterpart of the development described by Palmer. The victories of secondary teachers sometimes seemed more about accepting greater responsibilities than facilitating political engagement. In the cases of the BCTF and OTF, codes of ethics, disciplining power over members, and disinclination to strike can all add up to a defense of the status quo.

Francis S. Chase, founding Dean of the Graduate School in Education at the University of Chicago, offers insight into the effects of increased political participation by teachers. During the 1950s

Chase studied teacher morale and concluded that, despite satisfaction from increased educational planning and policy-making, many teachers felt that "participation is encouraged only for the sake of securing assent to decisions already made [that] may produce more dissatisfaction than satisfaction."[42] Canadian administrators described the growing responsibilities of the teacher, but not necessarily increased liberties. J.G. Althouse was representative of most educators when he paraphrased the words of Fred Clarke from *Freedom in the Educative Society*, published in 1946, in a talk to the Toronto board in 1950: "Freedom is a continuing conquest and discipline is the strategy by which that conquest is assured."[43] He went on to state that schools and democracy function best when individuals have choice but that duty, sacrifice, and responsibilities come before rights. Similarly, Frank MacKinnon steadfastly championed greater trust in teachers' abilities, but in an effort to demand time and resources to work harder.[44] He was not suggesting anyone spill the apple cart.

Implicit in the participatory democracy embraced by the postwar education system was a hierarchical system of authority. The federation and its members were still at the bottom. The Teaching Profession Act in Ontario was very clear in delineating teachers' duties, including compliance with the act, co-operation with authorities, and respect for the board of trustees. There was little mention of government's obligations to its teachers.[45] Similarly, British Columbia's *Public Schools Report* demonstrated a complex bureaucratic web of controls concerning teaching materials, examinations, and staffing, with little reflection of the voices of teachers.[46] While Robert Stamp overstates Ontario's postwar education as "dictatorial," he correctly emphasizes the Department of Education's final control over almost all aspects of teachers' work.[47] There was certainly a pyramid of power in Ontario and British Columbia systems. The Department of Education and its representative, the superintendent, dictated to inspectors, principals, and department heads, who then oversaw how classroom teachers, who were ultimately accountable to the public, communicated.[48] The state was offering only benevolence rather than autonomy to its teaching force. Classroom teachers, both men and women, worked within an environment that acquiesced to a stronger voice for teachers' federations, but did not alter the organizational structure that centralized authority in the hands of a few.

Male teachers at least had access to the ladder of the educational hierarchy. While historians may debate the extent to which the state afforded teachers as a group greater political influence during this era, there is little dispute that women were denied the same authority. The gender hierarchy of postwar education systems in both provinces is statistically stark. In an analysis of the positions held by women in the field of education for the 1954–55 school year, the BCTF accounted for thirteen principals, ten vice-principals, two inspectors, and two directors in the Department of Education for the province.[49] While the percentage this represents for all principals is unclear from the BCTF's study, records show that on average women comprised less than one percent of provincial inspectors and directors.[50] These positions were almost certainly held in the elementary level and the inspectors were confined to the "female" subject areas of home economics and girls' physical education. There were no women principals in Vancouver schools at the time, despite the fact that women accounted for two-thirds to three-quarters of the total teaching population in that city. Statistics were comparable in Toronto. In 1950 the board had 106 principals; women made up only six percent of the total. At the secondary level, the numbers negligibly improved, with women accounting for eleven percent of the eighteen principals.[51] From 1930 until 1970 the numbers remained constant at two women principals, not doubling to four until 1980.[52]

Furthermore, the position of department head (not made official in Vancouver secondary schools until 1957), was primarily held by men in both cities.[53] Headships generally reflected the gender hierarchy of subject matters. Like inspectorships, department headships were usually only given to women to oversee other women in fields like home economics and physical education. Subjects with greater prestige, from history to the sciences, were overwhelmingly governed by men. Of course an occasional woman, such as Tilly Rolston, Minister of Education for British Columbia in the 1950s, achieved top positions of educational authority.[54] Rolston was an individual success story that could have promoted the discourse of educational democracy. She was not representative, however, of the gendered politics of the age. Ultimately women were democracy's workers and men were its managers.[55] The embeddedness of this binary is evident from the 1962 book on *The Canadian School Principal*, in which masculine pronouns designated principals and feminine pronouns the teachers they were presumed to govern.[56]

Men and women were thus integrated into the school's laboratory of participatory democracy in different and fundamentally unequal ways. Their roles reflected societal and organizational "understandings about the respective worth and function of males and females."[57] Womanhood remained tied to the private sphere, and manhood to the public. The result was a gender order within Toronto and Vancouver secondary school systems whereby the aspirations and qualifications of women teachers were constricted. With men as the preferred candidates, women were considered lucky to have professional jobs. Equity policies, including the elimination of the marriage bar and equal remuneration, reflected widespread assumptions that secondary teaching, at least as long as the opportunities were constrained, was suitable for women. It was not, however, embraced as an avenue through which women would upset the prevailing gender order.[58]

Women provided the special skills of nurturer and moral benefactor for secondary school students. Committed to the vocation of teaching with these skills, and thus service to the community, "good" women teachers were not credited with desires for promotion, status, and monetary rewards. The commonplace assumption was that women found reward enough in their service to their communities. J.G. Althouse set the moral tone in an address to graduating student teachers in the mid-1950s: "service is something he would willingly do for nothing."[59] Of course, unlike the women in his audience, he did not have to face the hard reality of earning less than male colleagues. Many male administrators took a similarly high road, effectively undermining the moral authority of any among the rank and file in the profession who openly professed a desire for money and power. These were not to be publicly applauded in institutions committed to the postwar ideal of individual pursuits for community benefit.

Even if by chance women had such ambitions, they were believed to be bereft of the required masculine qualifications, namely, rationality and objective knowledge. An OTF column in the April 1949 issue of the *Educational Courier* suggested that women themselves were responsible for the limited opportunities available for them: "there is a tendency to complain that men usurp the better positions, and it is true that at present time nearly all the places outside the regular classrooms are held by men; but it is also true that men tend to improve their qualifications and compete for these positions, while few women do so."[60] Administrators, politicians, and even teachers' federation representatives regularly questioned the commitment of female secondary teachers, since they were believed to have primary obligations as wives and mothers. Men, in contrast, were tempted to consider teaching by promises of quick promotion, especially if they chose primary schools.[61] In his 1947 *Maclean's* article, "Why Teachers Quit," Max Braithwaite argued that men's high rate of departure was fueled by lack of opportunities for advancement. He quoted a man who rejected teaching mathematics for the navy because he would never earn enough unless he had better odds for promotion: "I've got to become a principal ... about one chance in forty."[62] No similar concern was expressed about female attrition in the profession: Braithwaite explained they simply left "to get married."[63]

In addition to uncovering masculinist justification of male promotions, Cecilia Reynolds' study of male and female principals from 1940 to 1980 in Ontario confirms that the organizational culture of schools limited administrative roles for women. The education system was still loosely structured enough that men's promotion was largely an informal process, where it was as much "who you know," or your connection with male administrators, as "what you know."[64] The editor of *The B.C. Teacher* acknowledged promotional closure, referring specifically to Vancouver, in a 1948 article: "The best principalships are only open to half a dozen men who have toiled through the road of seniority and mediocrity ... Our educational inbreeding is becoming more and more pronounced."[65] Women, or indeed any marginalized population without insider connections, were left to fill less desirable spaces. The occasional women who obtained principalships were also placed in the least prestigious schools, typically those in less populous, rural areas.[66] Limits on the authority of women who pursued administration were signaled as early as 1925 in British Columbia, with Putnam and Weir's *Survey of the School System*. They argued that a woman might suit a role as associate principal, "chosen because of her special fitness to act as an advisor to girls. It would be, of course, distinctly understood that the title of 'associate principal' carried no administrative power except in relation to female students."[67] Whatever the educational restructuring proposed by such ostensible progressives, the message was clear: women should not govern men.

Teachers' federations did not significantly challenge the prevailing gender culture, despite mostly supporting the elevation of women's overall status in teaching. The BCTF and the OTF/OSSTF perpetuated

women's relative position at the bottom of the teacher hierarchy
during the 1940s and '50s. Like administrators of the period, many
federation representatives questioned women's commitment to the
profession, scrutinized their moral behaviour, and neglected to
address issues that closed off promotion, such as maternity leave.[68]
It would be another decade or more before federations seriously
questioned the relatively low status of women teachers compared to
their male managers.[69] On occasion, the federations fought the
demotion of a female employee. In one case, the OTF supported a
woman's refusal to resign from her principalship because she was
being demoted, instead of promoted to a larger school, to make
room for a male principal with less experience.[70] Such defense may
well have reflected the political influence of the FWTAO for women
elementary teachers, a form of support absent in British Columbia.
Overall, however, postwar women were left discursively and structurally without formal political authority while finding themselves
with the new found "freedom" to teach.

THE CONTENT OF "DEMOCRATIC" PARTICIPATION

Included in these freedoms to teach was increased responsibility for
curriculum development. As the first chapter explained, this change
occurred in Ontario through the 1949 "Porter Plan." Although
scaled back in the later stages of implementation, it was still a move
towards teachers working locally to develop curriculum, rather than
simply following prescriptions from on high. Less extensive policy
reform took place in British Columbia, but by 1961 teachers had
officially designated positions on all provincial programming committees.[71] Educational authorities supported the general concept of
teachers' participation, as part of their duties in shaping educational
content.[72] New tasks were to be cherished: "local staffs can acquire
recognized, significant control over the nature of the curriculum they
administer; they can experience worthwhile personal professional
growth from working with their colleagues ... and they can realize
the satisfactions derived from the knowledge that they are the most
important influences."[73] The gendered implications inherent in this
message for postwar participatory "democracy" in schools becomes
clear when viewed from the perspective of many female staff.

Few of the women interviewed referred to working on provincial
policy-making committees. The concept of greater ownership over

curriculum was, however, very present in discussions of their daily work environments. For the most part, they did not interpret such initiatives as a desirable devolution but an onerous obligation added to an already busy work schedule. This characterization is perhaps clearest in discussions of the extracurricular duties that regularly overshadowed their course work. In fact, they insisted that ownership over curriculum could not be simply defined according to Ministry initiatives, as meaningful curriculum extended well beyond the classroom. Beverley Hurst commented: "We did much more than just teach during the day." To Sophie Canning, extracurricular activities meant "You were going all day." As a group, the women recalled providing extra help for students in the morning, supervision at lunch and after school activities, no spare time for preparation, and many late nights and long weekends marking or preparing special events like gymnastic demonstrations, Mother's Day teas, and fashion shows.

Meanwhile their male colleagues, while possibly also overworked, escaped the same level of duties.[74] Most of the women interviewed implied that men retained more control over their lives. Reflecting on her role in the Home Economics Association in Vancouver, Catharine Darby remembered that: "They [men] were nine to five and when it came to the extracurricular women generally got the heavy load." Phoebe McKenzie recalled bringing this point to the attention of her Toronto colleagues at a staff meeting. She was agitated that the men on staff, particularly the administrators, did not supervise dances and asked "why there were no men on duty Friday night. Lots of people would like to know why neither the principal nor one of the vice-principals was on duty." The women provided many answers to Phoebe's question in their interviews.

Among those answers were that administrators did not expect men to plan social events for the school as they lacked the requisite skills and were assumed to have families that needed their attention. Catharine explained that women were "dumped on as far as extracurricular, more than men, because the men would say they had to get home to cut the grass – women had the sense of responsibility." The narratives reveal that educational officials interpreted extra responsibilities for women teachers as a "natural" complement to their efforts in classrooms. Some women rationalized such discrimination, using biological arguments of the period. Sadie Chow remembered men who just said "Hey, my day's finished at five after

three and that's all the board's paying me for," but women were willing to put in long hours because they are "multi-taskers ... I think by
virtue of what innately is our makeup."

More unusual was the recognition that male administrators confirmed gender bias and ultimately their own control by designating
extracurricular duties to women. Ellen Stewart's principal wanted a
gymnastics display for the community, or what she referred to as "a
big show so that he would appear to be the great principal." The
principal was content to leave it up to Ellen to implement his idea,
despite the fact that the school's gymnasium was under construction.
Catharine Darby recounted her principal's decision to teach his first
course in Latin: a decision that resulted in her having to help him
during her spare time. She said: "unfortunately, it was my spare
period – in my preparation period – I think I taught about ninety
percent of it ... totally unnecessary, but I was given a few perks to
make up for it." Catharine further commented that because men
were in charge they often allocated themselves the smallest classes,
the least troublesome students, and the lightest workload. Some
women noted that this lighter workload trickled down from
administrators to a male hierarchy in subject areas among teachers.
Specifically, women mentioned that men often taught science and
math, courses that did not involve as much marking as did female-
dominated often language-based subjects. Ellen, who taught physical education, English, and social studies, explained the lack of
women in sciences at the time thus: "You see, marking science and
marking math is a piece of cake ... marking English and social studies can be a big job, so the men aren't going to give away the easy
jobs." Her story was very common. The women were at once describing the old boys' network of school culture and women's exclusion
from formal decision-making powers.

When discussing their role in programming, some women openly
acknowledged they were apolitical. When asked if she was politically active in those days, Sophie Canning emphatically answered
"No!" She went on to explain that her teaching and community
engagement prevented involvement with her federation or any major
planning within the school. Abigail Sears was remembering the
equal-pay issue of the day when she claimed to have almost "no
interest in all the political stuff going on ... but I was so busy."
Referring to gender conflicts in the school, Claire Anderson stated:
"I suppose those things were going on but I was always so busy." All

the women related their demanding schedules to their lack of formal authority and thus political weakness within the school and, more generally, in the education system. All they felt that they could control was teaching in the classroom, rather than more broad-based educational concerns. Abigail followed her earlier comments on this subject by clarifying that "I was interested in teaching. I wasn't interested in all this political stuff; a lot of my peers felt the same way."

When specifically questioned about curriculum development in the traditional sense of course content, the interviewees first described it as a completely top-down process. Karen Phillips explained that the Ontario Ministry said "here are the books you are going to read this year, and that's it. It was very restrictive." Alma Erickson shared these sentiments: "there was a curriculum we had to cover so that was your responsibility ... it was sent out by the government [and] each grade had to cover a certain amount of material and that was it." Karen and Alma were both fairly insistent that central regulations structured, and curbed, the topics, timelines, and activities for teachers' lessons.

In particular, most women noted that examinations set hard-to-escape conditions. Although the Hope Commission had called for a de-emphasis on examinations to allow for more freedom in the curriculum, senior exams remained in Ontario until the 1960s, and department-based general exams were the norm through the better part of the 1950s.[75] British Columbia's Chant Commission expressed a renewed faith in external examinations and many of its recommendations were implemented in the early 1960s.[76] Senior matriculation examinations remained mandatory in both jurisdictions. Fran Thompson was just one teacher who described needing to teach to the departmental exams, exams over which she had little influence. She recalled that a grade twelve exam in history was set by the male department head and the vice-principal one year, and it contained "detailed questions on it about military battles that I hadn't taught. I don't think it was in the textbook."[77] Fran asserted that because examinations were taken so seriously and strictly, she believed it to be unethical to inform her students of these questions. She explained: "I was really sorry. I knew it wasn't fair but couldn't do anything about it." Fran justified her compliance because she was an "obedient, law-abiding person who followed the rules." Following this self-characterization, she recounted a story in which she was successful with her students by wandering off prescribed content.

Acknowledging that she often wanted to teach material that was "not just textbook or set by the exam," she described one of her grade nine classes thus: "I got on the great plague. I knew that there were some wonderful descriptions so I took a whole week out of the set curriculum ... They absolutely adored it but somehow or other I didn't feel I had much freedom to do that."

Phoebe McKenzie recounted a story in which the democracy she was asked to teach did not correspond with her own experience. She recalled: "We got notices from the board in the fifties to emphasize the importance of democracy. We were told to be sure to show that democracy is the preferred type of government ... the democratic society is the preferred society." Phoebe remembered being encouraged to add her own personal knowledge, and not simply rely on the text. In response, "I taught the rise of Modern Russia. Now when we were studying Communism ... when we were through studying it, we had a big blackboard summary with characteristics of Communism and we would fill the whole front board and part of the side board. I had my own classroom so I would leave it on. We would go over it again." Phoebe was aware that she was crossing important boundaries: "I was told that you could never do that in New York. Americans were absolutely scared skinny of Communism. Even to this day, you know, one of the reasons they don't have Medicare is that it is socialized medicine." Her story is unique among those interviewed. She was one of the only persons to admit that personal politics informed lesson content. In demonstration of her own sentiments, Phoebe further recalled that trials of communists also took place in Canada during the period, and a good friend's husband was tried and imprisoned.

Newspapers of the period reveal a steady public surveillance of communist activities among teachers and other influential members of the education system in Toronto and Vancouver. Reporters cited Toronto teachers who attended communist rallies and school board candidates with communist affiliations.[78] These reports were also found in Vancouver newspapers, with added accusations that CCF and former communists taught socialism in schools.[79] One teacher, Keith Ralston, was pushed into the spotlight in 1957 when Archie Gibbs, a member of the provincial legislature, accused the Social Credit government led by W.A.C. Bennett of hiring known "Reds."[80] Ralston, who admitted to having past communist affiliations, was the victim of a public panic that leftist teachers were producing children who came home "imbued with leanings toward non-democratic forms of government" or worse, "poisoning the mind of youth against democracy."[81] Anyone who seemed less than compliant to the dominant order within schools could be smeared by such charges.

All the women in this study denied partisan ties. While Ellen Stewart mentioned her socialist father and Sophie Canning admitted that she liked some aspects of Communism, most emphasized the importance of presenting themselves as apolitical to their students. Catharine Darby insisted that people are wrong when they assume all teachers were left-leaning. Instead, she explained, you had to resist influencing students; "you had to be careful of the slant that you were portraying ... you couldn't say that this was yes, no, or whatever ... regardless of what you thought, you had to be careful." The common surveillance of teachers' political affiliations explains, in part, why the women interviewed resisted questions that might have designated their past actions or beliefs as rebellious or defiant.[82] They left themselves some room to maneuver, however, demonstrating that they were not mere marionettes. As Phoebe McKenzie noted, she was the "master of my own classroom, with my own expectations." Her narrative, like those of the others, speaks to the contradictions that defined their participation in the school's laboratory of "democracy." The education community expected them to follow their prescribed duties while at the same time to exhibit initiative and autonomy as professionals, and to do both within a cooperative, teamwork environment. The majority of interviewees described subtle negotiations of this tension, acknowledging their dutiful fulfillment of responsibilities even as they described their efforts to preserve autonomy.

Although Karen Phillips described the curriculum as prescriptive, she quickly noted: "It was the books and not the lessons. I covered twice as much because it was too restrictive. They had no modern stuff at all, so I introduced them to and assigned them other things to read." Interestingly, the particular reading Karen used to illustrate her enrichment was, as she described, "about a young rebellious guy who explored." She did not provide the title of the book, but her message was clear; alternative options were there. Later in the conversation, Karen quietly discussed her bold use of a book that was, as she designated it, "blacklisted." She explained: "Certain books were blacklisted from the English department or from the curriculum because of

a certain influence they thought wasn't appropriate ... to do with
McCarthyism, Communism, etc. ... I had all of my students read
Catcher in the Rye, not part of the curriculum but they were all
expected to read it." While one cannot be sure in what ways she
understood the book to be blacklisted, *Catcher in the Rye* was not on
the recommended text list from the Department of Education.[83]
Despite her awareness of surveillance and of the fears about seditious
activities in the McCarthy era, Karen's decision signified the bold,
unofficial steps she took to direct her students' learning. Her story
also illustrates that, while teachers were encouraged to be individuals
and have a strong influence on their students, lesson content was
intended to preserve the government's educational agenda.

Most interviewees argued that they took the prescribed material
and "enhanced it" with what Sadie Chow referred to as her "own
secrets" or their own pace, extra materials, and particular method of
teaching. Beverley Hurst, for example, repeatedly implied that the
content and structure of her lesson were determined by external
authorities. At a later point in the interview, Beverley was asked:
"Did the principal or the government or you determine what happened in the classroom?" Without vocalizing her response, Beverley
slowly raised her right hand index finger and firmly pointed it into
her own chest. Even decades later she could not verbalize her own
manipulation of the system; she still pretended to embrace Ministry
objectives. Nonetheless, she knew that she had set an agenda that
accommodated her own class, views, and workload. Mostly, the
women were able to accomplish what they believed was necessary
according to their obligations both to the government and their students, while still retaining certain autonomy. Muriel Fraser made
this argument when she stated: "I stuck to the curriculum. I think we
managed to finish it well, but then I talked to them a lot about trav-
els. You see, I would go overseas, because you knew French and
German ... I brought in a lot of stuff." Sophie Canning explained
that her expertise, particularly in dance, helped determine course
content. She recalled at one point teaching English and using music
and movement to help students with writing exercises. Typically,
these women teachers demonstrated control through how the content was covered and not the content per se. According to them, the
emphases and pace they set were influential in their students' learning. These women had what historian Rebecca Coulter refers to as
"power in practice."[84]

Everyday localized control was the women's primary form of influence upon the curriculum. More confrontational measures were not entirely out of reach, though such actions were not without consequences. When Claire Anderson first arrived at her secondary school, it quickly became apparent that the course materials, time on the field, and equipment were all insufficient compared to the men's program. She described a long campaign for equitable distribution of the budget and having great successes with the girls' sports teams thereafter. As a result, however, she remembered: "the men teachers, I had a bad time ... they would just 'poo poo' me or they would plan something to have the gym and it wasn't their turn." Claire recalled going to the principal regarding these incidents and offering her resignation. Although she did not leave, Claire noted that these same teachers drove another female colleague out of the school. Catharine Darby, a home economics teacher, shared a more ominous story relating to her expressions of authority within a Vancouver secondary school. Throughout our conversation, she kept returning to "threats" and an "incident." While still cryptic, towards the end of the interview she confessed that she had received veiled threats during an anonymous late night telephone call. The reason was that men felt "women were pushing for too much," and she, in particular, was "doing too much" and getting too many perks. Catharine and Claire were among the few women who gave specific illustrations of the intimidation and harassment that could accompany agitation for equality. Other women told stories of less disturbing disagreements with administrators about better curriculum resources, desired courses, and lesson plans. Some admitted threatening to leave or even resigning to achieve positions of greater authority. This type of mobility might well have been effective given the teacher shortage of the period.

Distinct differences in power and expressions of autonomy existed between interviewees promoted to full or assistant headships, and those who were not. Over half the women interviewed were promoted, well beyond the average. Promotions, which were comparable for both regions, were given almost entirely within female-dominated subjects, and in this sampling did not extend to principalships. As a general rule, those promoted were unmarried or at the very least without children. Most of the interviewees promoted were physical, home economics, or languages teachers, and only two women, both from Vancouver, were both mothers and administrators.

Typically, the interviewees who had advanced professionally also expressed having had greater opportunity to insert their own ideas into the content and methods of their classes, and do so in a cooperative and collegial environment. Those who were not promoted, like Fran Thompson, found "no sharing resources between teachers, or lesson plans ... no, all my teaching totally by myself." Alma Erickson, the only woman teaching in the math department of her secondary school, explained that she "had to do her own thing." June West argued, in fact, that she was glad she "wasn't a part of any team-teaching because to prepare took a lot of preparation already. I was pretty much left alone to teach as I thought I should teach." According to many who did not take on an administrative role, collaboration with colleagues was either non-existent or simply extra work. Given their workloads, and thus their limited opportunities for collaboration, they may have been dissuaded from being team players, which restricted possible promotion.

In contrast, Elizabeth MacKay, a department head, described a school environment in which "you got along well because I think there was teamwork mostly in departments ... administration and teachers communicated." Elizabeth recalled opportunities to meet other female heads of physical education departments as part of a city-wide association. They could "do a lot of chatting and discussing ... because of that association we moved from entirely inter-form competition to inter-school." Similarly, Karen Phillips connected her administrative position to her participation in broader initiatives. Feelings of relative autonomy and creative license emerged in her recollection of participating in curriculum-planning sessions with the OSSTF. She described this work as "making many advances ... all sorts of committees prepared booklets on curriculum." Karen even managed to create a more supportive environment for her colleagues by assisting with in-service training or educational conferences. Given Elizabeth's and Karen's confidence in affecting their school environments, it is not surprising that these women recalled positive responses from officials to their decision-making. Clearly, the hierarchal structure of the educational system was not defined simply by gender; the women themselves participated at a variety of levels. The difference in their perspectives is therefore understandable. Department heads wielded authority, in large part, as extensions of centralized, male-dominated authorities. No issue makes this difference more vivid than discussions regarding inspections or supervision visits that evaluated teachers' instructional practices.

SUPERVISING AN EGALITARIAN SCHOOL

In an effort to ensure that the secondary school reflected democratic practices, educational officials demanded changes not only to curriculum development but also to inspection procedures. Inspectors were now to offer friendly assistance rather than autocratic judgment. To facilitate the shift, the governments of Ontario and British Columbia permitted larger school districts to appoint their own municipal inspectors or superintendents to provide community-based and personalized support for improving instruction.[85] The prime goals were to initiate self-supervision as a way to strengthen teachers and to set an example for students' learning and participation as citizens.[86] The traditional annual inspection by board-appointed specialists was becoming rare. Inspectors or superintendents in the 1950s were thus instructed to appraise not only teachers' performance and student success, but also internal methods of supervision.[87] Specifically in British Columbia, a policy of teacher-consultants implemented peer supervision toward the end of the period. The Toronto board suggested similar sympathies in its 1961 publication, *A Survey on Supervisory Practices of Persons in Personal Communication with Classroom Teachers*, which insisted that "probably most supervision is provided by teachers for other teachers."[88] However instituted, such views suggest that visits of any sorts were to provide positive support for professional improvement. The old days of intimidation were supposed to be gone.

The women interviewed for this book asserted that, in their experience, teachers never oversaw each other's classes as the new concept of supervision suggested they should do. They viewed the non-collegial, authoritative forms of inspection to which they were subjected as interference and intimidation, and as representing a lack of trust in their knowledge and character. Inspections were not co-operative moments but oppositional incidents in which people took sides. The department head loomed as an adversary rather than a partner in the improvement of instruction. Beth Merle, a department head, explained this tension: "Well, some teachers didn't take very kindly to sharing their lessons or ideas, and as head you sometimes had to do things about lessons that you would see." June West, who was not a department head, illustrated the potentially adversarial relationship between supervisor and supervisee. She recalled: "One inspector I thought was not very wise, there was this one occasion where I was teaching basketball and she brought the head of the department in and was suggesting some things I was doing that the head of the department might do ... it was putting me in a bad position." June's reflections signify a common and special difficulty for women. How do women exert authority while being applauded as nurturers and not disciplinarians? They would face even greater pressure against male authorities. Even the powers of female department heads were far less than those of the male principals, inspectors, and superintendents to whom they were responsible.

For different reasons, all the women interviewed remembered tension-filled encounters with external, male inspectors. Inspections were stressful, "intimidating," and "bad" as weaknesses were identified.[89] Inspectors and principals graded performance according to a scale in a way reminiscent of an elementary school report card, with categories ranging from skills to relationships, and ratings from superior to unsatisfactory.[90] Evaluations included items ranging from a woman's appearance to her curriculum. According to those interviewed, visits did not support democracy or exchange; they represented little more than top-down dictation. A hierarchical relationship was conveyed, since inspectors rarely spoke to the teachers about instructional techniques, and provided written evaluations only to principals. Elizabeth MacKay explained: "You probably got inspected about once a year. They might tell you they would like to come into your class at such and such a time or they might just walk in. They may give comments, but they usually just walked out." Muriel Fraser commented sarcastically about visits: "It was always a great day when the inspector came around. It made you nervous and you knew you were up for inspection and you tried your best. Then there would be a great get-together afterwards between the inspector and the principal. They may come around at the end of the day and say what they thought." Negative responses helped prompt the OTF to recommend to the Hope Commission that "a copy of the Inspector's annual report on each teacher should be made available to the teacher concerned."[91] The federation also wanted suggestions for improvement to be made to individual teachers and that grading be discontinued.[92] British Columbia's Department of Education incorporated the BCTF's similar recommendations for regulating supervision in its 1958 *Rules and Regulations* governing public instruction. This document defined and restricted the power of supervisors and added that a "supervisor shall not evaluate the work of any teacher on a written report."[93] While changes occurred by the end of the period, relations between inspectors and teachers still remained distant, with teachers often unaware of complaints made by inspectors to educational officials.

Not surprisingly, many of those interviewed remained uncertain about what had transpired. A number presumed negative reports to account for a lack of promotion, increments in yearly pay, or permanent certificates. Fran Thompson made regular threats to quit based on an inspector's refusal to approve a permanent certificate, and thus higher pay and more job security. Phoebe McKenzie explained the contingency of security on the inspector's report: "If you taught successfully for two years, the inspector would decide to sign your certificate. That meant you had your permanent certificate." From the perspective of those evaluated, inspectors appeared to exert rather than share authority. Abigail Sears was rare in admitting to a negative report from a principal who supervised her work. As she explained, he did not approve of her using mornings to prepare for classes instead of fulfilling counselling duties in the office. She stated: "I have the report still from that principal and it was the most scathing report."

Adversarial relations existed despite initiatives by school boards and federations to improve inspections. The Toronto board, and its association of supervisors, in consultation with principals, inspectors, and male and female teachers, undertook their *Survey of Supervisory Practices* with teachers' feedback to understand better the dynamics of such communications.[94] The survey, which began in 1959, found that teachers wanted to know the purposes of criticisms, as well as visual and verbal demonstrations of changes demanded.[95] A survey of teachers conducted the same year by the BCTF's Supervision Practices Committee came to comparable conclusions. The twenty-five percent of provincial teachers who responded suggested supervisors tried to impose too much uniformity, provided conflicting advice, and needed more training in their duties.[96] While many believed that supervisors could be constructive, the consensus was that advice was more useful than evaluation.

The women teachers interviewed may have agreed in principle with such conclusions, but they argued that the inspectors' suggestions were essentially useless and inconsequential to the improvement of their instructional techniques. This opinion seemed fueled by the fact that inspectors were men who were supposed to be experts in teaching, but were in fact largely ignorant about the specialties of the women they observed. Jessie Russell asserted that supervision taught her little about teaching girls physical education: "there would be an inspector but he didn't have a clue about rhythmics or gymnastics." Beverley Hurst questioned the inspector's authority when she explained: "We never worried too much about those chaps because they were maths and physics people and they didn't really know ... they wouldn't really understand the makeup of the lesson the way they would in science and math. I mean they were nice people but ..." Even the prestige of scientific knowledge did not compromise her authority in female-dominated subjects such as languages.

Fran Thompson similarly recalled inspectors as administrative types out of touch with the classroom. She illustrated this point in a story about a Friday afternoon in which a "white-haired man ... an inspector came in and sat during the first half of my class, then he left his seat and did this extraordinary noisily energetic thing where he fired off questions." The inspector thought she needed "more pep to get the kids excited about all this ... he made a big thing about it ... fire a question here, fire a question there ... make that person answer." Fran stated that "wasn't my style. I quietly taught things and if you didn't put your hand up, I didn't ask you." Fran laughed, with great satisfaction, at what the students said on Monday, "We don't know what that guy was doing. Do you mind if we go back over the lesson we did on Friday?" Claire Anderson said that she indulged her principal's interest in teaching physical education and even flattered him as a strategy to get what she wanted. At one point, Claire received golf equipment because the principal loved golf and wanted students to learn the sport. When the principal came in the gymnasium, she told the class "take a moment because I want you to come here and see [the principal]; now he is a real golfer." She followed by quickly stating with laughter: "Oh yeah, that worked all right." By putting him on the spot, she asserted her superiority in instruction. The majority of the women interviewed believed that, despite the potential for negative reports, supervisors were ultimately of little consequence to their teaching. The common strategy was simply to humour them by showing inspectors or principals what they wanted to see and then continue to teach in ways they themselves deemed most effective.

The women, as a group, developed similar strategies to foil surprise visits from external authorities: a plan in which all members of schools were involved. It began, as June West noted, with teachers secretly letting each other know that the inspectors were in the school so they could prepare their lessons accordingly. June remembered: "Someone in the office would know the inspector arrived and would get the book and pass it to the teachers. That was the signal when the book got passed around and the teachers would pass it to each other." Jessie Russell described the school becoming a buzz with "the rumour that the inspector's coming today." Marion Hayes' and Beth Merle's narratives confirm such shared responses. Both recalled teachers putting on lessons for the inspector that were polished and practised from years past. Marion explained: "You got to know what some of them liked. Then, of course, you got these people that they said taught the same lesson every time." Beth, like Marion, implied that these secretive practices occurred, but she did not directly associate herself with them. She stated: "I know of teachers who always taught the same lesson for inspectors. The kids knew it." Lessons for inspectors not only prompted insider conspiracies among teachers but student complicity. As Muriel Fraser noted, "You made a special effort for that day. I used to talk to the kids and explain what was going on and they would rally around. They always behaved for those days." Teachers, students, and even office workers seemed to support each other in defining the classroom as a place where the teacher, not an external observer, would determine the practices. After all, as Phoebe McKenzie concluded in her narrative: "I'm going to tell you something. If there is going to be any improvement in education, it is going to be right in the classroom. The greatest value in the whole educational system is a darn good teacher in the classroom."

In the face of such determination and resolve, it might be hard to understand why many women claimed they did not make more radical demands, such as asking for promotion to the position of principal or inspector. Most interviewees simply realized that promotion was not really an option for their sex. Without identifying her own desire for advancement, June West stated: "Now they [women] have the opportunity. Then they didn't, so there was no point in wasting energy on that." Other women, who admitted to thinking about administration, may not have agitated because they feared seeming to be troublemakers in a period of hyper-patriotism. Teachers were inclined to choose more subtle expressions of dissatisfaction with official doctrines. In addition, promotions were not seen as an unqualified benefit since they might threaten security. Staying in a familiar setting and in a known role enabled many of the women to effectively shape their work environments. Common among the women was talk of "stability" and "staying put." Abigail Sears, for example, commented: "I felt equal [nevertheless] accepting that any promotions ... the men would have them and I wasn't interested ... they [women] weren't thinking in terms of promotion – they stayed." Grace Logan described her own immobility as itself a strategy for internal school promotion: "a lot of teachers moved around from one place to another but I stayed put and eventually became head of department and I got more pay for that."

In many ways, women teachers agreed with having a quasi-hierarchal power structure in the school. A firm pecking order, from their perspective, meant that they knew the rules they could quietly negotiate. Many interviewees spoke of their principals with respect and admiration, characterizing them as "benevolent dictators," or "military-like, who ran a tight ship."[97] Muriel Fraser's principal was a war veteran who emulated military structure to organize his secondary school. Muriel described him as an "ex-World War One Colonel ... a very strong wonderful man" who "ruled with an iron hand. He sent out daily orders and told us to 'kill your own snakes.'" Muriel laughed at the memory. Donna Weber's principal "called an assembly the first week he was there and told us we were to call him 'Colonel.' We were to recognize the ranks of all the other men on the staff who had been in the service and we were to call them by their rank." She nevertheless referred to him as pleasant, and someone who brought order to the school. Donna also remembered non-accommodation: nobody called the men by rank, "we just laughed, 'squadron leader what's his name.'" For them, as with the other women interviewees, principals who ruled in such a way, while perhaps overly authoritative, provided a healthy respect for a hierarchical structure in which members fulfilled defined duties. This was perceived to support teachers because principals kept to their administrative offices and out of classrooms. Such arrangements provided a clear message to students that teachers commanded classrooms and merited respect.

Some of the women brought similar authoritarian organization into their own spaces. Beth Merle seemed proud that her students were "scared to death" of her oral examinations in French. Sophie Canning, in a matter-of-fact tone, recounted using "the stick" to make a loud slapping noise on desks to teach students an important lesson in respect. For such professionals, hierarchy translated into better working and learning conditions. Few recalled embracing initiatives that would provide a more independent, democratic learning environment for students. Grace Logan argued that pupils did not respond well to new ventures: "I taught the same way I was taught … I expect lessons were pretty dull … they [students] were used to thinking certain ways and they didn't want it changed, thank you very much." Catharine Darby also commented that she avoided the "latest methods" because she "did things her own way." Despite gender discrimination, or perhaps even in part because of it, the familiar, orderly, and even traditional seemed most comfortable for these women in postwar classrooms.

As many insisted, "there were no gender differences I couldn't handle," or "I didn't feel gender discrimination because women just did what was needed."[98] Not only did the interviewees seem to lack the language with which to discuss any desires they might have had for more power or control, they also rejected tactics associated with union activism or public displays of dissatisfaction as personally untenable. Still worse, they saw them as destructive of the negotiation of workable authority in the postwar secondary schools of Toronto and Vancouver. Participation in the production of a "democratic" school, for these women, did not come from the pursuit of power but in another important way, as service providers.

The hierarchal structure of the school was both beneficial and detrimental to women teachers. They had to negotiate the tensions of upholding an inequitable school structure while simultaneously committing themselves to public democracy. The experience for the interviewees, like that shown in research conducted on women university teachers, meant at times a painful "bifurcated consciousness."[99] Despite insufficient recognition and rewards, in other words the lack of a meritocracy, they laboured hard as service providers and remained apolitical. Other choices presumably would have meant a short stay in the profession. The sampling of interviewees for this book reflects only those women who were not radical dissenters and therefore were able to succeed within the system. Nonetheless, they provide voice for all those who attempted to discover opportunities, wherever possible, for control over their work. Despite describing the failure of the Toronto and Vancouver secondary school to be democratic, they clearly communicated their sense of competence, empowerment, and ownership when it came to their own jobs. Women teachers were able to exercise power, albeit ultimately limited, through informal and localized means. Their narratives demonstrate that liberal democracy's disguise of the norms of inequality may be somewhat vulnerable to the "powers of the weak."[100] The women teachers readily declared, however, that greater battles had to be won in order to gain equality that would match political authority with responsibility. To bring about this revolution, postwar rhetoric of liberal democracy required women to assume public roles as authorities: roles denied to female teachers who were simultaneously idealized and scrutinized for their work as apolitical nurturers.

Conclusion

Postwar Canadian schools embodied a normative social contract. Women teachers worked in the name of a liberal democracy that offered a citizenship at once abstract and androgynous, and limiting and conservative. Their position in Toronto and Vancouver secondary schools illustrates the centrality of gender to the democratic project as it was understood in the tumultuous decades after the Second World War.

In accordance with a postwar national agenda, teachers were to ensure that students experienced "choice" in burgeoning curriculum options, "freedom" through personal growth of character, and "autonomy" in their lessons in civics. These core goals, with their presumptions of neutrality and objectivity, informed the vast majority of educators, whether progressive or traditionalist. Unanimity in support of such commitments masked the secondary school as a hegemonic institution that produced a highly diversified student body and teaching workforce, both of which were believed central to the victory of the West in the Cold War. Democratic fictions supplied regulatory discourses for a country seeking capitalist, white, Christian, nuclear family "normality." Such normality was the order of the day after the horrors of war, and in the face of massive social change, including a rise in immigration, the perceived growth of sexual "deviants," and an increase in women as paid labourers. The nation employed schools to promise security by categorizing students as leaders or workers based on their supposed capacity for knowledge and morality. This classification directed students to roles as citizens that similarly presumed a hierarchy of performance.

Teachers provided the conduits for "democratic" codes of conduct. Gender would be an arbiter for teachers' democratic functions. For women teachers, this meant being responsible for teaching a separate spheres ideology that assumed their inferiority as professionals without the ability for rational knowledge. In effect, women became reproductive, rather than productive, agents for the moral fortitude of the nation. Their role was to endorse male leadership. Within this model, women lacked political agency in the public sphere; their power was essentially private, rooted in domestic personal relations. Not surprisingly, they were rarely candidates for promotion in the educational system where their tenure was conditional on their performance of normative gender codes that gave preference to men. Predominately male authorities took for granted that women teachers needed regular surveillance to perform their duties.

Women knew how they were expected to behave and often performed accordingly. The women interviewed personified detached, objective, rational professionalism in an attempt to capture the privilege granted to masculine teachers. At the same time, they understood the necessity to adhere to rigid standards of social propriety. Daily embodiment of respectable femininity characterized a significant portion of their performance. Of course, their oral histories suggest that some teachers found ways to resist the codes that constrained them. They discussed forms of resistance from teaching subversive lessons to acting out non-dominant versions of femininity. The women interviewed were creative agents who struggled to find ways to reconcile patriarchal educational systems with their personal needs. Historians have assumed that the undemocratic school system was purely oppressive for women teachers. These narratives suggest, however, that their intimate knowledge of schools gave women opportunities to exert authority. In contrast, postwar educational authorities assumed that it was inspection visits and curriculum development initiatives which empowered women teachers. Many of this study's participants characterized these schemes as interference by male administrators. They disregarded such interference and focused on their own authority in the classroom.

The reflections of women teachers stand at the centre of this book on the history of and relationships between gender, education, and democracy. Henry Giroux suggests that we must engage with women's everyday and particular identities, voices, and experiences if we are to counter organized knowledge that maintains masculinist governance.[1] This is the analytic framework for oral histories of women teaching in Toronto and Vancouver schools after the Second World War. This book employs feminist theory that seeks to infuse modernist concerns for social structure and common oppression with poststructuralism's concern for hierarchies of identification and difference. Oral histories reveal how a woman teacher's motherhood, or even her speech, exposed a supposed lack of professionalism; how pants symbolized the destruction of domestic harmony; and how a Chinese-Canadian woman teaching home economics was perceived to disrupt an Anglo-Celtic national identity. Women's private identities informed their public roles in ways that were believed to require external governance. Even as they were charged with teaching directives of citizenship, they ultimately were to confirm male power.

Occasional acts of resistance were hard pressed to overcome this gendered reality. Just as the goals for postwar education were riddled with contradictions, these women teachers themselves emerge as complicated figures. They were neither entirely traditionalist nor progressive, neither heroes nor villains, neither typical nor atypical. In this respect, they were much like others around them. It is the power of this ordinariness, in their everyday knowledges, languages, and identities, which postwar officials sought to direct in channels that would affirm gender hierarchies. Ultimately, this ordinariness was influential in shaping Canada after the Second World War.

Democracy's Angels hopes to further a feminist appreciation of educational history by placing a spotlight on secondary school teachers. While this research explores bureaucratic structures in the mid-twentieth century, like earlier studies of nineteenth-century education it also examines what teachers actually did in their classrooms, including lesson plans, grading, and discipline. This approach takes for granted that schools are a site for labour history and that women need to be understood as workers.[2] This book also addresses the sometimes regional expression of teaching and education, a factor that few studies have recognized subsequent to Alison Prentice and Marta Danylewycz's pioneering comparative study of the teaching forces in Ontario and Quebec.[3] *Democracy's Angels* suggests that regional differences did not ultimately compromise overarching commitment to national goals. Across the country, women teachers served to affirm the democratic agenda to maintain Canada's mosaic, both gendered and vertical.[4]

The topic of gender and educational democracy has been largely overlooked by historians, in part because of the success of liberal ideology and the power of democratic rhetoric in privatizing women's voices even when present in public institutions. In deconstructing the discourses and principles that shaped postwar Canada, this work challenges the liberal basis of politics in the interests of gender equality. This book problematizes democracy, while supporting Chantal Mouffe's call for "radical democracy." Radical democracy calls for a flexible, pluralist citizenship that allows for expression of antagonistic social identities, while holding on to the fundamental assertions of liberty and equality.[5] It is toward this end that this study takes seriously Madeleine Arnot and Jo-Anne Dillabough's call for education research that employs feminist political theory to deconstruct the everyday practices of schooling.[6] Such theory helps expose the gendered codes built into the educational foundations of postwar democracy. *Democracy's Angels* suggests that historical studies can work with feminist theory to reveal the strategies and contextual factors that build fictional, universalizing narratives of masculine citizenship. Such historical assessments can explore how individuals and groups have struggled over spans of time, with successes and failures, for greater equality. The goal for future work in the educational history of gendered democracy should be to explore the full range of differences that underlay the country's social contract for citizenship.[7] Once that story is known, we will be able to share the confidence of one of my subjects who in her eighties, and despite all the setbacks she encountered in her own career, still insists on the value of her profession: "Try teaching ... you can really make a difference there."[8]

Biographical Sketches

TORONTO WOMEN TEACHERS

Muriel Fraser (pseudonym)

Muriel was born in 1919. At the time her family lived in New Brunswick, where her father was a professor at Mount Allison University. They moved to Ontario when Muriel was twelve because her father began to teach at the University of Western Ontario. Her mother was a graduate of medicine from the University of Toronto and worked as an anaesthetist and hospital administrator, or volunteered in the field. The family was of Irish heritage, above average income, and attended the Methodist Church (which later became The United Church of Canada). Muriel got her undergraduate degree from the University of Western Ontario in 1941 at the age of twenty-two. After her Ontario College of Education training in 1941, she taught French and German at a Toronto secondary school. In the late 1940s and early '50s, Muriel studied French at the Sorbonne and completed her master of arts in the United States. She eventually became the head of the languages department at the same Toronto school where she had been teaching and stayed there until 1968, at which time she worked as a French consultant with the Board of Education. She retired in the late 1970s. Muriel did not marry nor did she have children.

Marion Hayes (pseudonym)

Born in 1921 and raised in Ontario, Marion was part of a cattle-farming family of Scottish, Irish and English ancestry. Her father died in 1927, when she was just six years old. Marion's mother had been a teacher before marriage and resumed teaching after the death of her husband. The family, which included Marion's younger brother and sister, had only a modest income. After graduating from high school in 1940, Marion completed her bachelor of arts degree in history, with minors in political science and economics. She taught history and English following her graduation in 1944, and obtained her teacher training during the 1944 and 1945 summer sessions at the Ontario College of Education. Marion had teaching positions in the late 1940s and early '50s in rural areas just outside of Toronto. She began teaching in a Metropolitan Toronto school in 1952, and retired from that school in the early 1980s. Marion did not seek a promotion beyond the classroom during her career. She did not marry nor did she have children.

Beverley Hurst (pseudonym)

Beverley was born in Ontario during the year 1919. Growing up in a rural area, she and her family were of middle to upper socioeconomic status and Catholic, with an Irish heritage. Beverley's father worked as an elementary teacher briefly and then became a civil servant. Her mother was a public school teacher prior to marriage. The oldest of three sisters, Beverley graduated from high school at the age of seventeen and subsequently attended the University of Toronto for her undergraduate degree, which she completed in 1940. She completed her Ontario College of Education training in 1941, specializing in modern languages. Teaching mostly German and French, as well as some Latin classes, Beverley began her career in the 1940s at schools in eastern Ontario. From 1944 to 1977 she taught at two Toronto secondary schools. During that time Beverley periodically studied in France, and studied many summers in Quebec. She obtained a promotion to the head of the languages department at the Toronto school in which she taught. Beverley did not marry nor have children. She retired from the education system in the late 1970s.

Melanie Kilburn (pseudonym)

Born in 1928 and raised in Ottawa, Melanie was the youngest of four girls and a boy. Both of her parents graduated from Queen's

University. Her father owned a local store and eventually a patent firm. Her mother was a musician and kept the books for their store. Relative to the area, the family was upper socioeconomic in status. Melanie was of Scottish heritage and her family regularly attended The United Church of Canada. Melanie entered Queen's University at eighteen and majored in history, politics, and English. She graduated in 1949 and worked for the next two years as a secretary while living with her sister in Toronto. At the same time, she undertook graduate studies at the University of Toronto. In the 1951–52 academic year, Melanie enrolled in the Ontario College of Education. Subsequently, she was qualified to teach history, English, and physical education. She would enrol in two summer courses to obtain her specialist qualification in physical education. Melanie began and ended her classroom teaching career at a Toronto secondary school from 1953 to 1957. At the end of this period, Melanie married and gave birth to two sons. The family had moved to Quebec, where she worked as an inspector of student teachers for an elementary school until they moved back to the Toronto area in 1980.

Elizabeth MacKay (pseudonym)

Elizabeth was born in 1915 and raised in northern Ontario. She was the youngest of four children, with two older sisters and an older brother. Her father was a teacher and the principal of a normal school, her mother a piano teacher before marriage, and her two sisters were also briefly employed as teachers. Elizabeth defined her background as German and English. Her family was middle class and heavily involved in The United Church of Canada. Elizabeth graduated from high school at the age of eighteen in 1933. She achieved her diploma from the Margaret Eaton School of Health and Education in Toronto after two years of study from 1933 to 1935. Elizabeth moved to Atlantic Canada and taught physical education from 1935 to 1937 at a private school for girls. She completed her undergraduate degree in science and music from Mount Allison University in 1941. Following her degree, Elizabeth enrolled in the Ontario College of Education from 1942 to 1943, and completed half the year before taking on a teaching position at a southern Ontario secondary school. She then taught in a Toronto school for thirty-four years, from 1943 to 1977, when she retired. She primarily taught physical education, with some classes in English. She did not obtain an administrative position during her career. Elizabeth did not marry nor did she have children.

Phoebe McKenzie (pseudonym)

Born in 1914, Phoebe lived in eastern Ontario throughout her childhood. Her father was the owner of a local store, and her mother a milliner prior to marriage. She has one sister, younger by six years. Phoebe's family was of English, Irish, and Dutch heritage. Relative to others in the area, her family was quite prosperous. She attended the University of Toronto in 1932, majoring in English and history. After graduating in 1936, she completed her year of teacher training at the Ontario College of Education in 1937. She obtained teaching positions in both the Scarborough and Brockville regions during the late 1930s. Phoebe was married in 1940 at the age of twenty-five. In the early 1940s she taught at a Toronto secondary school, with time off in the later part of the decade to have two children. She resumed teaching at a different Toronto school in 1951 until she retired in the late 1970s. Her husband taught at that same school throughout the 1950s, and passed away in 1992. Phoebe was a classroom teacher, and did not accept an administrative position during her career.

Beth Merle (pseudonym)

Beth was born in southern Ontario in 1923. Her father worked for General Motors, and her mother worked as a lamp-shade maker prior to marriage. She had one sister who was three years younger than her. The family was politically conservative, with an above-average income for the area. Her family background was English and Scottish. Beth began her undergraduate degree in 1943 at the University of Toronto, residing at University College. She graduated at the age of twenty-four and then, in 1947, she attended the Ontario College of Education. Beth taught at a number of secondary schools in the areas of Oshawa, Etobicoke, and Toronto throughout the late 1940s and 1950s. While she taught classes in Spanish and English, her primary field was French. Beth was a department head for modern languages. In the mid-1950s, Beth studied at the Sorbonne in France. She taught summer courses for teachers in training and, later in her career, took a position with the Ministry of Education to develop curriculum. Beth did not marry nor did she have children. She retired in the early 1980s.

Karen Phillips (pseudonym)

Karen was born in 1919 in northern Ontario. Her father was the supervisor of the local post office and her mother was a full-time housewife. Karen did not have any siblings. Of Gaelic ancestry, her middle-class family belonged to The United Church of Canada. Karen completed her undergraduate degree at the University of Toronto from 1938 to 1942. She majored in English and minored in languages. Karen would continue her schooling throughout her years as a teacher by completing a master of arts and a doctor of philosophy. Following her undergraduate degree, she enrolled in the Ontario College of Education. Karen obtained her first job in a Toronto secondary school in 1943. She was married in 1947, which was her last year at that school. Karen did not have children. She began a new position at a different Toronto secondary school the following year and remained there until 1963. She was the head of the English department at that school, and left to join the board of education in the language studies division. She worked with the board until her retirement in the mid-1980s.

Fran Thompson (pseudonym)

Fran was born in the eastern United States in 1934, and moved to Toronto at the age of five. Her immediate family consisted of her father, who ran warehouses, her mother, who sold dresses prior to marriage, and a sister who was five years her senior. A conservative upper-class family, they were heavily involved in both the Episcopalian Church and The United Church of Canada. Fran attended Smith College in Massachusetts when she was seventeen years of age. After graduating with a major in English literature in 1955, she completed her honours year in history at the University of Toronto. She would obtain her master of arts in 1957 and her doctor of philosophy in the 1960s. Fran's first teaching job was with a private school in Toronto from 1956 to 1957. In 1958, she obtained her teacher training at the Ontario College of Education in order to acquire a job with the public secondary school system in Toronto. She taught in the system until the mid-1960s, when her teaching career was temporarily placed on hold while she had two sons. She ended her teaching career at the secondary level in the 1960s, but continued teaching at the university level for decades.

June West (pseudonym)

June was born in 1928 in southern Ontario. She moved to Toronto at the age of two or three years old. June resided permanently in Toronto, living in a middle-class neighbourhood. Her father worked as a small trade businessman. June had two younger brothers. The family was of Scottish, Irish, and English ancestry and attended the local United Church. In the fall of 1946, June entered the University of Toronto's Victoria College. She graduated in 1950 and then attended the Ontario College of Education. Graduating in the spring of 1951, at the age of twenty-three, June obtained her first job at a Toronto secondary school. She stayed there until 1954 teaching history, English, and physical education. June switched to a different Toronto school from 1954 until 1963. She would continue to be a classroom teacher in two more Toronto-area secondary schools throughout the 1960s and into the early 1970s. In the early 1970s, June completed her master of arts degree and accepted a position with the Ministry of Education. She retired from the education system in the late 1970s. June did not marry nor did she have children.

VANCOUVER WOMEN TEACHERS

Claire Anderson (pseudonym)

In 1920, Claire was born in California. She moved with her family to Vancouver around 1928. Her father started a printing business while her mother, who worked with the Edmonton press prior to marriage, was a homemaker. They were respectively of Scottish and Irish ancestry. Her family, including two brothers and one sister, attended Baptist churches. Claire later became a part of The United Church of Canada. She graduated from grade twelve at a Vancouver secondary school in 1939. Over the next couple of years Claire would finish her senior matriculation, take night courses, coach sports for teaching experience, and work odd jobs in order to attend Normal School in Vancouver. Her first teaching position in 1942, which lasted a year, was at a rural elementary school. She would subsequently teach at another rural school and at a technical high school just outside Vancouver. In 1948, Claire got a physical education teaching position at a Vancouver secondary school; she would stay at that school until retirement in the early 1980s. During those years, Claire's mother died and her father lived with her from 1955 until his passing in 1966. Claire did not marry nor did she have children.

Sophie Canning (pseudonym)

Sophie was born in 1927 and grew up around the Vancouver area. Her father was a construction worker and her mother assisted with the bookkeeping at the construction company. Sophie's ancestry is British and Dutch. She is a self-identified lesbian who has been in a relationship for over twenty years. She graduated from a Vancouver high school and then played sports professionally to pay for the bachelor of physical education program at the University of British Columbia. After graduating from university in 1949, Sophie attended normal school for one year, but immediately obtained her first position as a physical education teacher at the secondary level in Vancouver. She would leave that school after a decade and begin a new position at a Vancouver secondary school in 1960. She left secondary teaching in 1966 to head a specialist program at a Vancouver elementary school while teaching university. She retired from teaching in the mid-1970s to pursue other interests.

Sadie Chow (pseudonym)

In 1929, Sadie was born in the interior of British Columbia. Her father emigrated from China to work for the Canadian Pacific Railway and later mined gold and farmed. Her mother, who was also Chinese, was a homemaker until Sadie's father died in 1945, and she sold vegetables to local stores. Sadie was one of thirteen children in her family. She moved to Vancouver in 1947 to enrol at the University of British Columbia in the School of Home Economics. She left university within two years to find employment. She accepted a teaching position in the interior region on a temporary certificate for two years before returning to university and graduating in 1952. Sadie completed summer school courses for teacher training over the next three years while working as a teacher in and around her home town. After an interim position as a home economics teacher on Vancouver Island, Sadie obtained a job in 1956 at a Vancouver secondary school, where she stayed until 1963. During that period, she married and had her first child. Her husband ran a restaurant in

Vancouver. Subsequently Sadie had another child and taught home economics at two other Vancouver secondary schools, becoming head of department at one. She eventually returned to the first secondary school at which she taught and retired from there in the mid-1980s.

Catharine Darby (pseudonym)

An only child, Catharine was born in 1919 in Manitoba. Her family was English and middle class. Her father worked as an engineer and her mother worked as a homemaker. Catharine graduated from secondary school and university in the late 1930s. Following her undergraduate degree, she moved to Vancouver. She attended the University of British Columbia in 1942–43 for her teacher training. Her teaching areas were science, math, and home economics. She worked at a secondary school just outside of Vancouver for a number of years. In 1947, Catharine moved to a Vancouver secondary school; she stayed there for thirteen years until transferring to another secondary school in the city. After three years in that position, she transferred for a third and final time to another school in the area, where she became department head. She retired in the late 1970s. Catharine did not marry nor did she have children.

Alma Erickson (pseudonym)

Alma was born in 1918 Saskatchewan to a Swedish mother and father. She had two brothers. Alma's father worked many jobs after leaving the Swedish army, including farming on the prairies and becoming an engineer on fishing boats in British Columbia. Her mother did not work outside of the home. Alma graduated from a Vancouver secondary school in 1936 and enrolled at the University of British Columbia to study math and sciences. She graduated in 1940 and continued her teacher training for another year at the university. Alma's first four years of employment were during wartime in rural communities, where she taught a variety of subjects and age levels. She married in 1944 and stopped teaching. Alma moved for a short time with her husband, who worked as an engineer, to Manitoba. Then they returned to Vancouver, where she worked as a substitute teacher at many secondary schools. She also briefly worked for a private school in the area during 1947. Alma gave birth to a son in 1948 and a daughter in 1952. With the illness of her husband, Alma returned to full-time teaching in 1957 until her retirement in the late 1970s. She taught math and sciences at two Vancouver secondary schools over that period.

Grace Logan (pseudonym)

The sole child of a Scottish family, Grace was born in 1919 in Alberta. Her family was Methodist and then became part of The United Church with church union in 1925. Her family was working class, with her mother working as a homemaker and her father pursuing various jobs, including military service. Grace's family moved to Vancouver before she completed elementary school. She graduated from a Vancouver secondary school in 1936 and completed senior matriculation from a different school in the area the following year. Grace attended the University of British Columbia from 1937 to 1941 and majored in Latin, which was her primary teaching subject. She took her education training from the university the following year and continued summer-school courses to obtain her Bachelor of Education some years later. Her first jobs, from 1942 to 1945, were in rural communities teaching elementary and secondary students a variety of subjects. She then returned to Vancouver where she taught French for two years to men who had returned from the war. In 1947, Grace became a language teacher at a technical school in Vancouver. She retired from the head of department position of that school in the late 1960s. She did not marry nor did she have children.

Jessie Russell (pseudonym)

Jessie was born on Vancouver Island in 1924. She grew up and graduated from high school in that area. Her mother, of English background, was one of many generations of teachers. Her father, of Scottish background, had worked in coal mines, but once the family moved to Vancouver he worked for the city. Jessie attended Normal School in Victoria for her teacher training in 1943–44 . She spent the following three years attending summer school to obtain her specialist certificate in physical education. Over those years, she taught junior high school students in Vancouver and elementary students in areas just outside the city. From 1948 to 1954 Jessie left teaching to marry and have three children. She returned to teaching for a few years as an elementary teacher and then a physical education consultant with the Vancouver School Board. In 1957, Jessie started teaching physical education at a Vancouver secondary school. She joined another Vancouver secondary school in the late 1960s, from which she retired in the late 1980s.

Abigail Sears (pseudonym)

In 1922, Abigail was born on Vancouver Island. Her parents were both English. Her father worked as a logger and her mother worked on the farm on which they lived. She graduated from high school in that area and then went to the University of British Columbia for one year. During that time her father passed away, and Abigail needed to raise money for more university. She attended Normal School in Vancouver the following year. Her first job, which lasted one year, was at the elementary level in a rural mining town. For the 1943–44 school year, Abigail obtained a position at a Vancouver secondary school. That same year she married a man in the navy. Shortly after marriage she became pregnant with the first of her four children. Abigail stopped teaching then but continued to take summer school courses in Victoria in order to receive a permanent elementary certificate. She returned to teaching as a physical education, English, and guidance teacher at a Vancouver secondary school. She remained at that secondary school from 1958 to 1971, leaving to work at two other secondary schools in the area, and acting as an area counsellor for elementary schools until her retirement in 1980. During that period, she was promoted to head of department and received a master's degree at a university in the United States. Upon retirement from the Vancouver School Board, Abigail dedicated her time to teaching at the University of British Columbia until the mid-1990s.

Ellen Stewart (pseudonym)

Ellen was born in a city an hour from Vancouver in 1924, but was raised with her sisters and brothers in the city. Her father ran a logging business and her mother was a homemaker. Ellen is of Irish and Scottish descent, with family ties to both the Roman Catholic and Methodist churches. Her father passed away in 1938. Upon graduation from a Vancouver secondary school, Ellen attended the University of British Columbia from 1942–43 until 1946–47, where she took courses in history, art, and English. She went for a year of teacher training, followed by three years of summer courses to get her bachelor of education. Ellen accepted a secondary teaching position in a school on Vancouver Island for one year and then filled a position at a Vancouver secondary school from 1949 to 1955. She taught physical education, English, and social studies. For the following six years Ellen worked in three more secondary schools in Vancouver, at one of which she was appointed to head of department for a year. In the early 1960s she married, and retired from full-time teaching. Her husband worked in the food distribution industry and they did not have any children. Ellen accepted supply positions over the next decade.

Donna Weber (pseudonym)

Donna was born in Vancouver in the year 1929 to a father of German descent and a mother of English and Irish heritage. Donna is the oldest of three children in the family. Her mother worked as a teacher and her father worked for the British Columbia Electric Railway. Her mother insisted the family attend the Anglican Church regularly, but Donna would leave organized religion later in life. She graduated from a Vancouver secondary school in 1947. She obtained both her bachelor in physical education and her teaching training at the University of British Columbia from 1947 to 1952. Donna immediately received a position at a Vancouver secondary school teaching physical education and a course titled "Effective Living." Donna left secondary teaching after four years to pursue her master of arts at a university in the United States. Upon completing this degree, she taught physical education at the University of British Columbia until her retirement in the mid-1990s. Donna received her doctor of philosophy during her time teaching at the post-secondary level. She did not marry nor did she have children.

Notes

INTRODUCTION

1 The range of definitions of democracy in education is very wide. See, for example, Osborne, *Teaching for Democratic Citizenship* and Westheimer, "Democratic Dogma."

2 Arnot and Dillabough, "Introduction," in *Challenging Democracy*, 3. See also Heater, *A History of Education for Citizenship*.

3 Ibid., 4.

4 Dillabough and Arnot, "Feminist Political Frameworks"; Arnot and Dillabough, "Feminist Politics and Democratic Values in Education."

5 See two books by Pateman, *The Sexual Contract* and *The Disorder of Women*.

6 Phillips, *Engendering Democracy*

7 Adamoski, Chunn, and Menzies (editors), *Contesting Canadian Citizenship*.

8 Arnot and Dillabough, "Introduction," *Challenging Democracy*, 4.

9 Yuval-Davis, *Gender and Nation*. See also Yuval-Davis and Werbner (editors), *Women, Citizenship and Difference*; Phillips, *Democracy and Difference*; Young, *Inclusion and Democracy*.

10 Yuval-Davis, "Women, Citizenship and Difference," 4–5, as quoted by Arnot and Dillabough, "Feminist Politics and Democratic Values in Education," 164.

11 Arnot and Dillabough, "Introduction," *Challenging Democracy*, 5.

12 See, for example, Luke and Gore (editors), *Feminisms and Critical Pedagogy*; Kenway, Willis, and Blackmore, *Answering Back*; Coulter, "Doing Gender in Canadian Schools."

13 Walkerdine and Lucey, *Democracy in the Kitchen*. See also Walkerdine, *Schoolgirl Fictions*.

14 Dillabough, "Women in Teacher Education." See also Dillabough, "Gender Politics and Conceptions of the Modern Teacher."

15 Phimister, "The Principal and the School," 103, quoted by Stamp, *The Schools of Ontario*, 183.

16 Foucault, *Discipline and Punish*. See a similar application of Foucault for issues of post-war governance in Gleason, *Normalizing the Ideal*, 8.

17 Gramsci, *Selections from the Prison Notebooks* and *Selections from Cultural Writings*.

18 Gramsci, *Selections from the Prison Notebooks*, as cited by Andrew Ross, *No Respect*, 55.

19 Ibid.

20 Tillotson, *The Public at Play*. A strategy of containment in the United States during the postwar period is discussed by May in *Homeward Bound*. Traumatic changes included the return of military men and strained familial relations; women being expected to leave the workforce but continuing to work due to the flourishing economy; an unprecedented baby boom; a shift in the marketplace from a producer-based economy to a consumer-focus; waves of immigration; the threat of the atomic bomb; and a global intelligence race, typified by the launch of the Russian satellite Sputnik. These changes are explored by Owram in *Born at the Right Time*.

21 Tillotson, *The Public at Play*, 4–6.

22 Porter, "Women and Income Security in the Post-War Period"; Prentice, "Workers, Mothers, Reds"; Tillotson, "Human Rights Law as Prism."

23 "Fordism" is a term used by scholars to refer to post-Second World War labour management strategies used by the state and capital. Ford provided workers with higher wages and shorter hours in return for increased efficiency and workplace calm. These accommodations were extended primarily to white, male, unionized workers. See Sangster, "We No Longer Respect the Law," 47. For definitions of Fordism, see Bryan Palmer, *Working-Class Experience*.

24 Tillotson, *The Public at Play*, 9.

25 Johnson, *A Brief History of Canadian Education*; Stamp, *The Schools of Ontario*; Sutherland, "The Triumph of Formalism."

26 Gidney, *From Hope to Harris*, 30. See also a number of articles in Wilson and Jones (editors), *Schooling and Society in 20th Century British Columbia*.

27 Gaskell, *The Problems and Professionalism of Women Elementary Public School Teachers in Ontario, 1944–1954*, 32–42.

28 Dillabough, "Women in Teacher Education," 180–1.

29 See, for example, Gidney and Lawr, "Who Ran the Schools?" and Sutherland, *Children in English Canadian Society.*

30 Prentice and Theobald, "The Historiography of Women Teachers." See also Prentice, "The Feminization of Teaching in British North America and Canada"; Danylewycz, Light, and Prentice, "The Evolution of the Sexual Division of Labour in Teaching"; Danylewycz and Prentice, "Teachers, Gender and Bureaucratizing School Systems in Nineteenth-Century Montreal and Toronto."

31 Rousmaniere, *City Teachers.*

32 See, for example, French, *High Button Bootstraps* and Staton and Light, *Speak with Their Own Voices.* For an associational history of Catholic women teachers in Quebec, see Fahmy-Eid and Dumont (editors), *Maîtresses de maison, maîtresses d'école.*

33 Coulter and Harper (editors), *History Is Hers.* See, for example, Reynolds, "In the Right Place at the Right Time"; Reynolds and Smaller, "Ontario School Teachers: A Gendered View of the 1930s"; Reynolds, "Hegemony and Hierarchy"; Cavanagh, "The Heterosexualization of the Ontario Woman Teacher in Postwar Period"; Cavanagh, "Female-Teacher Gender and Sexuality in Twentieth-Century Ontario, Canada." See also Khayatt, *Lesbian Teachers* and Gelman, "The 'Feminization' of the High School."

34 Barman, *Sojourning Sisters.*

35 See appendix for a biographical overview of each interviewee.

36 Staton and Light, *Speak with Their Own Voices,* 130. They argue that the demographics of women teachers remained fairly consistent over a long period: most were white, Anglo-Saxon, protestant, and from lower to middle class families. The main change during this period was the increase in the number of married women teaching, as cited by Reynolds, "Hegemony and Hierarchy," 111–17. Reynolds' statistics show that in 1961, seventy-two percent of women teachers were British, followed by a small percentage with French and German backgrounds.

37 See, for example, Fraser and Nicholson, "Social Criticism without Philosophy." For a fuller explanation of my theoretical analysis of women teachers' oral histories, see Llewellyn, "When Oral Historians Listen to Teachers."

38 Theobald, "Teachers, Memory and Oral History," 21.

39 See, for example, Casey, "Why Do Progressive Women Activists Leave Teaching?" and Passerini, "Women's Personal Narratives."

40 Derrida, *Of Grammatology.*

41 See, for example, Quantz, "The Complex Vision of Female Teachers and the Failure of Unionization in the 1930s."

42 Rousmaniere, *City Teachers*, 1–2.

43 Harding, "Conclusion," 182–4; Spalter-Roth and Hartmann, "Small Happiness," 334–6.

44 Spalter-Roth and Hartmann, 340–1.

45 Haraway, *Simians, Cyborgs, and Women*, 191.

46 Ibid., 188.

47 Ibid., 187.

48 Parr, "Gender History and Historical Practice." For an example of a seemingly transparent story, see Rinehart, *Mortal in the Immortal Profession*. Rinehart's book is a product of the time in which it was written, when post-modern questions were not at the forefront of historical inquiry.

49 Thompson, *Voice of the Past*, 90.

50 Wolf, "Situating Feminist Dilemmas in Fieldwork," 2–3. See also Measor and Sikes, "Visiting Lives"; Gluck and Patai, (editors) *Women's Words*.

51 See, for example, Casey, *I Answer with My Life*. For information on shared interpretation in oral history, see High, Ndejuru, and O'Hare (editors), "Sharing Authority."

52 Barrett, "Words and Things," 202–3.

53 For example, critiques of Butler, *Gender Troubles*.

54 Casey, *I Answer with My Life*, 31.

55 Bakhtin, *The Dialogic Imagination*, as quoted by Casey, *I Answer with My Life*, 20–1.

56 Popular Memory Group, "Popular Memory," 228–34. See also Sewell, "The Concept(s) of Culture"; Munro, *Subject to Fiction*; Nelson, "From One-Room Schoolhouse to the Graded School"; Nelson, "Using Oral Case Histories to Reconstruct the Experiences of Women Teachers in Vermont."

57 Harstock, "The Feminist Standpoint," 159–60; Smith, *The Everyday World as Problematic*, 111. See also Collins, "Learning from the Outsider Within."

58 Smith, *The Everyday World as Problematic*, 141.

59 Barrett, "Words and Things," 210.

60 Mohanty, "Under Western Eyes," 54.

61 Bakhtin, *The Dialogic Imagination*, as paraphrased by Casey, *I Answer with My Life*, 26.

62 See, for example, Weiler, *Country Schoolwomen* and Rousmaniere, "Where Haley Stood." See also Bloom, "Stories of One's Own."

63 Weiler, "Remembering and Representing Life Choices," 44–6. See also Weiler, "Reflections on Writing a History of Women Teachers."

64 Foucault, "Prison Talk," 39.

65 Mauthner and Doucet, "Reflections on a Voice-centred Relational Method," 125–33.

66 Sangster, "Telling Our Stories," 317.
67 Ibid.

CHAPTER ONE

1 Johnson, *A Brief History of Canadian Education*; Stamp, *The Schools of Ontario*; Sutherland, "The Triumph of Formalism."
2 Stamp, *The Schools of Ontario*, 193. See also Stamp, "Growing Up Progressive?" 321–31.
3 Axelrod, "Beyond the Progressive Education Debate"; Gidney, *From Hope to Harris*.
4 Gidney, *From Hope to Harris*, 31.
5 Ibid., 30.
6 Dewey, *Experience and Education*, 34. See also Dewey, *School and Society* and *Democracy and Education*.
7 Axelrod, "Beyond the Progressive Education Debate."
8 There exists on-going debate, particularly in the United States, concerning competing strands of progressivism. Scholars have identified two primary strands: the liberal pedagogical progressives and the conservative administrative progressives. Most educators agree that more radical groups of progressives had a limited presence in schools, particularly in first part of the last century, with administrative reforms dominant. Furthermore, as David Labaree notes, pedagogical and administrative progressives, for all their differences, shared many beliefs and often worked together. See Labaree, "The Ed School's Romance with Progressivism." For more information on progressive strands in Canada, see also Patterson, "Progressive Education"; von Heyking, "Selling Progressive Education to Albertans, 1935–1953"; and Coulter, "Getting Things Done."
9 See, for example, Tillotson, *The Public at Play*; Sangster, *Transforming Labour*; Finkel, *Social Policy and Political Practice in Canada*.
10 Dewey, *Experience and Education*.
11 Swift, "Pendulum or Synthesis?" 83–4. See also Swift, *Trends in Canadian Education*.
12 Chant, "A Canadian Education," 15.
13 Gleason, *Normalizing the Ideal*, 8. She bases this definition on Foucault, *The History of Sexuality*, and Weeks, "Foucault for Historians," 106–19.
14 Owram, *Born at the Right Time*; Tillotson, *The Public at Play*; Gleason, *Normalizing the Ideal*, Adams, *The Trouble with Normal*.
15 Mann, "G.M. Weir and H.B. King," 115.
16 MacKenzie, "Providing for Individual Differences in Secondary Education in British Columbia"; Fleming and Conway, "Setting Standards in the

West," 303–4. The regional difference is attributable in part to the early influence of progressives George Weir and Harold Putnam. See Putnam and Weir, *Survey of the School System*.

17 Campbell, *Curriculum Trends in Canadian Education*, 96–7.

18 Wisenthal, "Summary of Total Full-Time Enrolment."

19 Gidney, *From Hope to Harris*, 9.

20 Lyons, Randhawa, and Paulson, "The Development of Vocational Education in Canada," 142. See also Addy, "Vocational and Industrial Education," 135.

21 Ontario Institute for Studies in Education of the University of Toronto, Ontario Historical Education Collection (OISE/UT, OHEC), Toronto Board of Education, Director of Education, *Report on the Experimental and Newer Aspects of Schools Work by the Toronto Board of Education*, 1951, 5; 1952, 37–9.

22 CVA, Public School Records, Vancouver School Board, *Board of School Trustees Annual Report, 1951–1952*.

23 Addy, "Vocational and Industrial Education," 136.

24 Morgan, "Secondary Education," 124. See also Evans, *Composite High Schools in Canada*.

25 CVA, H.B. Smith, "Ten Years of Secondary Education," *Board of School Trustees Annual Report, 1959–60*.

26 MacKenzie, "Providing for Individual Differences in Secondary Education in British Columbia," 33–6.

27 TDSBA, Toronto Board of Education, *Year Book* (1954), 12. For a listing and map of the collegiate institutes in the Toronto and Metropolitan areas, see the Ontario Secondary School Teachers' Federation provincial newsletter, *The Bulletin*, November 1957 and November 1959.

28 TDSBA, C.C. Goldring, "Appendix: Trends in Education," Toronto Board of Education, *Board Minutes*, 6 January 1950. See also Goldring, "Today's Secondary School Students."

29 OISE/UT, OHEC, *Report on the Experimental and Newer Aspects of Schools*, 8–10.

30 Johnson, *A History of Public Education in British Columbia*, 188; Chant, "A Canadian Education," 15.

31 Stamp, *The Schools of Ontario*, 183; OISE/UT, OHEC, Canadian Teachers' Federation, "Information Notes – Pupil Retention in Canadian Schools," *Pupil Retention in Canadian Schools* (Ottawa: Canadian Teachers' Federation Research Division, January 1957).

32 OISE/UT, OHEC, *Pupil Retention in Canadian Schools*; Johnson, *A History of Public Education in British Columbia*, 188; CVA, Vancouver School Board, *Board of School Trustees Annual Report, 1952–1958*.

33 Ralph W. Tyler, "Facing Up to the Big Issues," *The B.C. Teacher*, January 1953, 155.

34 Fleming, *Ontario's Educative Society*, as quoted by Smaller, "Vocational Training in Ontario's Secondary Schools," 14.

35 Johnson, *A History of Public Education in British Columbia*, 184. Toronto officials stated in their 1953 annual report that schools were finding it difficult to obtain consent from parents to limit academic course options for those grade nine students who had limited ability or ambition. OISE/UT, OHEC, *Report on the Experimental and Newer Aspects of Schools*, 3–4.

36 Benavot, "The Rise and Decline of Vocational Education," as cited by Smaller in "Vocational Training in Ontario's Secondary Schools," 10. For information on the history of streaming in Ontario schools see Curtis, Livingstone, and Smaller, *Stacking the Deck*.

37 Hansen, "Comprehensive Secondary Schools," 1.

38 Dorothy Thompson, *Globe and Mail*, 15 November 1957, as cited by Hume and Taylor in *Trouble in the School*, 12.

39 "Weir Says BC Youth Get Equal to Best," *News Herald*, 24 January 1947.

40 "One Student in Five Is 'Wasting School's Time,'" *Vancouver Herald*, 4 Februrary 1957. This was a Canadian Press story that came out of Toronto.

41 Barzun, "The Battle over Brains in Democratic Education," 115.

42 Neatby, *A Temperate Dispute*, 19.

43 Ibid.

44 Ibid., 12. See also Neatby, *So Little for the Mind*.

45 Stevenson, "Developing Public Education in Post-War Canada to 1960"; Johnson, *A Brief History of Canadian Education*, 170–1; Myers, "From Hope to Hall-Dennis," 11–14.

46 Province of Ontario, *Report of the Royal Commission on Education* (Toronto: King's Printer, 1950), 34.

47 Stamp, *The Schools of Ontario*, 193.

48 Province of British Columbia, *Report of the Royal Commission on Education* (Victoria: The Queen's Printer, 1960), 17–18.

49 Ibid., 264–360.

50 Johnson, *A History of Public Education in British Columbia*, 257–67.

51 Education officials during this period did not have available to them the language of educational opportunity. Equality of opportunity entered the vernacular of educators after James Coleman and his colleagues' use of the term in 1966. See Coleman et. al., *Equality of Educational Opportunity*.

52 Gidney, *From Hope to Harris*, 15 and 28. See also Phillips, *Public Secondary Education in Canada.*

53 "How to Guide Pupils Outlined by Goldring," *Globe and Mail*, 9 February 1959.

54 William F. Russell, "Education Can Save Democracy," *The Bulletin*, April 1950, 65.

55 Ibid.

56 Paul R. Hanna, "The Educational Outlook at Mid-Century," *The B.C. Teacher*, January 1951, 152.

57 Morgan, "Secondary Education," 123.

58 Adams, *The Trouble with Normal*, 40–1.

59 J.D.M. Griffin, "The Contribution of Child Psychiatry to Mental Hygiene," *Canadian Public Health Journal* 29 (November 1998), quoted by Gleason, *Normalizing the Ideal*, 119.

60 Ibid.

61 OISE/UT, OHEC, *Report on the Experimental and Newer Aspects of Schools*, 31–2.

62 TDSBA, Toronto Board of Education, *Annual Report – The Board of Education for the City of Toronto Reports to the Citizens for the Academic Year, 1960–1961*, 13.

63 OISE/UT, OHEC, *Report on the Experimental and Newer Aspects of Schools*; Toronto Board of Education, *Annual Report, 1960–1961*.

64 Province of British Columbia, Department of Education, *Public Schools Report* (Annual). (Victoria: The King's Printer, 1945), 126–7.

65 Johnson, *A History o f Public Education in British Columbia*, 186.

66 Gleason, *Normalizing the Ideal*, 119.

67 OISE/UT, OHEC, *Report on the Experimental and Newer Aspects of Schools*, 20–2; TDSBA, Toronto District School Board, *Annual Report, 1960–1961*, 13.

68 OISE/UT, OHEC, *Report on the Experimental and Newer Aspects of Schools*, 20–4.

69 "Psychiatry Costs More at Schools," *Toronto Sun*, 2 March 1959.

70 British Columbia, *Public Schools Report, 1955–1956*, 143–6; Fleming and Conway, "Setting Standards in the West," 303–4.

71 Mann, "G.M. Weir and H.B. King," 99.

72 Gleason, *Normalizing the Ideal*, 130.

73 Ibid., 119–20.

74 Adams, *The Trouble with Normal*, 42.

75 Ibid.

76 Campbell, *Curriculum Trends in Canadian Education*, 44–6.

77 Ibid., 47.

78 Province of British Columbia, Department of Education, *Effective Living* (Victoria: The King's Printer, 1950), 132–64.

79 Ibid., 132–64.

80 OISE/UT, OHEC, Department of Education, *Courses of Study* (Toronto: The Queen's Printer, 1954).

81 Stanley, "White Supremacy and the Rhetoric of Educational Indoctrination."

82 Igartua, "What Nation, Which People?"

83 Parr, "Introduction," in *A Diversity of Women*, 5.

84 Strong-Boag, "Canada's Wage-Earning Wives and the Construction of the Middle Class," 7; Adams, *The Trouble with Normal*, 26.

85 "Girls in Slacks Spark a Furore," *The Province*, 22 December 1956.

86 See, for example, Iacovetta, "Recipes for Democracy?"

87 W.E. Blatz, "Your Child – and Sex," *Maclean's Magazine*, 1 January 1945, 37–9, as cited by Adams, *The Trouble with Normal*, 75.

88 Adams, *The Trouble with Normal*, 21.

89 Ibid., 41.

90 Chant, "A Canadian Education," 18; Canadian Youth Commission, *Youth Challenges the Educators*. For more on the commission, see Gauvreau, "The Protracted Birth of the Canadian 'Teenager.'"

91 TDSBA, Toronto Board of Education, *Board Minutes*, 6 January 1950, 138.

92 Ibid.

93 Province of Ontario, *Royal Commission on Education*, Chapter 4, "Social, Spiritual and Other Aspects of Education," as cited by Stewart, *The 1955 Status of Recommendations in the Report of the Royal Commission on Education in Ontario*, 48–50. See also Axelrod, "Beyond the Progressive Education Debate," 237; Gidney and Millar, "The Christian Recessional in Ontario's Public Schools"; Sable, "George Drew and the Rabbis."

94 Putnam and Weir, *Survey of the School System*, 53–5.

95 Moriah Shaw, "Bible Study," *Homeroom: British Columbia's History of Education Website* http://www.viu.ca/homeroom/content/topics/programs/bible.htm.

96 London, "Lay Control in Public Education," 240.

97 Ibid.

98 McLaren, "'New Canadians' or 'Slaves of Satan'?"; Raptis, "Implementing Integrated Education Policy for On-Reserve Aboriginal Children in British Columbia," 121 and 136; Johnson, *A History of Public Education in British Columbia*, 138–47. Raptis demonstrates that integration of Aboriginal children into public schools began when the British Columbia government closed day schools starting in 1947. The provincial government legalized integration with amendment to the School Act in 1949 that

allowed school boards and the province to share costs with Indian Affairs for the education of Aboriginal children. Most on-reserve children would not attend off-reserve public schools until revision to the Indian Act in 1951 to educate Indian children in association with other children whenever possible. Johnson notes that while the integration of Aboriginal students would primarily take place in rural schools, public enrolment figures went from 1,200 in 1952 to 3,788 in 1961.

99 Neatby, *A Temperate Dispute*, 11–12.

100 Philip Deane, "Character, Not Missiles, Is the Challenge," *Globe and Mail*, 25 January 1958, as cited by Hume and Taylor, *Trouble in the School*, 173. See Bestor, *Educational Wastelands*.

101 See, for example, Althouse, *Addresses*, 63. See also Althouse, *Structures and Aims of Canadian Education*.

102 See, for example, Adams, *The Trouble with Normal*, 88–9 (images) and 142.

103 E.J. Palmer, "Democracy in School Life: Report of the Schools Committee of the Association for Education in Citizenship," *The Bulletin*, February 1951, 24.

104 Ibid, 25.

105 Flower, "The Larger School Unit in Canada," 37. See also Paton, "Democracy's Challenge to Our Schools," 5.

106 Flower, "The Larger School Unit in Canada," 37.

107 English, "The Reorganized System of Local School Administration in British Columbia," 44.

108 Maxwell A. Cameron, *Report of the Commission of Inquiry into Educational Finance*, 83–7, as quoted by Johnson, *A History of Education in British Columbia*, 128.

109 Johnson, *A History of Education in British Columbia*, 125–9.

110 Ibid., 131. See also English, "The Reorganized System of Local School Administration in British Columbia," 41.

111 English, "The Reorganized System of Local School Administration in British Columbia," 42–4.

112 Stamp, *The Schools of Ontario*, 184. See also Baird, *Educational Finance and Administration for Ontario*.

113 Ibid., 185.

114 Province of Ontario, *Report of the Royal Commission on Education*, Chapters 10 and 11; Stevenson, "Developing Public Education in Post-War Canada to 1960," 387; Johnson, *A Brief History of Canadian Education*, 114–16. The Toronto Metropolitan School Board emerged in 1953 from urban and suburban municipalities, including the city of Toronto, the towns of Leaside and Weston, the villages of Forest Hill and

Swansea, the Lakeshore district, and East York, North York, Etobicoke, York, and Scarborough townships. Newnham and Nease, *The Professional Teacher in Ontario*, 35. For more information on the creation of metropolitan governance see McCordic, "An Experiment in Metropolitan Government."

115 Fleming and Hutton, "School Boards, District Consolidation, and Educational Governance in British Columbia, 1872–1995," 1–22; Gidney, *From Hope to Harris*, 7.

116 English, "The Reorganized System of Local School Administration in British Columbia," 43.

117 "What We Said," *The B.C. Teacher*, December 1959, 132.

118 Province of Ontario, *Report of the Royal Commission on Education*, Chapters 10 and 11; Stevenson, "Developing Public Education in Post-War Canada to 1960," 387.

119 Althouse, *Addresses*, 117–18, as cited by Stamp, *The Schools of Ontario*, 187.

120 Flower, "Supervision in School Systems," 54–5 and 61. See also Ricker, *Teachers, Trustees, and Policy*.

121 While Vancouver and larger cities in British Columbia were granted the right to appoint their own superintendents, the rest of the province would not secure local control until 1973 with an amendment to the Public Schools Act. The amendment gave school boards with an enrolment of twenty thousand pupils the right to employ, discharge, and define duties for superintendents. See Fleming, "'Our Boys in the Field,'" 298–9.

122 English, "The Reorganized System of Local School Administration in British Columbia," 44.

123 Province of British Columbia, *Manual of School Law*, 7, as cited by British Columbia Teachers' Federation, "What We Said," 133; *Partial List of Acts Pertaining to the Administration of Education in Ontario* (Ontario: The Queen's Printer, 1954), 86–90.

124 Althouse, *Addresses*, 148; *Report on the Experimental and Newer Aspects of Schools*, 2–3.

125 Johnson, *A History of Public Education in British Columbia*, 156.

126 W.D. Douglas, "The Principal and Supervision and Inspection," *The Bulletin*, 31 May 1957, 141; Booth, "Some Basic Aims and Recent Trends in Secondary Education," 46–7.

127 Flower, "The New Principal," 69.

128 Ibid., 71; Flower, "Supervision in School Systems," 56–7.

129 Booth, "Some Basic Aims and Recent Trends in Secondary Education," 44.

130 Ibid., 45.

131 For examples of supervision concerns in British Columbia see "Editorial – Rating Scales," *The B.C. Teacher*, December 1947, 87–8; "Teacher Blacklist Charge under Probe," *Vancouver Sun*, 28 September 1951; CVA, Vancouver Public School Records, "Principal Reports on Teachers: Teacher Absences, and Teacher Exchange to Toronto," *Minutes of School Principals' Meetings*, February 28, 1956.

132 "What We Said," 146.

133 "Education 1959," *The B.C. Teacher*, May–June 1959, 389.

134 Ibid., 84–5.

135 Stamp, *The Schools of Ontario*, 190.

136 Ibid., 190.

137 D.L. Pritchard, "Curriculum Planning in Ontario," *The B.C. Teacher*, December 1952, 113–14.

138 Ibid.

139 Morrison, "Curriculum Construction," 89–90.

140 Myers, "From Hope to Hall-Dennis," 16.

141 L.S. Beattie, "Group Planning and Teacher Participation in Curriculum Revision," *The Bulletin*, June 1951, 120.

142 Stamp, *The Schools of Ontario*, 191.

143 Campbell, *Curriculum Trends in Education*, 101–7.

144 Johnson, *A History of Public Education in British Columbia*, 253.

145 "Education 1959," *The B.C. Teacher*, May–June 1959, 389.

146 Johnson, *A History of Public Education in British Columbia*, 253.

147 Flower, "Supervision in School Systems," 53.

148 MacKinnon, *The Politics of Education*, 3–4.

149 Ibid., 24–42.

150 Ibid, 86–7.

151 Ibid., 8 and 82.

152 OISE/UT, OHEC, *Report on the Experimental and Newer Aspects of Schools*, 5.

153 Chris Crombie, "New Approach to School Problem," *Vancouver Sun*, 13 September 1950.

154 TDSBA, Toronto Board of Education, *Annual Report, 1960–1961*; CVA, Vancouver School Board, *Board of School Trustees Annual Report, 1959–1969*.

155 George Roberts, "What Do 'They' Mean?" *The Bulletin*, October 1950, 189.

156 George Roberts, "What's Wrong with Our Teachers?" *The Bulletin*, December 1959, 393.

157 Ibid., 392–3.

158 Palmer, *Working-Class Experience*, 269.
159 Mann, "G.M. Weir and H.B. King," 115.

CHAPTER TWO

1 See, for example, Arnot and Dillabough, "Feminist Politics and Democratic Values in Education"; Walkerdine and Lucey, *Democracy in the Kitchen*; Arnot, *Reproducing Gender*; Weiler, *Women Teaching for Change*.
2 Coole, *Women in Political Theory*, 18.
3 Clark, "The Rights of Women," as cited by Dillabough, "Gender, Politics and Conceptions of the Modern Teacher," 377.
4 Pateman, *The Sexual Contract*; Pateman, *The Disorder of Women*.
5 Dillabough, "Gender, Politics and Conceptions of the Modern Teacher," 373–94.
6 Ibid., 380. See Walkerdine and Lucey, *Democracy in the Kitchen*, 200.
7 Casey, "Teacher as Mother," 301–20.
8 Dillabough, "Gender, Politics and Conceptions of the Modern Teacher," 381.
9 Ibid., 375.
10 Gaskell, *The Problems and Professionalism*, 32–42. See, for example, Aikenhead, "Research on the Teacher Shortage."
11 Weir, *Sacrificial Logics*, 66.
12 Neatby, *A Temperate Dispute*, 53–73.
13 Newnham and Nease, *The Professional Teacher in Ontario*, 8.
14 Ibid., 8; Neatby, *A Temperate Dispute*, 54–9.
15 For example, progressive educator Donalda Dickie, a recognized leader in teacher-education who authored the textbook *The Enterprise in Theory and Practice*, believed in teaching based on child-centered instruction *and* the mastering of knowledge and skills. Coulter, "Getting Things Done," 686–9. See Dickie, *The Enterprise in Theory and Practice*.
16 J.L. Ord, "The Qualities of a Good Teacher," *The Bulletin*, September 1959, 199–200 and 238.
17 Edgar Dale, "The Education of Teachers," *The B.C. Teacher*, April 1959, 249–350.
18 Ibid., 350. Even though women comprised three-quarters of the teaching force across Canada, the generic teacher was always referred to with the male pronoun. See Reynolds, "Hegemony and Hierarchy," 114. She noted that in 1951, women comprised seventy-three percent and men twenty-eight percent of the teaching workforce in the country (statistics were rounded up in the original source). This would change by 1971, when women were sixty-six percent and men thirty-four percent.

19 Newnham and Nease, *The Professional Teacher in Ontario*, 8.

20 Neatby, *A Temperate Dispute*, 54–9.

21 Scarfe, "The Aims of Education in a Free Society," 69. The emphasis is mine.

22 Ibid., 71.

23 Katz, "The Crisis in Education – Part 1," 9.

24 Interview with Donna Weber.

25 Interview with Catharine Darby.

26 Interview with Phoebe McKenzie.

27 Interviews with Karen Phillips and Melanie Kilburn.

28 Interview with Sophie Canning.

29 Gidney, *From Hope to Harris*, 11; Gaskell, *The Problems and Professionalism*, 60.

30 Interview with June West.

31 Reynolds, "Hegemony and Hierarchy," 106–7.

32 Ibid.

33 Similar stories were told by Toronto interviewees Muriel Fraser, Karen Phillips, and Elizabeth MacKay.

34 Interview with Sadie Chow.

35 Reynolds, "Hegemony and Hierarchy," 103. See also Smith, "Teacher Training." Newnham and Nease, *The Professional Teacher in Ontario*, 38–59, speaks to the specific paths to certification for all levels of teachers in Ontario. For an outline of the certification requirements for British Columbia teachers, see Johnson, *A History of Public Education in British Columbia*, 209–23.

36 Interview with Alma Erickson.

37 Interview with Beth Merle.

38 Acker, *Gendered Education*; Cavanagh, "The Heterosexualization of the Ontario Woman Teacher in the Postwar Period."

39 Rich, "Gender Positioning in Teacher Education in England," 137: see also Davies, "The Sociology of Professions and the Profession of Gender," 672.

40 TDSBA, *Year Book*, 1954; CVA, Public School Records, *Vancouver Personnel and Research Subject Files*, Loc. 59–A–1, File 18, "Calculations of Married Women on Staff, School Term 1956–1957."

41 Canadian Education Association, *Report on the Status of the Teaching Profession*; LaZerte, *Teacher Education in Canada*.

42 LaZerte, *Teacher Education in Canada*, as cited by L. John Prior, "Teaching and Professionalism," *The B.C. Teacher*, November 1959.

43 Johnson, *A History of Public Education in British Columbia*, 221–2.

44 Smith, "Teacher Training," 166.

45 Archives of Ontario, "Teacher Training," http://www.archives.gov.on.ca/
    english/exhibits/education/teachers.htm. See, for more information,
    Department of Education, Teacher Education Branch Records, RG 32–19,
    1945–1960.
46 Hickman, "The Preparation of Teachers," 49–52.
47 Ibid., 49–50.
48 Ibid., 51.
49 Ibid., 50.
50 Government of Canada, *Survey of Elementary and Secondary Education*,
    as cited by "Education 1959," 388.
51 Newnham and Nease, *The Professional Teacher in Ontario*, 38–59.
52 Interview with Claire Anderson.
53 Interview with Fran Thompson.
54 Interview with Grace Logan.
55 Braithwaite, "Why Teachers Quit."
56 Rivers and Jackson, "Teacher Supply in Canada," 20. See also Fleming,
    *Estimates of Teacher Supply and Demand in Ontario Secondary Schools
    for 1957–1972.*
57 "Next Year – B.C. Short of Teachers by 1,700," *Vancouver Sun*, 5 March
    1955.
58 Rivers and Jackson, "Teacher Supply in Canada," 10.
59 Smith, "Teacher Training," 168; French, *High Button Bootstraps*, 142;
    Stamp, *The Schools of Ontario*, 199.
60 "Amount of B.C. Teachers Not Qualified for Positions," *Vancouver Sun*,
    21 February 21, 1947.
61 "Many Teachers Take Summer Courses," *The Bulletin*, September 1954,
    165.
62 Smith, "Teacher Training," 168.
63 Province of Ontario, Department of Education, *Report of the Minister of
    Education* as quoted by Gaskell, *The Problems and Professionalism*, 157.
64 "B.C. Teachers Not Qualified for Positions."
65 The employment of women in education was similar to national trends in
    which women's participation in paid labour reached over thirty percent,
    with over half married, which was a higher percentage than in any previ-
    ous peacetime. See, for example, Strong-Boag, "Canada's Wage-Earning
    Wives," 7.
66 TDSBA, Toronto District School Board, *Year Book*, 1954, 12.
67 *Vancouver Personnel and Research Subject Files*, Loc. 59–A–1, File 18,
    "Calculations of Married Women on Staff, School Term 1956–1957."
    These statistics are not exact, as many women would not denote

themselves as Miss or Mrs and instead used initials. Furthermore, many
women did not reveal to the board that they were married because it
would affect their employment status. The fact that education officials
were specifically recording the numbers of married women speaks to their
uneasy inclusion into the profession. For more on the position of married
women teachers in British Columbia, see Shopland, *Status of Married
Women Teachers in the Province of British Columbia.*

68 "Married Women Teacher Survey," *The B.C. Teacher*, March 1946, 206.
For more information on the informal segregation of men and women in
teacher education at the Ontario College Education, see Reynolds,
"Hegemony and Hierarchy," 103–5.

69 Johnson, *A History of Public Education in British Columbia*, 219.

70 Ibid.

71 *Globe and Mail*, 23 January 1959.

72 "What We Said," *The B.C. Teacher*, September-October 1959, 14.

73 Cavanagh, "The Heterosexualization of the Ontario Woman Teacher,"
65–9; Cavanagh, "Female-Teacher Gender and Sexuality in Twentieth-
Century Ontario, Canada," 113–34.

74 Staton and Light, *Speak with Their Own Voices*, 143–4; CVA, *Vancouver
Personnel and Research Subject Files*, Loc. 59–A–1, File 18, "*Report to
Personnel Committee, February 7th 1955*, Status of Married Women as
Teachers." Furthermore, in British Columbia women's mandatory retire-
ment age of sixty was revised to equal that of men at age sixty-five.

75 Khosla, King, and Read, *The Unrecognized Majority.*

76 Ibid., 40.

77 Gaskell, *The Problems and Professionalism*, 31–2.

78 Khoslad et. al., *The Unrecognized Majority*, 40. They show that in 1945
men were paid $2,118 and women were paid $1,361. By 1954–55 the pay
for men was $4,136 and for women $3,362.

79 Interview with Abigail Sears.

80 Smith, "Teacher Training," 168

81 Johnson, *A Brief History of Canadian Education*, 164.

82 Aikenhead, "Research on the Teacher Shortage," 37–9.

83 Interview with Marion Hayes.

84 Aikenhead, "Research on Teacher Shortage," 38. The number of men in
the education labour force steadily increased after 1921. Cecilia Reynolds
argues that this was due, in part, to the increasing prestige of the profession as it began to require more credentials. She notes, however, that this
mostly took place in the rapidly expanding administration and not in the
classroom. In 1940, approximately twenty percent of the secondary staff

was assigned to manage; by 1980 this number was almost fifty percent. See Reynolds, "Hierarchy and Hegemony," 98–9.

85 Aikenhead, "Research on Teacher Shortage," 38.

86 See, for example, interview with Sadie Chow and interview with Alma Erickson.

87 Interview with Beverley Hurst.

88 Aikenhead, "Research on Teacher Shortage," 37–8.

89 Braithwaite, "Why Teachers Quit," 10.

90 Aileen Campbell, "Pay Equality Hurts School," *The Province*, 22 September 1958.

91 Roberts, "What's Wrong with Our Teachers?" *The Bulletin*, 394.

92 Ibid.

93 Labbatt, *Always a Journey*, 46–51. Before the inception of the Elementary Teachers' Federation of Ontario in 1998, elementary teachers had gendered affiliates: the Federation of Women Teachers' Associations in Ontario (FWTAO) and the Ontario Public School Men Teachers' Federation (OPSMTF).

94 "Patrick McGivney Toronto Head Teachers' Federation," *Telegram*, 25 September 1952. Other articles include: Robert Adams, "Teachers Opposing Plan for Uniform Salaries in Metro," *Toronto Daily Star*, 17 January 1959; "Teachers Resent Uniform Pay Plan Boycott Meeting," *Toronto Daily Star*, 29 January 1959.

95 "Board Won't Pay More Pence, Marriage's but Indulgence," *The Province*, 14 February 1957.

96 Gaskell, *The Problems and Professionalism*, 36.

97 Ibid., 37–8.

98 Eileen Gladman, "Problems in Professional Conduct," *The Bulletin*, May 1959, 145.

99 Gaskell, *The Problems and Professionalism*, 32.

100 Ibid., 38–9.

101 Ibid., 41–2.

102 "Some Ethical Considerations," *The B.C. Teacher*, February 1955, 199; "Married Women Teachers Urged To Be 'Fair,'" *News Herald*, 26 February, 1955.

103 Ibid.

104 CVA, Vancouver Public School Records, *Minutes of School Principals' Meetings*, Loc. 74-A-6, "Reports on Teachers, Public Relations and Leaves of Absences," 12 February 1959; Vancouver Public School Records, *Minutes of School Principals' Meetings*, Loc. 74-A-6, "Married Women and Extra-Curricular Activities," 28 May 1959; "Hints to Job-Seekers,"

The B.C. Teacher, May–June 1951, 333; "Recruitment and Selection of Teachers," *The B.C. Teacher*, November 1952, 61; "Teachers Told Not To Quit Classrooms for Honeymoons," *Vancouver Sun*, 29 April 1952.

105 "Some Ethical Considerations," *The B.C. Teacher*, February 1955, 199.
106 "Hints to Job-Seekers," *The B.C. Teacher*, May-June, 1951, 333.
107 Interview with Jessie Russell.
108 Rich, "Gender Positioning in Teacher Education," 145.
109 Ibid.

CHAPTER THREE

1 See, for example, Yuval-Davis, *Gender and Nation* and Martin, "Excluding Women from the Educational Realm."
2 Martin, "Excluding Women from the Educational Realm," as cited by Arnot and Dillabough, "Feminist Politics and Democratic Values in Education," 165.
3 Arnot and Dillabough, "Feminist Politics and Democratic Values in Education," 164.
4 Walkerdine, "Post-structuralist Theory and Everyday Social Practices," 177, as quoted by Arnot and Dillabough, "Feminist Politics and Democratic Values in Education," 177.
5 Walkerdine and Lucey, *Democracy in the Kitchen*.
6 Yuval-Davis, *Gender and Nation*, 45.
7 Cavanagh, "The Gender of Professionalism and Occupational Closure," 55.
8 Ibid.
9 Glazer and Slater, *Unequal Colleagues*, 232, as quoted by Cavanaugh, "The Gender of Professionalism and Occupational Closure," 55. For contemporary work on appearance, teachers and pedagogy, see Weber and Mitchell, *"That's Funny, You Don't Look Like a Teacher."*
10 Butler, *Gender Trouble*, as cited by McPherson, "The Case of the Kissing Nurse," 181.
11 Butler, "Performative Acts and Gender Constitution," 282.
12 McPherson, "The Case of the Kissing Nurse," 181.
13 Ibid.
14 See, for example, Mitchinson, *The Nature of Their Bodies* and Kelm, *Colonizing Bodies*.
15 Paton, *Concern and Competence*, 3. See, for example, Watts, "Character Education in the Secondary Schools of Alberta."
16 Ralph W. Tyler, "Facing Up to the Big Issues," *The B.C. Teacher*, 151.
17 Ibid.

18 Adams, *The Trouble with Normal*, 20.
19 Province of Ontario, *Report of The Royal Commission on Education*, 28–31, as cited by Mariana Valverde, "Building Anti-Delinquent Communities," 37.
20 Frank Wilson, "Ethics in a Free Society," *The B.C. Teacher*, April 1955, 304.
21 H.L. Tracy, "In Praise of Teachers," *The Bulletin*, October 1951, 162.
22 Sidney Katz, "The Crisis in Education – Part 2," 49.
23 Scarfe, "The Aims of Education," 72; See also Scarfe, *A Philosophy of Education*.
24 "The Teacher," *The B.C. Teacher*, February 1953, 197.
25 Ibid.
26 Althouse., *Addresses*, 203.
27 Ibid., 201.
28 Norman McLeod, "Taking Stock," *The Bulletin*, 15 December 1957, 358.
29 Ibid., 359–60.
30 "Are You a Weak Teacher?" *The B.C. Teacher*, February 1946, 186.
31 Ibid., 186–8.
32 Ibid., 188.
33 Theobald, "Teachers, Memory and Oral History," 17–18.
34 Gaskell, *The Problems and Professionalism*, 111–17.
35 Ibid., 111.
36 S.R. Laycock, "You Can't Get Away From Discipline," 7, quoted in Gleason, *Normalizing the Ideal*, 124–5. See also Laycock, "Teaching – A Job in Human Relations," 77–80.
37 Laycock, "Professional Ethics and Mental Health," *The B.C. Teacher*, May–June 1957, 397–8. See also, by the same author, "Your Job in Public Relations," *The B.C. Teacher*, January 1955, 152–4 and "Invest in Good Teachers," *The B.C. Teacher*, January 1957, 210–11.
38 Gleason, *Normalizing the Ideal*, 3–18 and 124–5.
39 Dr Charles G. Stogdill, "Warn Parents: Allow Child to Think for Self," *Telegram*, 7 October 1952.
40 Althouse, *Addresses*, 146 and 205.
41 "City's Experienced Teachers Not Guilty of Talking Too Much," *The Province*, 9 April 1955.
42 May Hill Arbuthnot, "Teachers Are People," *The B.C. Teacher*, May–June 1946, 325.
43 Ibid.
44 Interview with Ellen Stewart.
45 "British Columbia Teachers' Federation Code of Ethics," *The B.C. Teacher*, September-October 1946, 9; "C.T.F. Adopts National Code of

Ethics," *The B.C. Teacher*, November 1947, 55. The Canadian Teachers' Federation adopted a code of ethics for teachers' organizations across the country, including the BCTF and OSSTF. See also Gaskell, *The Problems and Professionalism*, 168.

46 For example, see Laycock, "Professional Ethics and Mental Health," *The B.C. Teacher*, 397.

47 Gleason, *Normalizing the Ideal*, 119–39. Gleason outlines psychologists' definitions of the "normal" child and the "good" teacher in the postwar era. She argues that teachers often rejected these definitions. For example, most teachers did not believe that a quiet, reclusive student was a problem or abnormal.

48 Adams, *The Trouble with Normal*, 86–91 and 109–11.

49 Macomber, *Teaching in the Modern Secondary School*, 253–4.

50 Pierson, *"They're Still Women after All."*

51 McPherson, "The Case of the Kissing Nurse," 190.

52 Ibid., 191–3.

53 "Girls in Slacks Spark a Furore," *The Province*, 22 December 1956.

54 "Tight Clothes in Dirty Thirties Never Raised Teachers' Eyebrows," *The Province*, 9 September 1958; "'Naughty Nylon' Problem Invades City Schools," *The Province*, 28 May 1952.

55 Cavanagh, "The Heterosexualization of the Ontario Woman Teacher." See also Reynolds, "Too Limiting a Liberation"; Oram, "Embittered, Sexless or Homosexual"; Oram, "Serving Two Masters?" On the moral panic about lesbians, see, for example, Lillian Federman, *Odd Girls and Twilight Lovers*.

56 Cavanagh, "The Heterosexualization of the Ontario Woman Teacher," 66.

57 Khayatt, *Lesbian Teachers*, 21–6. For work on the dominance of heterosexual discourses in contemporary schooling, see Lather, *Getting Smart* and Epstein and Johnson, *Schooling Sexualities*.

58 See Strange, *Toronto's Girl Problem*.

59 Popenoe, "Better Teachers, Biologically Speaking," 5, as quoted in Cavanaugh, "The Heterosexualization of the Ontario Woman Teacher," 67.

60 Cavanaugh, "The Heterosexualization of the Ontario Woman Teacher," 67.

61 "Cupid So Busy Can't Get Enough P.T. Teachers" and "See Kindergarten Spot to Choose Motherly Wife," *Globe and Mail*, 9 January 1952.

62 "Pretty, New Teachers," *Vancouver Sun*, 15 September 1950.

63 "It's Still Education Week," *Vancouver Sun*, 6 March 1952.

64 CVA, Public School Records, *Vancouver Personnel and Research Subject Files*, Loc. 58-F-1, File 18, "Proceedings of the CEA – Kellogg Vancouver Metropolitan Zone Conference Held at the University of British

Columbia," 3 November1955. For more on the historical and cultural representations of teaching, see, for example, Biklen, *School Work*.

65 Arbuthnot, "Teachers Are People," *The B.C. Teacher*, May–June 1946.

66 See Khayatt, *Lesbian Teachers*, 11–32.

67 Adams, *The Trouble with Normal*, 21.

68 Morgan, "Secondary Education," 125.

69 Frank Wilson, "Education and Civilization," *The B.C. Teacher*, December 1953, 113.

70 Ibid.

71 Rousmaniere, "Where Haley Stood," 153. See also Sangster, *Earning Respect*.

72 Ibid.

73 Gaskell, *The Problems and Professionalism*, 33; Reynolds, "Hegemony and Hierarchy," 116–17. Reynolds statistics for Ontario show that in 1941, eighty-two percent of women teachers were of British origin and in 1961 that number had only dropped to seventy-two percent.

74 Iacovetta, "Recipes for Demoracy?" 301. See also Iacovetta, "Remaking Their Lives" and *Gatekeepers*.

75 Ibid., 301–2.

76 Ibid., 302.

CHAPTER FOUR

1 This chapter uses Shirley Tillotson's concept of postwar participatory democracy as a serious attempt to implement an ideal of rule by "the people" that was limited by the liberal tendency to produce greater bureaucracy and leadership by "experts." See Tillotson, *The Public at Play*, 5–6.

2 Arnot and Dillabough, "Feminist Politics and Democratic Values in Education," 162–5.

3 Martin, "Excluding Women from the Educational Realm," as cited by Arnot and Dillabough, "Feminist Politics and Democratic Values in Education," 165.

4 Pateman, *The Disorder of Women*; Pateman, "Equality, Difference and Subordination."

5 Blackmore, *Troubling Women*; Kinnear, *In Subordination*; Smyth, Acker, Bourne, and Prentice (editors), *Challenging Professions*.

6 Young, "Gender as Seriality," as cited by Arnot and Dillabough, "Feminist Politics and Democratic Values in Education," 165.

7 Gidney, *From Hope to Harris*, 11–12; Watts, "Decentralized Curriculum Building," 22–3. See also CVA, Public School Records, *Vancouver School*

Board Reports, 1945–1960; TDSBA, Toronto Board of Education, *Annual Reports*, 1950–1960.

8 Watts, "Decentralized Curriculum Building," 22–3.

9 Ibid.

10 Scarfe, "The Aims of Education," 72–3. See also Bruner, *The Process of Education* and Bender, *The Top-One-Per-Cent Policy*.

11 Paton, *Concern and Competence*, 94.

12 Dewey, *Experience and Education*, 10.

13 Paton, *Concern and Competence*, 94.

14 Laycock, "What Kind of Teachers Do We Need?" *The B.C. Teacher*, April 1948, 257; Laycock, "Toward Better Teaching," *The B.C. Teacher*, September–October 1949, 11–15.

15 Watts, "Decentralizing Curriculum Building," 21; Paton, *Concern and Competence*, 73.

16 Scarfe, "The Aims of Education," 84.

17 Neatby, *A Temperate Dispute*, 21.

18 Scarfe, "The Aims of Education," 75.

19 Ibid.

20 Newnham and Nease, *The Professional Teacher in Ontario*, 212–20. The OTF oversaw the Ontario Secondary School Teachers' Federation, Federation of Women Teachers' Associations in Ontario, Ontario Public School Men Teachers' Federation, Ontario English Catholic Teachers' Association and Association des Enseignants Franco-Ontariens.

21 Reynolds, "Hegemony and Hierarchy," 109.

22 Gidney, *From Hope to Harris*, 22.

23 Gaskell, *The Problems and Professionalism*, 28.

24 Gidney, *From Hope to Harris*, 22–3.

25 Gaskell, *The Problems and Professionalism*, 123–4 and 133.

26 Ibid., 162.

27 David L. Tough, "Licensing is Coming," *The Bulletin*, March 1954, 53–4.

28 Johnson, *A History of Public Education in British Columbia*, 239–44.

29 BCTFA, BCTF Library, *Historical Reviews and Dissertations*, Bruneau, "*Still Pleased to Teach*," 31.

30 Johnson, *A History of Public Education in British Columbia*, 249–50.

31 Bruneau, "*Still Pleased to Teach*," 50.

32 Johnson, *A History of Public Education in British Columbia*, 244–7.

33 Ibid., 251–2.

34 "Ruling to Permit Teachers on Municipal Council Asked," *The Province*, 6 April 1945; "Teacher Shortage," *The B.C. Teacher*, November 1946.

35 CVA, Public School Records, Special Committees' Correspondence and Reports, Loc. 59–B–2, File 14, Special Committee #25 – To Set a Policy for Employees Seeking Public Office, "Report to Special Board Meeting, September 2nd, 1958." See also "Who Should Be on Council?" *The B.C. Teacher*, January 1959, 210.

36 D.S. Hamilton, "The Crux of Freedom," *The B.C. Teacher*, November 1945, 65.

37 "Teacher Shortage," *The B.C. Teacher*, November 1946, 53. See also "The Canadian Teachers' Federation National Policy," *The B.C. Teacher*, November 1946, 68–9.

38 See, for example, Ozga and Lawn, *Teachers, Professionalism and Class*; Bessant and Spaull, *Teachers in Conflict*; Bessant and Spaull, *Politics of Schooling*.

39 Apple, "Work, Class and Teaching."

40 Palmer, *Working-Class Experience*, 269–77.

41 Ibid., 277.

42 Chase, *Education Faces New Demands*, as cited by "The Teacher and Policy Making: How Democratic Can You Get?" *The B.C. Teacher*, December 1952, 102–4 and 107.

43 TDSBA, *Board Minutes*, 6 January 1950, 139. See also Clarke, *Freedom in the Educative Society*.

44 MacKinnon, *The Politics of Education*, 82–8.

45 OISE/UT, OHEC, Department of Education, *The Teaching Profession Act* (Toronto: The King's Printer, 1944); Newnham and Nease, *The Professional Teacher in Ontario*, 3–13 and 198–9.

46 See, for example, British Columbia, Department of Education, *Public Schools Report, 1948–1949* and *1960–1961*; CVA, British Columbia, *Annual Report, 1948–1949* (Victoria: The King's Printer, 1950); CVA, British Columbia, *Annual Report, 1960–1961* (Victoria: The Queen's Printer, 1962).

47 Stamp, *The Schools of Ontario*, 200–1.

48 Gidney, *From Hope to Harris*, 9–36.

49 BCTFA, BCTF Official Records, *Women in Teaching*, "Analysis of Positions Held by Women in the Field of Education in B.C., 1954–1955," 1955.

50 BCTFA, BCTF Official Records, *BCTF Miscellaneous*, Loc. RG1, B36, File – List of School Inspectors and Secretaries of School Boards, "British Columbia School Inspectors, 1949–1950 and 1952–1953," 1953.

51 Reynolds, "Hegemony and Hierarchy," 111 and 115.

52 Ibid.

53 "More Posts of Responsibility," *The B.C. Teacher*, December 1957, 121–2.

54 Proom, "Tilly Jean Rolston." Rolston was British Columbia's first woman cabinet minister. As the Minister of Education she revamped *Effective Living*, introduced in 1950, to include a lesson on sex education.

55 Strober and Tyack, "Why Do Women Teach and Men Manage?"; Danylewycz, Light, and Prentice, "The Evolution of the Sexual Division of Labour in Teaching"; Danylewycz and Prentice, "Teachers, Gender and Bureaucratizing School Systems in Nineteenth Century Montreal and Toronto."

56 French, *High Button Boot Straps*, 130.

57 Mills, "Gender, Sexuality and Organizational Theory," 33, as cited by Reynolds, "In the Right Place at the Right Time," 133.

58 Reynolds, "In the Right Place at the Right Time," 134.

59 Althouse, *Addresses*, 200.

60 OTF Column, *Educational Courier*, April 1949, as cited by Gaskell, *The Problems and Professionalism*, 221.

61 Gaskell, *The Problems and Professionalism*, 212.

62 Braithwaite, "Why Teachers Quit," 10.

63 Ibid.

64 Reynolds, "In the Right Place at the Right Time," 137.

65 "Editorial: Who Should Make the Curriculum?" *The B.C. Teacher*, May–June 1948.

66 Gaskell, *The Problems and Professionalism*, 223–5.

67 Putnam and Weir, *A Survey of the School System of British Columbia*, 168.

68 French, *High Button Boot Straps*, 133.

69 For example, the BCTF in the 1970s undertook a serious study of the status of women teachers in the province. See BCTFA, BCTF Official Records, *Women in Teaching*.

70 Gaskell, *The Problems and Professionalism*, 223–5.

71 Johnson, *A History of Public Education in British Columbia*, 253.

72 L.S. Beattie, "Group Planning and Teacher Participation in Curriculum Revision," *The Bulletin*, June 1951, 120.

73 Love, "Where Do We Go from Here?" 31.

74 After an examination of a British woman's diary during the Second World War, Martin Lawn argues that women teachers' workloads increase during a time of national crisis. He concludes, contrary to this study, that this extra responsibility brought a measure of additional power. See "What Is the Teacher's Job?"

75 Province of Ontario, *Report of the Royal Commission on Education*, 89–90; Robert Gidney, *From Hope to Harris*, 14 and 20.

76 Province of British Columbia, *Report of the Royal Commission on Education*, 1960, 264–360; Johnson, *A History of Public Education in British Columbia*, 267.

77 See also interviews with Alma Erickson and Donna Weber.

78 In 1952 alone "City Teachers at Red Rally," *Telegram*, 26 September; "4 Communists Run for Council Posts 4 For School Board," *Telegram*, 11 November; "24 Seeking 14 Seats on Board of Education," *Globe and Mail*, 18 November. See also Clarke, "'Keep Communism out of Our Schools.'"

79 See, for examples, Paul St Pierre, "School Brings Socialism to Westons," *Vancouver Sun*, 14 September 1951; "Socialism Being Taught in Schools?" *Vancouver Sun*, 12 July 1945.

80 "Bennett Aroused at Charge 'Known Red' on School Staff," *Vancouver Sun*, 2 February 1957; "'I Was a Communist' City Teacher Admits," *The Province*, 13 February 1957; "Former Communist Teacher Keeps Job," *Vancouver Sun*, 19 February 1957; "Ex-Communist Teacher Charges Investigated," *The Province*, 14 February 1957. In this last article, R.F. Sharp, Superintendent of Schools, tries to calm fears about communist teachers by assuring the public that new teachers are required to take an oath of allegiance to the queen.

81 "Socialism Being Taught in Schools?"; "Paynter Hits CCF 'Teachers,'" *The Province*, 2 October 1945.

82 One may also surmise that the women teachers did not see themselves as defiant to authority because popular memory has designated the postwar era as a conformist period in history.

83 OISE/UT, OHEC, Department of Education, *Text Books Approved or Recommended for Use in Elementary and Secondary Schools* (Toronto: The Queen's Printer, 1955); OISE/UT, OHEC, Department of Education, *Text-books Aauthorized, Approved, and Recommended* (Toronto: The Queen's Printer, 1950–9); OISE/UT, OHEC, Department of Education, *Courses of Study, Grade XIII English* (Toronto: The Queen's Printer, 1954).

84 Coulter, "Getting Things Done," 678.

85 Johnson, *A Brief History of Canadian Education*, 106–8.

86 Booth, "Some Basic Aims and Recent Trends in Secondary Education," 44; Flower, "Supervision in School Systems," 58–9.

87 OISE/UT, OHEC, *Report on the Experimental and Newer Aspects of Schools*, 2–3.

88 OISE/UT, OHEC, Toronto Board of Education, *A Survey of Supervisory Practices of Persons in Personal Communication with Classroom Teacher* (Toronto: Toronto Board of Education, 1961), 1.

89 Interview with Jessie Russell; interview with Elizabeth MacKay; interview with June West; interview with Muriel Fraser; and interview with Grace Logan.

90 Douglas, "The Principal and Supervision and Inspection," *The Bulletin*, 31 May 1957, 141–2; "Editorial: Rating Scales," *The B.C. Teacher*, December 1947; CVA, Public School Records, *Principal Annual Reports*, Loc. 74–A–6, "Principal Reports on Teachers, February 28, 1956."

91 Gaskell, *The Problems and Professionalism*, 90.

92 Ibid., 91.

93 "What We Said," *The B.C. Teacher*, December 1959, 146.

94 Toronto Board of Education, *A Survey of Supervisory Practices*, 1961, 1–21.

95 Ibid., 14–16.

96 BCTF Supervision Practices Committee, "Of Teachers and Supervision," *The B.C. Teacher*, February 1960, 233–5.

97 Interview with June West; interview with Karen Phillips; interview with Ellen Stewart; interview with Grace Logan; and interview with Donna Weber.

98 Interview with Sadie Chow; interview with Grace Logan.

99 Acker and Feurverger, "Doing Good and Feeling Bad," 418.

100 Tillotson, *The Public at Play*, 159–60.

CONCLUSION

1 Giroux, *Postmodernism, Feminism and Cultural Politics*, as cited by Arnot and Dillabough, "Feminist Politics and Democratic Values in Education," 179.

2 Prentice and Theobald, "The Historiography of Women Teachers," 24.

3 Danylewycz and Prentice, "The Evolution of the Sexual Division of Labour in Teaching" and "Teachers, Gender and Bureaucratizing School Systems in Nineteenth-Century Montreal and Toronto."

4 John Porter's seminal text, *The Vertical Mosaic*, published in 1968, did not address gender.

5 Mouffe, "Feminism, Citizenship and Radical Democratic Politics."

6 Arnot and Dillabough, "Feminist Politics and Democratic Values in Education," 185.

7 Canadian educational historians need to build upon contemporary studies to explore the role of marginalized groups of women educators, particularly racial minority teachers, in twentieth-century citizenship debates. One example is Henry, *Taking Back Control*.

8 Interview with Beverley Hurst.

Bibliography

PRIMARY SOURCES

Interviews

Anderson, Claire (pseudonym). Interview by author. Vancouver, British Columbia, 13 May 2005.

Canning, Sophie (pseudonym). Interview by author. Salt Spring Island, British Columbia, 19 September 2005.

Chow, Sadie (pseudonym). Interview by author. Vancouver, British Columbia, 16 September 2005.

Darby, Catharine (pseudonym). Interview by author. Vancouver, British Columbia, 19 May 2005.

Erickson, Alma (pseudonym). Interview by author. Vancouver, British Columbia, 15 September 2005.

Fraser, Muriel (pseudonym). Interview by author. Toronto, Ontario, 1 December 2001.

Hayes, Marion (pseudonym). Interview by author. Toronto, Ontario, 27 November 2001.

Hurst, Beverley (pseudonym). Interview by author. Toronto, Ontario, 14 December 2001.

Kilburn, Melanie (pseudonym). Interview by author. Toronto, Ontario, 21 January 2002.

Logan, Grace (pseudonym). Interview by author. Vancouver, British Columbia, 19 September 2005.

MacKay, Elizabeth (pseudonym). Interview by author. Toronto, Ontario, 14 November 2001.

McKenzie, Phoebe (pseudonym). Interview by author. Toronto, Ontario, 16 November 2001.

Merle, Beth (pseudonym). Interview by author. Toronto, Ontario, 23 November 2001.
Phillips, Karen (pseudonym). Interview by author. Toronto, Ontario, 26 November 2001.
Russell, Jessie (pseudonym). Interview by author. Vancouver, British Columbia, 16 September 2005.
Sears, Abigail (pseudonym). Interview by author. Vancouver, British Columbia, 17 May 2005.
Stewart, Ellen (pseudonym). Interview by author. Vancouver, British Columbia, 13 September 2005.
Thompson, Fran (pseudonym). Interview by author. Toronto, Ontario, 20 November 2001.
West, June (pseudonym). Interview by author. Toronto, Ontario, 7 December 2001.
Weber, Donna (pseudonym). Interview by author. Vancouver, British Columbia, 22 May 2005.

Newspapers and Newsletters

B.C. Teacher, British Columbia Teachers' Federation Newsletter, 1945–1960
Bulletin, Ontario Secondary School Teachers' Federation, 1945–1960
Globe and Mail, 1950–1960
Telegram, 1945–1960
Toronto Daily Star, 1950–1960
Vancouver Province, 1945–1960
Vancouver Sun, 1945–1960
Vancouver News Herald, 1945–1957

Archives of Ontario (AO)

Department of Education. Teacher Education Branch Records. 1945–1960.
Lessons Learned: The Evolution of Education in Ontario, http://www.archives.gov.on.ca/english/exhibits/education/teachers.htm.

City of Vancouver Archives (CVA)

Public School Records. Board of School Trustees Annual Reports. 1945–1969.

Public School Records. *Minutes of School Principals' Meetings.*
1946–1959.
Public School Records. *Principal Annual Reports.* 1945–1960.
Public School Records. *Vancouver School Board Annual Reports.*
1945–1960.
Public School Records. *Vancouver Personnel and Research Subject Files.*
1945–1960.
Public School Records. *Special Committees' Correspondence and Reports.*
1945–1960.

British Columbia Teachers' Federation Archives (BCTFA)

BCTF Library. *Historical Reviews and Dissertations.*
BCTF Official Records. BCTF *Miscellaneous.* 1945–1960.
BCTF Official Records. *Files of Teachers' Salaries, Salary Agreements and
Arbitration.* 1945–1960.
BCTF Official Records. *Women in Teaching.* 1970–Present.

Toronto District School Board Sesquicentennial Museum and Archives (TDSBA)

Toronto Board of Education. *Annual Reports* (Board Officials).
1950–1960.
Toronto Board of Education. *Minutes.* 1945–1960.
Toronto Board of Education. *Year Book.* 1950–1955.

Ontario Institute for Studies in Education of the University of Toronto, Ontario Historical Education Collection (OISE/UT, OHEC)

Canadian Teachers' Federation. *Pupil Retention in Canadian Schools.*
Ottawa: Canadian Teachers' Federation Research Division, January
1957.
Department of Education. *Courses of Study.* Toronto: The Queen's Printer,
1954.
Department of Education. *The Teaching Profession Act.* Toronto: The
King's Printer, 1944.
Department of Education. *Text Books Approved or Recommended for
Use in Elementary and Secondary Schools.* Toronto: The Queen's
Printer, 1955.

Department of Education. *Text-books Authorized, Approved, and Recommended and Instructions Regarding Text-books for Public, Separate, Continuation and High Schools and Collegiate Institutes for the School Year, 1950–1959.* Toronto: The Queen's Printer, 1950–1959.

Province of Ontario. *Partial List of Acts Pertaining to the Administration of Education in* Ontario (Public Schools Act, Schools Administration Act, Secondary Schools and *Boards of Education Act, Department of Education Act).* Ontario: The Queen's Printer, 1954.

Toronto Board of Education, Director of Education. *Report on the Experimental and Newer Aspects of Schools Work by the Toronto Board of Education.* Ontario: The Queen's Printer, 1950–1955.

Toronto Board of Education. *A Survey of Supervisory Practices of Persons in Personal Communication with Classroom Teachers.* Toronto: Toronto Board of Education, 1961.

Books, Articles, and Reports

Althouse, J.G. *Structures and Aims of Canadian Education.* Toronto: W.J. Gage, 1949.

– *Addresses: A Selection of Addresses by the Late Chief Director of Education for Ontario, Covering the Years 1936–1956.* Toronto: W.J. Gage, 1958.

Addy, B.F. "Vocational and Industrial Education." In *Canadian Education Today: A Symposium,* edited by Joseph Katz. 126–36. Toronto: McGraw-Hill, 1956.

Aikenhead, J.D. "Research on the Teacher Shortage." In *Education: A Collection of Essays on Canadian Education, Volume 2, 1956–1958.* 37–9. Toronto: W.J. Gage, 1959.

Baird, Norman B. *Educational Finance and Administration for Ontario.* Toronto: Department of Research, Ontario College of Education, University of Toronto, 1952.

Barzun, Jacques. "The Battle over Brains in Democratic Education." *The University of Toronto Quarterly* 23, no. 2 (January 1954): 109–21.

Bender, Wilbur J. *The Top-One-Per-Cent Policy.* Cambridge, Mass.: Harvard University Press, 1961.

Bestor, Arthur. *Educational Wastelands: The Retreat from Learning in our Public Schools.* Urbana: University of Illinois Press, 1953.

Blatz, W.E. "Your Child – and Sex." *Maclean's Magazine* (January 1945): 37–9.

Braithwaite, Max. "Why Teachers Quit." *Maclean's Magazine* (January 1947): 9–13.

Booth, C.W. "Some Basic Aims and Recent Trends in Secondary Education." *Canadian Education* 14, no. 4 (1959): 35–50.

Bruner, J.S. *The Process of Education.* Cambridge, Mass.: Harvard University Press, 1960.

Campbell, H.L. *Curriculum Trends in Canadian Education.* Toronto: W.J. Gage, 1952.

Canadian Youth Commission. *Youth Challenges the Educators.* Toronto: Ryerson, 1946.

Canadian Education Association, Committee on the Status of the Teaching Profession (Chairman M.E. Lazerte). *Report on the Status of the Teaching Profession.* Toronto: Canadian Education Association, 1949.

Chant, S.N.F. "A Canadian Education." In *Canadian Education Today: A Symposium*, edited by Joseph Katz. 14–25. Toronto: McGraw-Hill, 1956.

Chase, Francis. S. *Education Faces New Demands.* Pittsburgh: University of Pittsburgh Press, 1956.

Clarke, Fred. *Freedom in the Educative Society.* London: University of London Press, 1948.

Dewey, John. *School and Society.* Chicago: University of Chicago Press, 1900.

– *Democracy and Education.* New York: MacMillan, 1916.

– *Experience and Education*, 60th Anniversary Edition. West Lafayette, Indiana: Kappa Delta Pi, 1998.

Dickie, Donalda J. *The Enterprise in Theory and Practice.* Toronto: W.J. Gage, 1940.

English, J.F.K. "The Reorganized System of Local School Administration in British Columbia." In *Education: A Collection of Essays on Canadian Education, Volume 2, 1956–1958.* 41–4. Toronto: W.J. Gage, 1959.

Evans, H.M. *Composite High Schools in Canada.* Edmonton: University of Alberta Monographs in Education 1, 1959.

Fleming, W.G. *Estimates of Teacher Supply and Demand in Ontario Secondary Schools for 1957–72.* Educational Research Series, Number 3. The Department of Educational Research, Ontario College of Education. Toronto: University of Toronto Press, 1956.

Flower, G.E. "The Larger School Unit in Canada." In *Education: A Collection of Essays on Canadian Education, Volume 1, 1954–1956.* 37–44. Toronto: W.J. Gage, 1956.

– "Supervision in School Systems." In *Canadian Education Today: A Symposium*, edited by Joseph Katz. 52–65. Toronto: McGraw-Hill, 1956.

– "The New Principal." In *Education: A Collection of Essays in Canadian Education, Volume 2, 1956–1958*. 69–72. Toronto: W.J. Gage, 1959.

Goldring, C.C. "Today's Secondary School Students." In *Education: A Collection of Essays on Canadian Education, Volume 2, 1956–1958*. 9–12. Toronto: W.J. Gage, 1959.

Government of Canada. *Survey of Elementary and Secondary Education*. Ottawa: Dominion Bureau of Statistics, 1958–1963.

Griffin, J.D.M. "The Contribution of Child Psychiatry to Mental Hygiene." *Canadian Public Health Journal* 29 (November 1938): 550–3.

Hickman, G.A. "The Preparation of Teachers." In *Education: A Collection of Essays on Canadian Education, Volume 2, 1956–1958*. 49–52. Toronto: W.J. Gage, 1959.

Hume, William E. and Harold F. Taylor. *Trouble in the School: Educators Cheat Your Child and the Nation*. Bracebridge, Ontario: Bracebridge Books, 1958.

Katz, Sidney. "The Crisis in Education – Part 1." *Maclean's Magazine* (March 1953): 7–9.

– "The Crisis in Education – Part 2." *Maclean's Magazine* (March 1953): 20–1 and 47–51.

Laycock, S.R. "You Can't Get Away from Discipline." *Educational Review of the New Brunswick Teachers' Federation* 60 (1946): 4–7.

– "Teaching – A Job in Human Relations." In *Education: A Collection of Essays on Canadian Education, Volume 2, 1956–1958*. 77–80. Toronto: W.J. Gage, 1959.

LaZerte, Milton E. *Teacher Education in Canada*. Toronto: W.J. Gage, 1950.

Love, R.J. "Where Do We Go from Here?" In *Education: A Collection of Essays on Canadian Education, Volume 3, 1958–1960*. 21–5. Toronto: W.J. Gage, 1960.

MacKenzie, D.B. "Providing for Individual Differences in Secondary Education in British Columbia." In *Education: A Collection of Essays on Canadian Education, Volume 1, 1954–1956*. 33–6. Toronto: W.J. Gage, 1956.

MacKinnon, Frank. *The Politics of Education: A Study of the Political Administration of the Public Schools*. Toronto: University of Toronto Press, 1960.

Macomber, Freeman Glenn. *Teaching in the Modern Secondary School*. Toronto: McGraw Hill, 1952.

Maxwell, Cameron A. *Report of the Commission of Inquiry into Educational Finance*. Victoria: The King's Printer, 1945.

McCordic, W.J. "An Experiment in Metropolitan Government." *Canadian Education* 14, no. 2 (1959): 3–15.

Morgan, Ewart H. "Secondary Education." In *Canadian Education Today: A Symposium*, edited by Joseph Katz. 114–25. Toronto: McGraw-Hill, 1956.

Morrison, Allan B. "Curriculum Construction." In *Canadian Education Today: A Symposium*, edited by Joseph Katz. 75–95. Toronto: McGraw-Hill, 1956.

Neatby, Hilda. *So Little for the Mind*. Toronto: Clark, Irwin, 1953.

– *A Temperate Dispute*. Toronto: Clark, Irwin, 1954.

Newnham, W.T. and A.S. Nease. *The Professional Teacher in Ontario: The Heritage, Responsibilities and Practices*. Toronto: The Ryerson Press, 1965.

Phillips, Charles E. *Public Secondary Education in Canada*. Toronto: W.J. Gage, 1955.

Phimister, Z.S. "The Principal and the School." *The School* (November 1947): 103.

Popenoe, Paul. "Better Teachers, Biologically Speaking." *Education Digest* 2, no.8 (1937): 4–5.

Province of British Columbia. *Manual of School Law*. Victoria: The Queen's Printer, 1958.

– *Report of the Royal Commission on Education*. (Chant Commission) Victoria: The Queen's Printer, 1960.

Province of British Columbia, Department of Education. *Effective Living*. Victoria: The King's Printer, 1950.

Province of British Columbia, Department of Education. *Public Schools Report* (Annual). Victoria: The King's/Queen's Printer, 1945–1960.

Province of Ontario. *Report of the Royal Commission on Education*. (Hope Commission) Toronto: The King's Printer, 1950.

Province of Ontario, Department of Education. *Report of the Minister of Education*. Toronto: The King's Printer, 1952.

Putnam, J. Harold and George M. Weir. *Survey of the School System of British Columbia*. Victoria: The King's Printer, 1925.

Rivers, F.S. and R.W.B. Jackson. "Teacher Supply in Canada." *Canadian Education* 3 (June 1953): 3–21.

Scarfe, Neville. *A Philosophy of Education*. Winnipeg: University of Manitoba Press, 1952.

– "The Aims of Education in a Free Society." In *The Second Canadian Conference on Education: A Report*, edited by Fred W. Price. 65–90. Toronto: University of Toronto Press, 1962.

Smith, Herbert Edgar. "Teacher Training." In *Canadian Education Today: A Symposium*, edited by Joseph Katz. 164–73. Toronto: McGraw-Hill, 1956.

Stewart, Edward E. *The 1955 Status of Recommendations in the Report of the Royal Commission on Education in Ontario, 1950*. Master's Thesis: University of Michigan, 1956.

Swift, W.H. "Pendulum or Synthesis?" In *Education: A Collection of Essays on Canadian Education, Volume 1, 1954–1956*. 81–4. Toronto: W.J. Gage, 1956.

– *Trends in Canadian Education*. Toronto: W.J. Gage, 1958.

Watts, Morrison. "Character Education in the Secondary Schools of Alberta." In *Education: A Collection of Essays on Canadian Education, Volume 2, 1956–1959*. 81–94. Toronto: W.J. Gage, 1959.

– "Decentralized Curriculum Building." In *Education: A Collection of Essays on Canadian Education, Volume 3, 1958–1960*. 27–31. Toronto: W.J. Gage, 1960.

Wisenthal, M. "Summary of Total Full-time Enrolment, by Level of Study, Related to Relevant Population, Canada, Selected Year, 1951 to 1975." *Historical Statistics of Canada*. Ottawa: Statistics Canada, 2003.

SECONDARY SOURCES

Acker, Sandra. *Gendered Education: Sociological Reflections on Women, Teaching and Feminism*. Buckingham: Open University Press, 1994.

– and Grace Feurverger. "Doing Good and Feeling Bad: The Work of Women University Teachers." *Cambridge Journal of Education* 26, no. 3 (1996): 401–22.

Adamoski, Robert, Dorothy E. Chunn, and Robert Menzies (editors). *Contesting Canadian Citizenship: Historical Readings*. Peterborough: Broadview Press, 2002.

Adams, Mary Louise. *The Trouble with Normal: Postwar Youth and the Construction of Heterosexuality*. Toronto: University of Toronto Press, 1994.

Altenbaugh, Richard. "Introduction." In *The Teacher's Voice: A Social History of Teaching in Twentieth Century America*, edited by Richard J. Altenbaugh. 1–5. London: Falmer Press, 1992.

Apple, Michael. "Work, Class and Teaching." In *Schoolwork: Approaches to the Labour Process of Teaching*, edited by Jenny Ozga. 101–15. Milton Keynes: Open University Press, 1988.

Arnot, Madeleine. "Introduction." In *Challenging Democracy: International Perspectives on Gender, Education and Citizenship*, edited by Madeleine Arnot and Jo-Anne Dillabough. 1–18. New York: Routledge, 2000.

– *Reproducing Gender: Essays on Educational Theory and Feminist Politics.* London: Routledge, 2002.

– and Jo-Anne Dillabough. "Feminist Politics and Democratic Values in Education." *Curriculum Inquiry* 29, no. 2 (1999): 159–89.

Axelrod, Paul. "Beyond the Progressive Education Debate: A Profile of Toronto Schooling in the 1950s." *Historical Studies in Education* 17, no. 2 (Fall 2005): 227–41.

Bakhtin, M. *The Dialogic Imagination.* Austin: University of Texas Press, 1981.

Barman, Jean. *Sojourning Sisters: The Lives and Letters of Jessie and Annie McQueen.* Toronto: University of Toronto Press, 2003.

Barrett, Michele. "Words and Things: Materialism and Method in Contemporary Feminist Analysis." In *Destabilizing Theory: Contemporary Feminist Debates*, edited by M. Barrett and A. Phillips. 201–19. Cambridge, UK: Polity Press, 1992.

Benavot, Aaron. "The Rise and Decline of Vocational Education." *Sociology of Education* 56, no. 2 (1983): 63–76.

Bessant, Bob and Andrew D. Spaull. *Teachers in Conflict.* Carlton, Victoria: Melbourne University Press, 1972.

– *Politics of Schooling.* Carlton, Victoria: Pitman Pacific Books, 1976.

Biklen, Sari Knopp. *School Work: Gender and the Cultural Construction of Teaching.* New York: Teachers College Press, 1995.

Blackmore, Jill. *Troubling Women: Feminism, Leadership and Educational Change.* Philadelphia: Open University Press, 1999.

Bloom, Leslie Rebecca. "Stories of One's Own: Nonunitary Subjectivity in Narrative Representation." *Qualitative Inquiry* 2, no.2 (1996): 176–88.

Bruneau, William A. 'Still Pleased to Teach:' A Thematic Study of British Columbia Teachers' Federation, 1917–1978. Vancouver: unpublished manuscript, 1984.

Butler, Judith. *Gender Trouble: Feminism and the Subversion of Identity.* New York: Routledge, Chapman, and Hall, 1990.

– "Performative Acts and Gender Constitution: An Essay in Phenomenology and Feminist Theory." In *Performing Feminisms: Feminist Critical Theory and Theatre*, edited by Sue-Ellen Case. 270–82. Baltimore: Johns Hopkins University Press, 1990.

Casey, Kathleen. "Teacher as Mother: Curriculum Theorizing in the Life Histories of Contemporary Women Teachers." *Cambridge Journal of Education* 20 (1990): 301–20.

– "Why Do Progressive Women Activists Leave Teaching?: Theory, Methodology, and Politics in Life-history Research." In *Studying Teachers' Lives*, edited by I. Goodson. 187–208. London: Routledge, 1992.

– *I Answer with My Life: Life Histories of Women Teachers Working for Social Change*. New York: Routledge, 1993.

Cavanagh, Sheila L. "The Heterosexualization of the Ontario Woman Teacher in the Postwar Period." *Canadian Women Studies* 18, no. 1 (1998): 65–9.

– "The Gender of Professionalism and Occupational Closure: The Management of Tenure Related Disputes by the 'Federation of Women Teachers' Associations of Ontario'1918–1949." *Gender and Education* 15, no. 1 (2003): 39–57.

– "Female-Teacher Gender and Sexuality in Twentieth-Century Ontario, Canada." *History of Education Quarterly* 45, no. 2 (2005): 247–73.

Clark, Lorenne M.G. "The Rights of Women: The Theory and Practice of the Ideology of Male Supremacy." In *Contemporary Issues in Political Philosophy*, edited by W.R. Shea and J. King-Farlow. 49–65. New York: Science History Publication, 1976.

Clarke, Frank K. "'Keep Communism out of Our Schools': Cold War Anti-Communism at the Toronto Board of Education, 1948–1951." *Labour/ Le Travail* 49 (Spring 2002): 93–120.

Collins, Patricia Hill. "Learning from the Outsider Within: The Sociological Significance of Black Feminist Thought." In *Feminist Approaches to Theory and Methodology: An Interdisciplinary Reader*, edited by S. Hesse-Biber, C. Gilmartin, and R. Lydenberg. 155–78. New York: Oxford University Press, 1999.

Connell, Richard W. *Gender and Power: Society, the Person and Sexual Politics*. Stanford: Stanford University Press, 1987.

Coole, Diana. *Women in Political Theory: From Ancient Misogyny to Contemporary Feminism*. Hertfordshire: Hearvester, Wheatsheaf, 1993.

Coulter, Rebecca Priegert. "Doing Gender in Canadian Schools: An Overview of the Policy and Practice Melange." In *Gender Issues in International Education: Beyond Policy and Practice*, edited by S. Erskine and M. Wilson. 113–29. New York: Garland Press, 1999.

– "Getting Things Done: Donalda J. Dickie and Leadership through Practice." *Canadian Journal of Education* 28, no. 3 (2005): 669–99.

– and Helen Harper (editors). *History is Hers: Women Educators in Twentieth Century Ontario*. Calgary: Detselig, 2005.

Curtis, Bruce, David W. Livingstone, and Harry Smaller. *Stacking the Deck: The Streaming of Working-Class Kids in Ontario Schools*. Toronto: Our Schools/Our Selves, 1992.

Danylewycz, Marta and Alison Prentice. "Teachers, Gender and Bureaucratizing School Systems in Nineteenth Century Montreal and Toronto." *History of Education Quarterly* 24, no. 1 (1984): 75–100.

Danylewycz, Marta, Beth Light, and Alison Prentice. "The Evolution of the Sexual Division of Labour in Teaching: A Nineteenth-Century Ontario and Quebec Case Study." *Histoire sociale/Society History* 16, no. 31 (1983): 81–109.

Davies, C. "The Sociology of Professions and the Profession of Gender." *Sociology* 30 (1996): 661–78.

Derrida, Jacques. *Of Grammatology*. Baltimore: Johns Hopkins University Press, 1976.

Dillabough, Jo-Anne. "Gender, Politics and Conceptions of the Modern Teacher: Women, Identity, and Professionalism." *British Journal of Sociology of Education* 20, no. 3 (1999): 374–94.

– "Women in Teacher Education: Their Struggles for Inclusion as 'Citizen Workers' in Late Modernity." In *Challenging Democracy: International Perspectives on Gender, Education and Citizenship*, edited by Madeleine Arnot and Jo-Anne Dillabough. 161–83. New York: Routledge, 2000.

– and Madeleine Arnot. "Feminist Political Frameworks: New Approaches to the Study of Gender, Citizenship and Education." In *Challenging Democracy: International Perspectives on Gender, Education and Citizenship*, edited by Madeleine Arnot and Jo-Anne Dillabough. 21–40. New York: Routledge, 2000.

Epstein, Debbie and Richard Johnson. *Schooling Sexualities*. Buckingham: Open University Press, 1998.

Fahmy-Eid, Nadia and Micheline Dumont (editors). *Maîtresses de maison, maîtresses d'école. Femmes, familles et éducation dans l'histoire du Québec*. Montréal: Boréal, 1983.

Federman, Lillian. *Odd Girls and Twilight Lovers: A History of Lesbian Life in Twentieth Century America*. New York: Penguin Books, 1991.

Finkel, Alvin. *Social Policy and Political Practice: A History*. Waterloo, Ontario: Wilfrid Laurier University Press, 2006.

Fleming, W.G. *Ontario's Educative Society, Volume 3: Schools, Pupils and Teachers*. Toronto: University of Toronto Press, 1972.

Fleming, Thomas. "'Our Boys in the Field': School Inspectors, Superintendents, and the Changing Character of School Leadership in British Columbia." In *Schools in the West: Essays in Canadian Educational History*, edited by Nancy M. Sheehan, J. Donald Wilson, and David C. Jones. 285–303. Calgary: Detselig, 1986.

– and David Conway. "Setting Standards in the West: C.B. Conway,
Science and School Reform in British Columbia, 1938–1974." *Canadian
Journal of Education* 21, no. 3 (1996): 294–317.

– and B. Hutton. "School Boards, District Consolidation, and Educational Governance in British Columbia, 1872–1995." *Canadian Journal of Educational Administration and Policy* 10 (January 1997):
1–22.

Foucault, Michel. *Discipline and Punish: The Birth of the Prison*. New
York: Vintage, 1979.

– "Prison Talk." In *Power/Knowledge: Selected Interviews and Other
Writings, 1972–1977*, edited by C. Gordon. 37–54. New York:
Pantheon Books, 1980.

– *The History of Sexuality, Volume I: An Introduction*. New York:
Vintage, 1990.

Fraser, Nancy and Linda Nicholson. "Social Criticism without Philosophy:
An Encounter between Feminism and Post-modernism." In *The
Postmodern Turn: New Perspectives on Social Theory*, edited by S.
Siedman. 242–61. Cambridge: Cambridge University Press, 1995.

French, Doris. *High Button Bootstraps: Federation of Women Teachers'
Associations of Ontario, 1918–1968*. Toronto: Ryerson, 1968.

Gaskell, Sandra. *The Problems and Professionalism of Women Elementary
Public School Teachers in Ontario, 1944–1954*. Ed.D. Dissertation:
Faculty of Education, University of Toronto, 1989.

Gauvreau, Michael. "The Protracted Birth of the Canadian 'Teenager':
Work, Citizenship and the Canadian Youth Commission, 1943–1955."
In *Cultures of Citizenship in Post-war Canada, 1940–1955*, edited by
Nancy Christie and Michael Gauvreau. 201–38. Montreal and
Kingston: McGill-Queen's University Press, 2003.

Gelman, Susan. "The 'Feminization' of the High School: Women
Secondary Teachers in Toronto, 1871–1930." *Historical Studies in
Education* 2 (1990): 119–48.

Gidney, Robert D. *From Hope to Harris: The Reshaping of Ontario's
Schools*. Toronto: University of Toronto Press, 1999.

– and Doug A. Lawr. "Who Ran the Schools? Local vs. Central Control of
Policy Making in Nineteenth-Century Ontario." *Ontario History* 67
(1980): 131–43.

– and Wynn P.J. Millar. "The Christian Recessional in Ontario's Public
Schools." In *Religion and Public Life in Canada: Historical and
Contemporary Perspectives*, edited by Marguerite Van Die. 275–93.
Toronto: University of Toronto Press, 2001.

Giroux, Henry. *Postmodernism, Feminism and Cultural Politics*. New York: SUNY, 1991.

Glazer, Penina M. and Miriam Slater. *Unequal Colleagues: The Entrance of Women into the Professions, 1890–1940*. New Jersey: Rutgers University Press, 1987.

Gleason, Mona. *Normalizing the Ideal: Psychology, Schooling and the Family in Postwar Canada*. Toronto: University of Toronto Press, 1999.

Gluck, Sherna-Berger and Daphne Patai (editors). *Women's Words: The Feminist Practice of Oral History*. New York: Routledge, 1991.

Gramsci, Antonio. *Selections from the Prison Notebooks*. New York: International Publishers, 1971.

– *Selections from Cultural Writings*. London: Lawrence and Wishart, 1979.

Hansen, Ron. *Comprehensive Secondary Schools: A Pilot Study of Two Ontario Schools Fifty Years after the Introduction of Comprehensive Programming* (Unpublished Report). London, Ontario: The University of Western Ontario, Faculty of Education, 2002.

Haraway, Donna. *Simians, Cyborgs, and Women: The Reinvention of Nature*. New York: Routledge, 1991.

Harding, Sandra. "Conclusion: Epistemological Questions." In *Feminism and Methodology*, edited by S. Harding. 181–90. Bloomington: Indiana University Press, 1987.

Harstock, Nancy. "The Feminist Standpoint: Developing the Ground for a Specifically Feminist Historical Materialism." In *Feminism and Methodology*, edited by S. Harding. 157–80. Bloomington: Indiana University Press, 1987.

Heater, Derek. *A History of Education for Citizenship*. New York: Routledge, 2004.

Henry, Annette. *Taking Back Control: African Canadian Women Teachers' Lives and Practices*. Albany: State University of New York Press, 1998.

High, Steven, Lisa Ndejuru, and Kristen O'Hare (editors). "Sharing Authority: Community-University Collaboration in Oral History, Digital Storytelling, and Engaged Scholarship." *Journal of Canadian Studies*, 43, no. 1 (2009).

Iacovetta, Franca. "Remaking Their Lives: Women Immigrants, Survivors, and Refugees." In *A Diversity of Women: Ontario, 1945–1980*, edited by Joy Parr. 135–67. Toronto: University of Toronto Press, 1995.

– "Recipes for Democracy? Gender, Family, and Making Female Citizens in Cold War Canada." In *Rethinking Canada: The Promise of Women's History*, 4th Edition, edited by Veronica Strong-Boag, Adele Perry, and Mona Gleason. 299–312. Oxford: Oxford University Press, 2002.

- *Gatekeepers: Reshaping Immigrant Lives in Cold War Canada.* Toronto: Between the Lines, 2006.

Igartua, José E. "What Nation, Which People? Representations of National Identity in English Canadian History Textbooks from 1945 to 1970." Unpublished Paper for CISH 2005.

Johnson, F. Henry. *A History of Public Education in British Columbia.* Vancouver: Publications Centre, University of British Columbia, 1964.

- *A Brief History of Canadian Education.* Toronto: McGraw-Hill, 1968.

Kelm, Mary-Ellen. *Colonizing Bodies: Aboriginal Health and Healing in British Columbia, 1900–1950.* Vancouver: UBC Press, 1998.

Kenway, Jane, Sue Willis, and Jill Blackmore. *Answering Back: Girls, Boys and Feminism in Schools.* New York: Routledge, 1998.

Khayatt, Madiha Didi. *Lesbian Teachers: An Invisible Presence.* Albany: State University of New York Press, 1992.

Khosla, Punham, Laura King, and Linda Read. *The Unrecognized Majority: A History of Women Teachers in British Columbia.* Vancouver: Status of Women Committee in British Columbia, British Columbia Teachers' Federation Collection, 1979.

Kinnear, Mary. *In Subordination: Professional Women, 1870–1970.* Montreal and Kingston: McGill-Queen's University Press, 1995.

Labaree, David F. "The Ed School's Romance with Progressivism." In *Brookings Papers on Education Policy,* edited by Diane Ravitch. 89–129. Washington: Brookings Institution Press, 2004.

Labatt, Mary. *Always a Journey: A History of the Federation of Women Teachers' Associations of Ontario, 1918–1993.* Toronto: Federation of Women Teachers' Associations of Ontario, 1993.

Lather, Patti. *Getting Smart.* New York: Routledge, 1992.

Lawn, Martin. "What Is the Teacher's Job? Work and Welfare in Elementary Teaching, 1940–1945." In *Teachers: The Culture and Politics of Work,* edited by M. Lawn and G. Grace. 50–64. London: Falmer Press, 1987.

Llewellyn, Kristina R. "When Oral Historians Listen to Teachers: Using Feminists' Findings." *Oral History Forum* 23 (2003): 89–112.

London, James. "Lay Control in Public Education: The British Columbia School Trustees Association, 1905–1946." In *School Leadership: Essays on the British Columbia Experience, 1872–1995,* edited by Thomas Fleming. 223–46. Mill Bay, British Columbia: Bendall Books, 2001.

Luke, Carmen and Jennifer Gore (editors). *Feminisms and Critical Pedagogy.* New York: Routledge, 1992.

Lyons, John E., Bikkars Randhawa, and Neil A. Paulson. "The Development of Vocational Education in Canada." *Canadian Journal of Education* 16, no.2 (1991): 137–50.

Mann, Jean. "G.M. Weir and H.B. King: Progressive Education or Education for the Progressive State?" In *Schooling and Society in 20th Century British Columbia*, edited by J. Donald Wilson and David C. Jones. 91–118. Calgary: Detselig, 1980.

Martin, Roland. "Excluding Women from the Educational Realm." In *The Education Feminism Reader*, edited by Lynda Stone. 105–121. New York: Routledge, 1994.

Mauthner, Natasha and Andrea Doucet. "Reflections on a Voice-centred Relational Method: Analyzing Maternal and Domestic Voices." In *Feminist Dilemmas in Qualitative Research: Public Knowledge and Private Lives*, edited by J. Ribbens and R. Edwards. 119–46. Thousand Oaks, CA: Sage, 1998.

May, Elaine Tyler. *Homeward Bound: American Families in the Cold War Era*. New York: Basic Books, 1988.

McLaren, John P.S. "'New Canadians' or 'Slaves of Satan'?: The Law and The Education of Doukhobor Children, 1911–1935." In *Children, Teachers and Schools in the History of British Columbia*, edited by Jean Barman, Neil Sutherland, and J. Donald Wilson. 147–60. Calgary: Detselig Enterprises, 1995.

McPherson, Kathryn. "'The Case of the Kissing Nurse': Femininity, Sexuality, and Canadian Nursing, 1900–1970." In *Gendered Pasts: Historical Essays in Femininity and Masculinity in Canada*, edited by Kathryn McPherson, Cecilia Morgan, and Nancy Forestell. 179–98. Toronto: Oxford University Press, 1999.

– *Bedside Matters: The Transformation of Canadian Nursing, 1900–1990*. Toronto: University of Toronto Press, 2003.

Measor, Lynda and Patricia Sikes. "Visiting Lives: Ethics and Methodology in Life History." In *Studying Teachers' Lives*, edited by I. Goodson. 209–33. London: Routledge, 1992.

Middleton, Sue. *Disciplining Sexuality: Foucault, Life Histories, and Education*. New York: Teachers College Press, 1998.

Mills, A. "Gender, Sexuality and Organizational Theory." In *The Sexuality of Organization*, edited by J. Hearn, D. Sheppard, P. Tancred-Sheriff, and G. Burrell. 29–44. London: Sage, 1989.

Mohanty, Chandra Talpade. "Under Western Eyes: Feminist Scholarship and Colonial Discourses." In *Third World Women and the Politics of*

Feminism, edited by C. Mohanty, A. Russo, and L. Torres. 51–80. Bloomington: Indiana University Press, 1991.

Mouffe, Chantal. "Feminism, Citizenship and Radical Democratic Politics." In *Feminists Theorize the Political*, edited by J. Butler and J. Scott. 369–84. New York: Routledge, 1992.

Munro, Peter. *Subject to Fiction: Women Teachers' Life History Narratives and the Cultural Politics of Resistance*. Buckingham: Open University Press, 1998.

Myers, Douglas. "From Hope to Hall-Dennis: The Official Report as an Instrument of Educational Reform." In *Means and Ends in Education: Comments on Living and Learning*, edited by Brian Crittenden. 11–24. Toronto: The Ontario Institute for Studies in Education, 1969.

Nelson, Margaret K. "From One-Room Schoolhouse to the Graded School: Teaching in Vermont, 1910–1950." *Frontiers* 7, no. 1 (1983): 14–20.

– "Using Oral Case Histories to Reconstruct the Experiences of Women Teachers in Vermont, 1900–1950." In *Studying Teachers' Lives*, edited by I. Goodson. 167–86. London: Routledge, 1992.

Oram, Alison. "Embittered, Sexless or Homosexual: Attacks on Spinster Teachers in 1918–1939." In *Not a Passing Phase: Reclaiming Lesbians in History 1840–1985*, edited by Lesbian History Group. 99–118. London: Women's Press, 1989.

– "Serving Two Masters? The Introduction of a Marriage Bar in Teaching in the 1920s." In *The Sexual Dynamics of History*, edited by Lesbian Feminist History Group. 134–48. London: Pluto Press, 1983.

Osborne, Ken. *Teaching for Democratic Citizenship*. Toronto: Our Schools/Ourselves, 1991.

Owram, Doug. *Born at the Right Time: A History of the Baby-Boom Generation*. Toronto: University of Toronto Press, 1996.

Ozga, Jenny and Martin Lawn. *Teachers, Professionalism and Class: A Study of Organized Teachers*. London: Falmer Press, 1981.

Palmer, Bryan D. *Working-Class Experience: Rethinking the History of Canadian Labour, 1800–1991*. Toronto: McClelland and Stewart, 1992.

Parr, Joy. "Introduction." In *A Diversity of Women: Ontario, 1945–1980*, edited by Joy Parr. 3–18. Toronto: University of Toronto Press, 1995.

– "Gender History and Historical Practice." In *Gender and History in Canada*, edited by Joy Parr and Mark Rosenfeld. 8–27. Toronto: Copp Clark, 1996.

Passerini, Luisa. "Women's Personal Narratives: Myths, Experiences, and Emotions." In *Interpreting Women's Lives: Feminist Theory and*

Personal Narratives, edited by Personal Narratives Group. 189–97.
Bloomington: Indiana University Press, 1989.

Pateman, Carole. *The Sexual Contract*. Cambridge: Polity Press, 1988.

– *The Disorder of Women: Democracy, Feminism and Political Theory*.
Stanford: Stanford University Press, 1989.

– "Equality, Difference and Subordination: The Politics of Motherhood
and Women's Citizenship." In *Beyond Equality and Difference:
Citizenship, Feminist Politics, Female Subjectivity*, edited by G. Bock
and S. James. 17–31. New York: Routledge, 1992.

Paton, J.M. *Concern and Competence in Canadian Education: Essays by
J.M. Paton*, edited by D.A. MacIver. Toronto: Guidance Centre, Faculty
of Education, University of Toronto, 1973.

Patterson, R.S. "Progressive Education: Impetus to Educational Change in
Alberta and Saskatchewan." In *Education in Canada: An Interpretation*,
edited by E. Brian Titley and P.J. Miller. 169–92. Calgary: Detselig, 1982.

Phillips, Anne. *Engendering Democracy*. Pennsylvania: Pennsylvania State
University Press, 1991.

– *Democracy and Difference*. Cambridge: Polity Press, 1993.

Pierson, Ruth Roach. *"They're Still Women after All: The Second World
War and Canadian Womanhood*. Toronto: McClelland and Stewart, 1986.

Popular Memory Group. "Popular Memory: Theory, Politics, Method." In
Making Histories: Studies in History-Writing and Politics, edited by R.
Johnson, G. McLennan, B. Schwartz, and D. Sutton. 205–52. London:
Hutchinson, 1982.

Porter, Ann. "Women and Income Security in the Post-War Period: The
Case of Unemployment Insurance, 1945–1962." *Labour/Le Travail* 31
(1993): 111–44.

Porter, John. *The Vertical Mosaic: An Analysis of Social Class and Power
in Canada*. Toronto: University of Toronto Press, 1968.

Prentice, Alison. "The Feminization of Teaching in British North America
and Canada: 1845–1875." *Histoire sociale/ Social History* 8 (1975):
5–20.

– and Marjorie Theobald. "The Historiography of Women Teachers: A
Retrospect." In *Women Who Taught: Perspectives on the History of
Women and Teaching*, edited by A. Prentice and M. Theobald. 3–33.
Toronto: University of Toronto Press, 1991.

– (editors). *Women Who Taught: Perspectives on the History of Women
and Teaching*. Toronto: University of Toronto Press, 1991.

Prentice, Susan. "Workers, Mothers, Reds: Toronto's Postwar Daycare
Fight." *Studies in Political Economy* 30 (1989): 115–44.

Proom, Juliette. "Tilly Jean Rolston: She Knew How to Throw a Party." In *Not Just Pin Money: Selected Essays on the History of Women's Work in British Columbia*, edited by Barbara K. Latham and Roberta J. Pazdro. 381–8. Victoria: Camosun College, 1984.

Quantz, Richard A. "Interpretive Method in Historical Research: Ethnography Reconsidered." In *The Teacher's Voice: A Social History of Teaching in Twentieth Century America*, edited by Richard J. Altenbaugh. 174–94. London: Falmer Press, 1992.

– "The Complex Vision of Female Teachers and the Failure of Unionization in the 1930s: An Oral History." In *The Teacher's Voice: A Social History of Teaching in Twentieth Century America*, edited by Richard J. Altenbaugh. 137–56. London: Falmer Press, 1992.

Raptis, Helen. "Implementing Integrated Education Policy for On-Reserve Aboriginal Children in British Columbia, 1951–1981." *Historical Studies in Education* 20, no. 1 (2008): 118–46.

Reinharz, Shulamit. "Neglected Voices and Excessive Demands in Feminist Research." *Qualitative Sociology* 16 (1993): 69–76.

Reynolds, Cecilia. "Hegemony and Hierarchy: Becoming a Teacher in Toronto, 1930–1980." *Historical Studies in Education* 2, no. 1 (1990): 95–118.

– "Too Limiting a Liberation: Discourse and Actuality in the Case of Married Women Teachers." In *Feminism and Education: A Canadian Perspective*, edited by Frieda Forman, Mary O'Brien, Jane Haddad, Dianne Hallman, and Philinda Masters. 145–68. Toronto: Centre for Women's Studies in Education, 1990.

– "In the Right Place at the Right Time: Rules of Control and Woman's Place in Ontario Schools, 1940–1980." *Canadian Journal of Education* 20, no. 2 (1995): 129–45.

– and Harry Smaller. "Ontario School Teachers: A Gendered View of the 1930s." *Historical Studies in Education* 6, no. 3 (1994): 151–69.

Rich, Emma. "Gender Positioning in Teacher Education in England: New Rhetoric, Old Realities." *International Studies in Sociology of Education* 11, no. 2 (2001): 131–56.

Ricker, Eric Williams. *Teachers, Trustees, and Policy: The Politics of Education in Ontario, 1945–1975*. PhD Dissertation: University of Toronto, 1981.

Rinehart, Alice Duffy. *Mortal in the Immortal Profession: An Oral History of Teaching*. New York: Irvington Publishers, 1983.

Ross, Andrew. *No Respect: Intellectuals and Popular Culture*. New York: Routledge, 1988.

Rousmaniere, Kate. *City Teachers: Teaching and School Reform in Historical Perspective*. New York: Teachers College Press, 1997.
– "Where Haley Stood: Margaret Haley, Teachers' Work, and the Problem of Teacher Identity." In *Telling Women's Lives: Narrative Inquiries in the History of Women's Education*, edited by Kathleen Weiler and Sue Middleton. 147–61. Philadelphia: Open University Press, 1999.
Sable, Martin. "George Drew and the Rabbis: Religious Education and Ontario's Public Schools." *Canadian Jewish Studies* 6 (1998): 25–53.
Sangster, Joan. *Earning Respect: The Lives of Working Women in Small-Town Ontario, 1920–1960*. Toronto: University of Toronto, 1995.
– "Telling Our Stories: Feminist Debates and the Use of Oral History." In *Rethinking Canada: The Promise of Women's History*, Third Edition, edited by V. Strong-Boag and A. Fellman. 304–21. Toronto: Oxford University Press, 1997.
– *Transforming Labour: Women and Work in Post-war Canada*. Toronto: University of Toronto Press, 2010.
– "'We No Longer Respect the Law': The Tilco Strike, Labour Injunctions, and the State." *Labour/Le Travail* 53 (Spring 2004): 47–87.
Sewell, William H. "The Concept(s) of Culture." In *Beyond the Cultural Turn: New Directions in the Study of Society and Culture*, edited by Victoria E. Bonnell and Lynn Hunt. 35–61. Berkeley and Los Angeles: University of California Press, 1999.
Shaw, Moriah. "Bible Study." *Homeroom: British Columbia's History of Education Website* http://www.viu.ca/homeroom/content/topics/programs/bible.htm.
Shopland, Stella. *Status of Married Women Teachers in the Province of British Columbia*. MA Thesis: University of Washington, 1957.
Smaller, Harry. "Vocational Training in Ontario's Secondary Schools: Past, Present – and Future?" *Training Matters: Works in Progress for the Labour Education and Training Research Network*. Toronto: York University, Centre for Research on Work and Training, April 2000.
Smith, Dorothy. *The Everyday World as Problematic*. Toronto: University of Toronto Press, 1987.
Smyth, Elizabeth, Sandra Acker, Paula Bourne, and Alison Prentice (editors). *Challenging Professions: Historical and Contemporary Perspectives on Women's Professional Work*. Toronto: University of Toronto Press, 1999.
Spalter-Roth, Roberta and Heidi Hartmann. "Small Happiness: The Feminist Struggle to Integrate Social Research with Social Activism." In *Feminist Approaches to Theory and Methodology*, edited by S.

Hesse-Biber, C. Gilmartin, and R. Lydenberg. 333–47. New York: Oxford University Press, 1999.

Stamp, Robert M. *The Schools of Ontario, 1876–1976*. Toronto: University of Toronto Press, 1982.

– "Growing Up Progressive? Part II: Going to High School in 1950s Ontario." *Historical Studies in Education* 17, no. 2 (Fall 2005): 321–31.

Stanley, Timothy J. "White Supremacy and the Rhetoric of Educational Indoctrination: A Canadian Case Study." In *Children, Teachers, and Schools in the History of British Columbia*, edited by Jean Barman, Neil Sutherland, and J. Donald Wilson. 39–56. Calgary: Detselig, 1995.

Staton, Patricia Anne and Beth Light. *Speak with Their Own Voices: A Documentary History of the Teachers of Ontario and the Women Elementary Public School Teachers in Ontario*. Toronto: Federation of Women Teachers' Associations of Ontario, 1987.

Stevenson, Hugh A. "Developing Public Education in Post-War Canada to 1960." In *Canadian Education: A History*, edited by J.D. Wilson, R. Stamp, and L.P. Audet. 386–415. Toronto: Prentice-Hall, 1970.

Strange, Carolyn. *Toronto's Girl Problem: The Perils and Pleasures of the City, 1880–1930*. Toronto: University of Toronto Press, 1995.

Strober, Myra and David Tyack. "Why Do Women Teach and Men Manage? A Report on Research on School." *Signs* 5 (Spring 1980): 494–503.

Strong-Boag, Veronica. "Canada's Wage-Earning Wives and the Construction of the Middle Class, 1945–1960." *Journal of Canadian Studies* 29, no. 3 (1994): 5–25.

Sutherland, Neil. *Children in English Canadian Society: Framing the Twentieth Century Consensus*. Toronto: University of Toronto Press, 1976.

– "The Triumph of Formalism." In *Children, Teachers and Schools in the History of British Columbia*, edited by Jean Barman, Neil Sutherland, and J. Donald Wilson. 101–24. Calgary: Detselig, 1995.

Theobald, Majorie. "Teachers, Memory and Oral History." In *Telling Women's Lives: Narrative Inquiries in the History of Women's Education*, edited by Kathleen Weiler and Sue Middleton. 9–24. Philadelphia: Open University Press, 1999.

Tillotson, Shirley. "Human Rights Law as Prism: Women's Organizations, Unions and Ontario's Female Employees Fair Remuneration Act, 1951." *Canadian Historical Review* 72 (1991): 532–57.

– *The Public at Play: Gender and Politics of Recreation in Post-War Ontario*. Toronto: University of Toronto Press, 2000.

Thompson, Paul. *Voice of the Past: Oral History*. Oxford: Oxford University Press, 1978.

Valverde, Mariana. "Building Anti-Delinquent Communities: Morality, Gender, and Generation in the City." In *A Diversity of Women: Ontario, 1945–1980*, edited by Joy Parr. 19–45. Toronto: University of Toronto Press, 1995.

Von Heyking, Amy. "Selling Progressive Education to Albertans, 1935–1953." *Historical Studies in Education* 10, nos.1 and 2 (1998): 67–84.

Walkerdine, Valerie. "Post-structuralist Theory and Everyday Social Practices: The Family and the School." In *Feminist Social Psychology: Developing Theory and Practice*, edited by Valerie Walkerdine. 57–76. Milton Keynes: Open University Press, 1986.

– *Schoolgirl Fictions*. London: Verso, 1990.

– and Helen Lucey. *Democracy in the Kitchen: Regulating Mothers and Making Daughters*. London: Virago, 1989.

Weber, Sandra and Claudia Mitchell. *"That's Funny, You Don't Look Like a Teacher": Interrogating Images and Identity in Popular Culture*. Washington: Falmer Press, 1995.

Weeks, Jeffery. "Foucault for Historians." *History Workshop* 14 (Autumn 1982): 106–19.

Weiler, Kathleen. *Women Teaching for Change*. Massachusetts: Bergin and Garvey, 1988.

– "Remembering and Representing Life Choices: A Critical Perspective on Teachers' Oral History Narratives." *Qualitative Studies in Education* 5, no. 1 (1992): 39–50.

– *Country Schoolwomen: Teaching in Rural California, 1850–1950*. Stanford: Stanford University Press, 1998.

– "Reflections on Writing a History of Women Teachers." In *Telling Women's Lives: Narrative Inquiries in the History of Women's Education*, edited by Kathleen Weiler and Sue Middleton. 43–59. Philadelphia: Open University Press, 1999.

Weir, Alison. *Sacrificial Logics: Feminist Theory and the Critique of Identity*. New York: Routledge, 1997.

Westheimer, Joel. "Democratic Dogma: There Is No One-Size-Fits-All Approach to Schooling for Democracy." *Our Schools/Ourselves* 15, no. 1 (2005): 25–30.

Wilson, J. Donald and David C. Jones (editors). *Schooling and Society in 20th Century British Columbia*. Calgary: Detselig, 1980.

Wolf, Diane L. "Situating Feminist Dilemmas in Fieldwork." In *Feminist Dilemmas in Fieldwork*, edited by D.L. Wolf. 1–55. Boulder: Westview Press, 1996.

Young, Iris Marion. "Gender as Seriality: Thinking about Women as a Social Collective." In *Social Postmodernism*, edited by L. Nicholson and S. Seidman. 187–215. Cambridge: Cambridge University Press, 1995.

– *Inclusion and Democracy*. New York: Oxford University Press, 2000.

Yuval-Davis, Nira. *Gender and Nation*. London: Sage Press, 1997.

– "Women, Citizenship and Difference." *Feminist Review* 57 (1997): 4–27.

– and Penina Werbner (editors). *Women, Citizenship and Difference (Postcolonial Encounters)*. New York: St Martin's Press, 1999.

Index